How to Be a Multi-Hyphenate in the Theatre Business

How to Be a Multi-Hyphenate in the Theatre Business empowers theatre professionals to take hold of their own careers and become successful 'multi-hyphenates' – artists with multiple proficiencies, often cross-pollinating each other to help flourish professional capabilities.

Discussing self-identity, networking, workflow, failure, passion, purpose, socially responsible artistry, social media, and the effects of COVID-19, Michael Kushner, award-winning theatre multi-hyphenate artist, sets the stage for artists of all disciplines and backgrounds to find personalized success in the theatre industry. Complete with informative and lively exercises and excerpts from Kushner's popular podcast and workshop, *Dear Multi-Hyphenate*, this book addresses questions such as How do we recover from a pandemic? How do we give more access to marginalized theatre creators? and What goes into producing our own projects? Featuring exclusive information from a myriad of theatre makers such as agents, managers, designers, actors, press representatives, producers, comedians, social media stars, writers, executive directors, CEOs, and lawyers, this book promotes the dismantling of gatekeeping and provides a specialized, hands-on experience to an innovative and lucrative approach to theatre making.

Featuring words and insight from Emmy and Golden Globe Winner Rachel Brosnahan, Colleen Ballinger, Tony Winner Tonya Pinkins, Tony Winner Randy Graff, Tony Winner Frances Ruffelle, Tony Nominee L Morgan Lee, Bob the Drag Queen, Olivier Award Winner Sophie Thompson, Carbonell Award Winning Elena Maria Garcia, Shakina Nayfack, The Skivvies, Tony Nominee Michael McElroy, Tony Winner Beowulf Boritt, Ann Harada, Mary Testa, Tony Winner Ken Davenport, and over one hundred other artists, *How to Be a Multi-Hyphenate in the Theatre Business* is an invaluable resource for theatre artists at any level in their careers, whether they are undergraduates, graduate students, professors, award-winning members of the theatre and film community, working professionals, high school students, or entrepreneurs.

Michael Kushner is New York City's leading multi-hyphenate and the executive producer of the Emmy-nominated series *Indoor Boys*. In true multi-hyphenate form, Michael served as the director of programming for The Green Room 42, providing the space with sold-out programming post-pandemic. He is the owner of Michael Kushner Photography and has been published in the *New York Times, Vogue, People, Playbill,* and more. He is also the creator of The Dressing Room Project, where he photographs actors prepping for their roles on and off Broadway. Michael holds a BFA in Musical Theatre from Ithaca

College, where he won the 2020 Outstanding Young Alumni Award. He is the founding member of Musical Theatre Factory, the Executive Producer of XaveMePlease (created by Wesley Taylor, Frameline 43 Festival Finalist), and the creator of the podcast Dear Multi-Hyphenate with Broadway Podcast Network. He is an active participant of Covenant House Sleep Out, as well as a performer and a member of the Actors' Equity Association.

How to Be a Multi-Hyphenate in the Theatre Business

Conversations, Advice, and Tips
from 'Dear Multi-Hyphenate'

Michael Kushner

Routledge
Taylor & Francis Group

NEW YORK AND LONDON

Front cover image: Michael Kushner Photography;
Back cover image: Daniel Nolen

First published 2023
by Routledge
605 Third Avenue, New York, NY 10158

and by Routledge
4 Park Square, Milton Park, Abingdon, Oxon, OX14 4RN

Routledge is an imprint of the Taylor & Francis Group, an informa business

Library of Congress Cataloging-in-Publication Data
Names: Kushner, Michael, author.
Title: How to be a multi-hyphenate in the theatre business : conversations,
    advice, and tips from 'Dear Multi-Hyphenate' / Michael Kushner.
    Other titles: Dear multi-hyphenate (Podcast)
Description: New York, NY : Routledge, 2023. | Includes bibliographical
    references and index.
Identifiers: LCCN 2022028976 (print) | LCCN 2022028977 (ebook) |
    ISBN 9781032184760 (hardback) | ISBN 9781032184159 (paperback) |
    ISBN 9781003254744 (ebook)
Subjects: LCSH: Theater—Vocational guidance.
Classification: LCC PN2074 .K87 2023 (print) | LCC PN2074 (ebook) |
    DDC 792.02/93—dc23/eng/20220815
LC record available at https://lccn.loc.gov/2022028976
LC ebook record available at https://lccn.loc.gov/2022028977

ISBN: 978-1-032-18476-0 (hbk)
ISBN: 978-1-032-18415-9 (pbk)
ISBN: 978-1-003-25474-4 (ebk)

DOI: 10.4324/9781003254744

Typeset in ITC Officina Sans
by Apex CoVantage, LLC

This book is dedicated to the artists who were, who are, and who will be.
For Remy, Sandwich, Doris, Penny, and Amy.

Contents

Foreword

There once was a boy who wanted to be part of the magical world of theatre. He stepped into my life with wide eyes, an eager heart, and a Dorothy Hamill haircut. This young man's journey began in the 2000s when I was a theatre educator in a prep school. In the spring of 2005, we were working on *Macbeth*, and I needed someone to play Macduff's son. I had no one. Michael, the young actor with the poorly chosen haircut had just started school, and he was in my Intro to Theatre class. I asked the young actor disguised with a Dorothy Hamill haircut if he would like to play the role, but before I could even finish my request, young Michael exclaimed as if while performing the perfect layback spin with a catch foot, "YES!"

His hair grew, thank goodness, and Michael stayed the course of being an actor. He was a sponge. *A sponge*. One is only a true sponge if they are present and with no hidden agenda. As an educator, I have identified the difference between who is really listening and who is pretending to listen – who doesn't give a crap and who can't wait till the bell rings so they can look at their phone and see how many "likes" they have on their really cool new nose ring.

He personified the improvisation guidelines of "yes and" and "sure, I'll try." Always eager to be, Michael had ideas. Michael was driven. Michael wanted more. But wanting more doesn't always mean you *need* more. One can always create more with less. *Can and a stick*. My father would tell us all we needed to play with was a can and a stick. I never understood what that meant as a child. I thought it was a really bad joke, and he just didn't want us to have the coolest toys. Now as an adult I realized he was a genius. When we have less, our imagination goes into overdrive. Everything can be a possibility.

I implement this philosophy in my class, and as stated before, those that really listened got it and continued to work with less to make more. Not only can we create with less, but we start reinventing ourselves while discovering that we don't have to be just the yellow crayon in the box, we can be more, and we can put two crayons together and create a new color we never knew we could be.

Reinventing oneself is terrifying, invigorating, and liberating all at the same time. Artistically reinventing oneself can be a daunting challenge. Sometimes we feel as if we are moving away from our dreams, from what we worked so hard for, and all that hard work was in vain. Our journey never shows us the rest stops until we have left the station and we look back. My exceptional student with the poor haircut dreamed and dreamed big. Musical theatre was his world, but a world lives in a universe where there are so many other possibilities. His universe moved about, and he discovered other galaxies. There he discovered other dreams that he would soon place in his own solar system. Our art should not be one thing, but many. It makes us a better and stronger artist and human being.

Multi-hyphenating our lives is what we actually do most. When we multi-hyphenate, we are feeding other artistic components of our lives. I am an actor. But I never could have become the actor I am today if I was not in tune with every aspect of myself. Michael's life mantra, "Sure, I'll try," opened the door to so many possibilities, so many *hyphens*. He fed his art, and his art is feeding him.

About Elena Maria Garcia:

Elena is a first-generation Cuban American artist/mami of two/working professional/creative chef/life coach/lawn manicurist/cleaning service/mechanic/school project engineer/cupboard stocker/hair stylist and colorist/chauffer/holistic healer/fortune teller/adjunct/Santa Claus/Easter Bunny/Tooth Fairy/and wife of 25 years. She is a three-time recipient of the Carbonell Award and was last seen at the Adrienne Arsht Center in her one-person show *Fuácata! or A Latina's Guide to Surviving the Universe*, which she cowrote with Stuart Meltzer of Zoetic Stage. She is the founder of Separate Checks Improv Troupe, Quien Sigue A Quien, and Big Purse and Matching Shoes. Elena has taught improvisation and acting for over 30 years, and currently teaches at Universal Acting, New World School of the Arts, Nova Southeastern University, and Florida International University. She is a member of the Screen Actors Guild and Actors' Equity. Elena would like to thank her daughters, Ana and Emma; her husband, Jerry; Mami; and her friends and students for their support. She dedicates her performance to her father, Dr. Francisco N. Garcia, and Tori Velle Fortney, whose love for the magic of theatre will go on.

Elena Maria Garcia

Acknowledgments

Special Thanks: Elena Maria Garcia, Nicholas Rohlfing, Ashley Kate Adams, Kimberly Faye Greenberg, Kara Johnson, Stacey Walker, Lucia Accorsi, Cynthia Henderson, mom, dad, Lizzie, Robin, Poppy, Ginette Molina, The Chipped Cup, and – of course – Rafael Jaen.

Prologue: A Note From the Author

"No casting director, no producer, no agent, no friend, no one can dictate your art. Multi-hyphenating allows you to have creative freedom, but it requires focus, goals, boundaries, and a tough, yet permeable skin. We can all do this."

Michael Kushner, Dear Multi-Hyphenate

When I first discovered the word *multi-hyphenate*, it was as if all the lights turned on. As of 2022, I've been in the industry for 22 years. As a theatre artist, there are moments when time stops. Discovering this word was one of them. It was a pivot – years before the word grew in popularity during the COVID-19 pandemic. For everyone who told me I couldn't do more than one thing, or for everyone who assured me I'm still finding my way – this word was my answer. It wasn't an answer to them, per se; it was an answer for me.

I've always said yes to creativity, but this word would be my ticket to doing so unapologetically. Even while I identified with other aspects of my artistry, tapping into those skills always risked judgment from others – something I've always feared. After growing up as an actor and then getting my BFA in musical theatre, I started a photography business because it interested me and provided extra income.

As the business expanded, I met with friends, audition buddies, artists I would casually work with, whomever, and they would look at me over their cocktail glass and ask with a derogatory tone: "So how is Michael Kushner Photography[1] going?" They'd have this grin that seemed to say, "I give it one month."

Who knows? Maybe that was me projecting my fear. Perhaps that was my psyche telling me I shouldn't be trying to juggle becoming a photographer on top of my acting. Maybe it was my shame that I was not as devoted to acting as I had thought. Or perhaps that person was just being a poop. But, when someone I've known most of my 22 years in the industry comes up to me at an event at which I was photographing and says, "You're doing *this* now?" I'm not sure it was *all* in my head . . .

After sticking with the business and landing some incredible opportunities in the Broadway community, I did notice derogatory attitudes start to come less and less. More praise. More interest. More following. People I had wished to simply meet one day were all of a sudden coming over to my apartment to photograph with me! It's interesting, but not a new lesson – artists constantly have to prove themselves in order to find support.

Despite the great experiences I was having, the moments where others would judge me ruined it. Yet, why was I allowing others to squash something in me that I had always known to be true? Not only do I want to do more than one thing. . . . I *do* more than one thing. From the moment I started in the theatre in 2000, I was in an environment that encouraged exploration.

Cynthia O'Brien, the artistic director of *Next Stop Broadway*,[2] a training center for young performers, established an environment where, even though I might have been acting in a show, I was also able to be a part of the writing process, the costuming process, and the directing process. Almost seamlessly, this outlook continued as I entered high school and Carbonell award-winning Elena Maria Garcia[3] – who wrote the Foreword – kept pressing on us to take control of our work with the idea that theatre can be made with a can and a stick, and *no one* can tell you when to start. So in sophomore year, we were assigned to write our own one-person shows for our final exams, and we would direct, design, and run our fellow classmates' productions. It was a way to learn about other proficiencies, get something done, and access different aspects of one's artistry for a common goal. Garcia also happens to be an incredible gardener, and ironically, she had planted the first seeds of the concept of multi-hyphenating in me. It just wasn't called that yet.

At Ithaca College,[4] I had the incredible Cynthia Henderson[5] as my freshman acting teacher who instilled technique and possibility in me. Cynthia has this fabulous way of combining the ethereal wonder of the Universe and the practical and commercial ideals of performance. She has found ways to build a science out of acting in an absolutely brilliant manner. She's a multi-hyphenate as well, balancing many proficiencies of her artistry and introducing concepts to me like self-focused work and *why* we do something. Understanding that our work should be placed on the other, I began to commit myself to projects that would reach and inspire different groups of people. By senior year, not only was I studying musical theatre, but I was also the student liaison of the Guest Artist committee, a teaching assistant to Henderson's Freshman Scene Study class, donating time as a guest artist choreographing at the Jewish Community Center,[6] and hosting *Best of Broadway* on Ithaca's radio station, WICB.[7] Even then, in the small college ecosystem, I was practicing to be a multi-hyphenate – to my knowledge there still was no name. We called it busy or confused.

After graduating from Ithaca, working consistently in regional theatre, becoming a member of Actors' Equity Association,[8] and moving to New York City, I continued the work I had always known to be true – soaking up all the information I could from whatever spaces I found myself in. I learned the basics of producing and the economics of a nonprofit start-up, thanks to being a founding member of Musical Theatre Factory.[9] I found myself backstage of Broadway shows capturing magical moments in the dressing room, thanks to creating *The Dressing Room Project*.[10] Finally, I would pay my bills and quit my for-now job, thanks to photography.

These efforts would constantly feed into themselves allowing me to continue experiencing, changing, and growing. Yet similar to when I met doubtful people in past cocktail parties – even though I found myself getting published in the *New York Times*[11] and *Vogue*,[12] producing award-winning theatrical events/web series, joining boards of nonprofits, starring in readings of new musicals, and continuing to expand my support system – an agent I wanted to work with told me I was lazy and "hadn't done much" to move my career forward. They waved my resume in my face saying they'd be in touch. While that seems *maddening*, and it was, it still served to be one of the more formative moments of my career. Why? Because even with this person's opinion of me, I was still growing and happier in my art than ever. When I'm genuinely happy – *no one* can take that away from me except myself. Unfortunately, there will always be bullies who want to take away other people's happiness. The only thing that will stop them in their tracks is if you're the train and you plow ahead.

While the agent interaction certainly hurt, my friend MaryJo McConnell[13] came up to me at an event. and we began to kibitz. When I told her what I was going through, she looked at me and said, "You are such a multi-hyphenate." Suddenly, all my wounds from interaction with the agent had healed. That's when this word became my identity. I love being an actor. I love being a producer. I love being a podcaster. I love being a photographer. I love being a writer. And not only am I each of these proficiencies, each one of these proficiencies support the other. I *am* a multi-hyphenate. I am not the first one, however, and I am not the only one to currently exist. But I am the only one who is dissecting this specific approach to art with a scientific eye. I am entirely curious about the ways that it worked for myself and others and the ways it will continually ebb and flow. I don't mean to sound like an infomercial, but I mean this when I say – if I can do it, *you* can do it.

While I will cover much about the different roles and opportunities in show business, this book is not about how to get an agent. This book is not about audition secrets. This book is not an exposé on all the drama in the theatre industry. Instead, we will uncover showbusiness artistic approaches from the perspective of the multi-hyphenate artist and the ways one can find agency in a very unstructured and unpredictable industry. This book is about access, the ability to find ways to access the industry, access the deepest parts of our artistry, and create access for others. The whole idea of being a multi-hyphenate is taking control of your artistry. It's about decision-making and understanding the tools to get your voice across, whether that's producing your own web series, writing a play, fundraising, and so on. It's about the responsibility of when to access your voice and how to access your voice. It's about understanding that no casting director, no producer, no agent, no friend, no one can dictate your art. Multi-hyphenating allows creative freedom, but it requires

focus, goals, boundaries, and a tough yet permeable skin. We can all do this.

In my efforts to keep show business moving in a forward motion, it is my responsibility to provide access to those around me who have not been able to benefit from the same privileges that have benefited me. Our industry is loaded with perspectives of all shapes and sizes, and in this book, you'll be meeting theatrical moguls and legends, all the way to people who are just starting. Some of the people you're going to hear from are not multi-hyphenates but still have insight that will prove useful. Experience is insight – and in the new territory of multi-hyphenating, all is welcome here. We don't judge at this cocktail party.

There are so many stories in the industry that go from Point A to Point B, but the gray matter in the middle, the connections, the emails, the meetings, the chance encounters – that's the meat and potatoes that cannot be taught in schools until this book. Along with the practical steps one can take to expand their multi-hyphenate identity, I plan to bring forward some of the most inspiring stories of courage, growth, once-in-a-lifetime opportunities, and moments of individuality that will help artists of any age understand that is never too late to start advocating for yourself and your artistry. While it seems we are in a world bogged down by competition, some people are genuinely interested in the success of others. Multi-hyphenating allows an artist to find those people and build something great together.

I could easily write an article or a blog post about multi-hyphenating, and I have, but the truth is, when it comes to multi-hyphenating, it's so much more than practical motions. Sure, there are many, and they are covered in this book, but the most important are understanding mindset, intention, and accessibility. It's sort of like when a theatre student begins their BFA training – the design major usually has to take an intro to acting class, and the acting major has to take an intro to design class. There are simply prerequisites we all have to understand before setting our art into motion. Once we commit ourselves to this, our art is fuller and more focused.

Once again, please understand that this book is written with the idea that artists come from all different types of environments, privileges, educational settings, and perspectives. For every avenue covered, there are million other ways. The multi-hyphenate journey is personal, and I believe there are a myriad of tools and perspectives to pick and choose from the start. I do not speak on anyone's experience (but my own) when it comes to navigating this industry – all I can do is provide insight, tips, tricks, and ideas to carry with us into this new venture of post-pandemic theatre-making.

Whether we've been putting on puppet shows for our families or daydreaming on the bus or wrapping blankets around ourselves to become characters – we've been putting on skits without permission since many of us can remember – why can't we continue to do that *and* get paid?

There is certainly no one way to find success in show business, but multi-hyphenation allows one to travel on a personal path and make individual decisions. While showbusiness can be incredibly impulsive and things can change at the drop of a hat, multi-hyphenation has proved to be the one aspect of it that promotes stability. Even after years of identifying as a multi-hyphenate, it wasn't until December 2019 that I realized how much agency it allowed me. **Agency** is the self-motivated act of permission an artist uses to protect themselves. Permission is something many artists don't know they have – when, in fact, it's our secret weapon.

Case in point, I had been asked to sing in a Feinstein's/54 Below[14] show and I was on my way to soundcheck; afterward, I would head to therapy a few streets down and then turn back around for the performance. Even in this instance when I was singing *Supercalifragilisticexpialidocious*[15] in a cabaret, I was incredibly grateful to do so. So, very much looking forward, I got off the train and walked toward Feinstein's/54 Below on 54th Street in Manhattan.

Because it was winter, it was about 5:30 p.m., and the sky was already pitch black. Even as a Jew, I happen to love New York City around Christmas time – there was a bounce in my step as I headed to the stage door when a call interrupted Bing Crosby[16] on my Spotify. It's a (212) number, which is the old-school area code of New York. You can no longer get the area code associated with your phone number, so when someone calls with a (212) number, it's usually Broadway or the hospital.

I picked up the phone. It was Idina Menzel's[17] team. Menzel was performing a big Christmas show at Carnegie Hall,[18] and they needed a photographer for the show and the after-party. I stopped dead in my tracks – I had always dreamed of such a phone call. The number of witch hats I bought from Target and bent to make like Susan Hilferty's[19] costume design in *Wicked*[20] is absurd. Wasn't I just in middle school doodling drawings of Elphaba on my notes in class? And now here I am . . . walking in Midtown, and I get a call from her team. Ironically, early that day I had a talk with myself. I promised myself that I would no longer be late to or cancel anything in my schedule the day of or the day before. I understood that I was beginning to develop a reputation in this industry, and I wanted to uphold it and set a good example. No matter what

came, I would stick to my commitment, and I would see it through.

"I'm sorry," I said to Menzel's team. "I'm not available. Thank you, though."

And I hung up. As I rounded the corner to 54 Below, I saw the lights of Broadway and stopped dead in my tracks. What was I doing? I felt my thirteen-year-old self pulling at my shirt saying, "Call them back." So I did.

"I'm so sorry – lapse of judgment," I said. "I'll be there. 7:30."

Remember, it was 5:30 pm. I called the producers of the Feinstein's/54 Below show, who happened to be two dear friends, Jen Sandler[21] and Ben Caplan,[22] and I explained the situation. They knew what this meant to me, what it would do for my career, and graciously let me go. Plus, I offered them a free headshot session to seal the deal. I then called my boyfriend and asked him to lay out a suit, charge my batteries, and pack my bags. I Lyfted up to my apartment, changed, kissed my boyfriend Remy and my puppy Sandwich for luck, threw on my bag, and got right back into the Lyft – heading to Carnegie Hall. In the Lyft, I realized I had just bowed out of a performance opportunity to photograph a show. I had started as a professional child actor and received my higher degree as a performance major – so, by that time, I had been in the industry for 19 years as a performer. I would never have thought I'd have made this decision to forego a performance opportunity and take photos. Looking out the window of my ride, I cracked a smile only Miranda Priestly from *The Devil Wears Prada*[23] would have been proud of.

In my photography studio hangs a photo of Menzel traipsing across the Carnegie Hall stage. It serves a reminder that if I hadn't listened to myself, if I hadn't accessed my truest want within myself, there would not only be a blank space on my wall but a blank space in me. Multi-hyphenating gives us the agency to make decisions and teaches us things about ourselves we didn't know were possible. It's not just a way of approaching art; it's art itself. And it's the most fulfilling, personal art there is.

Structure

How to be a Multi-Hyphenate in the Theatre Business: Conversations, Advice, and Tips from "Dear Multi-Hyphenate" provides exactly that: conversations, advice, and tips from industry professionals who identify as multi-hyphenate, do not identify as multi-hyphenate, cultivate multi-hyphenates, and benefit from other's being multi-hyphenates. *"Dear Multi-Hyphenate"* is the name of my podcast, my workshops, and my overall experiences and creations that revolve around multi-hyphenating. Additionally, every photograph accompanying the book's various parts was taken by me, the author, Michael Kushner, of Michael Kushner Photography. They illustrate many relevant points. While there is never one path for an artist, the structure of the book is meant to guide the artist through a journey of spiritual and tangible checkpoints so they can venture into their multi-hyphenate journey with a more focused framework.

The book is structured with four features:

> **Career Connection.** At the beginning of each chapter, a different career or experience will be featured to help inform the reader of diverse and new job opportunities in the theatre in the 21st century. These *Career Connections* will be tied into the following chapter to further the lesson in focus. Needless to say, the careers and art forms included in this book only cover a fraction of the types of artistic opportunities found in the theatre as there are endless possibilities to create and produce income.
>
> **The Chapter.** Each chapter opens access to an artist at any level who wants to broaden or strengthen their multi-hyphenate identity. While there is no one answer for any artist, the chapters provide tools to apply as well as insight from prominent industry professionals and their experiences.
>
> **Exercise.** Each chapter ends with a unique exercise to help implement the lessons covered. The exercises are meant for the artist to be able to make these lessons personal and applicable to their own multi-hyphenate identity.
>
> **In Conversation With.** To further explore how each chapter's lesson can be incorporated into an artist's

personal life, each chapter is paired with an excerpt from an episode of the podcast *Dear Multi-Hyphenate*, where a prominent industry professional recalls a personal account connected to the chapter's lesson.

Notes

1 www.michaelkushnerphotography.com/
2 www.thecentercs.com/events-tickets/education/next-stop-broadway
3 www.imdb.com/name/nm1470289/
4 www.ithaca.edu/academics/school-humanities-and-sciences/theatre-arts
5 www.ithaca.edu/faculty/chenderson
6 https://jcca.org/
7 www.iheart.com/live/92-wicb-ithaca-college-5244/
8 https://actorsequity.org/
9 https://mtf.nyc/
10 www.dressingroomproject.com/
11 www.nytimes.com/2016/08/09/theater/review-new-york-musical-festival-newtons-cradle.html
12 www.vogue.com/slideshow/broadway-with-love-a-benefit-concert-for-parkland-usa-gallery
13 www.maryjomcconnell.com/
14 https://54below.com/
15 https://en.wikipedia.org/wiki/Supercalifragilisticexpialidocious
16 https://en.wikipedia.org/wiki/Bing_Crosby
17 https://idinamenzel.com/
18 www.carnegiehall.org/
19 www.susanhilferty.com/
20 https://wickedthemusical.com/
21 https://54below.com/artists/jen-sandler/
22 www.bencaplanmusic.com/
23 www.imdb.com/title/tt0458352/

Cynthia Henderson

Introduction
The First Step

DOI: 10.4324/9781003254744-1

The opportunities in the theatre span a wide web of creativity, a balance of ego, point of view, action, and individuality. Over the thousands of years theatre has existed, it boils down to one objective: to tell a story. The ways in which one is able to tell a story have changed drastically and will continue to do so. In the 21st century, an artist has the capability and the responsibility to find their own ways to tell their individual stories. Therefore, there's one thing an artist must carry with them through the 21st century: *chutzpah*.

Despite the effects of COVID-19,[1] to still be invested in a career in the theatre is exactly that . . . chutzpah, a Yiddish term, pronounced ˈKHo͞otspə/, which means 'courage.' To still have dreams – one had to survive a global pandemic, an industry shutdown, Zoom[2] fatigue, unpack, process, and dismantle racist and anti-Semitic rhetoric, witness a Russian and Ukrainian war, the surge of the Omicron and other variants, plus undergo the side effects of both vaccinations and their boosters. To still hold one's head high and continue their journey is simply courageous.

The trick is . . . one must never, *ever* give up in show business. One must always be a voice for the voiceless. One must always defend their past, present, and future. One must always lead with what they know. Without artists, society is mirrorless, unempathetic, and clueless. It's an artist's job to speak from the heart, even when it feels like society has lost their own. Be a warrior.

Feeling overwhelmed? Unsure where to start? In the 21st century, theatre artistry is all about an individualistic point of view. It's about figuring out the ways to tell a story without relying on anyone else for permission.

If one is looking at an iceberg, one may not know that all they see is ⅛ of the iceberg above the water while ⅞ of the iceberg remains below; therefore, this mammoth structure is being propped up by huge support. How is it formed? How does it stay afloat? How do we prevent it from melting? The theatre is that iceberg.

By understanding how theatre in the 21st century is formed, how it stays afloat, and how to keep it from melting, one must have access. Today, **accessibility** is the act of creating lucrative and equitable opportunities for collaboration, opening up space for decentered or marginalized folks, and forming outreach. No more 'boys club.' No more paying one's way to the top. No more 'it's about who you know.' No more waiting for permission.

In the pandemic, the world experienced a massive identity crisis. Millions of people's jobs and lives were lost, a cultural war occurred between vaccinated people and anti-vaxxers, and the unpacking of systemic racism caused many to reflect on their own privilege. While systemic racism is an epidemic in the United States, the theatre business is not removed from that equation. The theatre is thought to be an inclusive, equitable space held for all who come through its stage door, and while many inhabitants of the community are forward thinkers, it is still an enterprise that profits off White supremacy, anti-Semitism, and the exploitation of people of color as well as members of the LGBTQIA+ community.

When it's put into perspective, theatre artists lost their livelihood during the pandemic and were deeply affected. The theatre is a billion-dollar enterprise affecting everyone from designers to actors to Lyft drivers to videographers. According to statista.com,[3] in the 2018/2019 season alone, the season *just* before the pandemic, the total revenue raked in by Broadway musicals and plays came out to be $1.83 billion (statista.com).

While the theatre industry rakes in almost $2 billion in one year, many theatre artists couldn't pay their rent and felt abandoned, unsafe, and scared.

An extremely unfortunate experience, it forced many people to look inward and reexamine their relationship to show business. For the first time, many artists in the theatre around the world collectively asked themselves, "Why?"

Why Do I Do What I Do?

Asking oneself a question like this is the first step in not only creating accessibility to oneself but also for others. With the pandemic taking away job security, artistic expression, and community – it is up to the artist to find it within themselves to rebuild and begin their next chapter. Collectively as a society, we will feel the aftereffects of the pandemic for years to come. Why not take the steps to begin to strengthen one's artistry and become resilient?

A question like "Why?" can be a terrifying experience. *Why?* Looking at someone who has committed their whole life to a specific job, suddenly they are asked *why* they do what they do and they cannot answer the question. It's just been that way forever; waking up at 6 a.m., filling up the gas tank and stopping at Dunkin' Donuts, showing up for work, taking their lunch break, heading home at 5 p.m.– rinse, lather, and repeat. Is there even time to stop and take stock?

There's certainly nothing wrong with that if it is fulfilling and brings joy. But if one is unaware of their unhappiness and is suddenly made conscious of their eagerness for a more productive and fulfilling life, it then spurs a snowball effect of self-discovery. They then begin to understand that they have not been engaged in their work for quite some time, and they have been skimming the surface of their own possibilities. Many begin to make out-of-character decisions and commit to grand decisions, possibly to overcompensate. Maybe *that's* why dad bought the Porsche.

According to a world poll conducted by *Gallup*,[4] "Only 15% of the world's one billion full-time workers are engaged at work. It is significantly better in the U.S., at around 30% engaged, but this still means that roughly 70% of American workers aren't engaged" (news.gallup.com Clifton, 2017).

That's a lot of people to be disengaged most of their day. What keeps someone in an unhappy workplace? Is it comfort keeping them at bay? Pay? Convenience? Fear? Whatever the reason, stagnant day-to-day activity is not few and far between; it's an epidemic. Seems foreboding, right? So, how can the terrifying question of *Why* be turned into something liberating?

The first step to finding accessibility from within is when the adverb *Why* becomes the noun *Why*. It's not flashy, it's not pretty, but it is important and will help one understand the power and the purpose a Why serves.

Cynthia Henderson,[5] author of *The Actor's Landscape*[6] and Ithaca College's first black tenured and full professor, focuses her acting training teachings on a character's motivation, or what she calls "The Why of it All." Henderson's perspective comes from the actor breathing life into a character, but the principle is applicable to any human being.

"You should be able to explain what you do, why you do it, how you do it – the 'Why' of it all – without a lot of jargon," Henderson says on Episode 11, "The Why of it All," of *Dear Multi-Hyphenate*.[7]

> Why do we do what we do? Acting is an exploration of the human condition. That's what it is. It's not about being someone you're not. It's actually delving deeply into the essence of who you are as a human being and expanding on that as if you're in this particular situation. But you also have to take into account everything the author gives you. You have to be a detective, find out why this person does what they do, and explore their humanity.

A person's Why doesn't just have to be kept to the stage and only used by actors. Yet, whether or not one calls it a goal, objective, or intention – the Why is meant to put someone's needs and wants front and center.

The Why is usually a sentence expressing a goal. In acting, the Why can be boiled down to what Konstantin Stanislavski[8] calls the character's Super Objective. The Super Objective is simply what the character wants throughout the story. *I want to achieve world peace. I want to rescue my family from poverty. I want to become a world-renowned writer.* All these statements are from the eyes of the character defining what they want out of life. Sometimes, the playwright maps it out clearly, and other times, the actor needs to fill in the blanks.

"I think about 'Why' a lot because obviously it changes in some ways every day, and some days it doesn't," says Tony-nominated director Leigh Silverman[9] (*Violet*,[10] *From Up Here*[11]).

> It's the only place I can be myself. I direct to try to understand the world in a different way. I look to theatre makers to hold up a mirror to myself and society, and it's been the place for me that has been the most hope, optimism, resolution.

Similar to any boat or building or medical discovery or coalition – art should have a strong foundation below, just like the iceberg. And that's exactly what a Why is. It's a foundation that strengthens an artist's point of view, in turn helping decision-making, commitment, and communication.

After opening Jane Wagner's[12] *The Search for Signs of Intelligent Life in the Universe* at The Shed[13] starring *Saturday Night Live*'s Cecily Strong,[14] Silverman continued the conversation of the importance of 'Why' on Episode 57 of *Dear Multi-Hyphenate*: "Leigh Silverman: What is Essential?"[15]

"You know," says Silverman,

> It's one of the things that has been most challenging about COVID, right, is that those things that we expected and wanted and thought would always be there from the theatre are not. It is, I think in the funhouse of this time, a very, very hard thing to feel like the job that you do and the way that you do it, and the life that you've chose[n] as your north star is not there . . . and not only a thing you always felt was essential, but you really start to understand the word essential and you understand it differently and you understand it doesn't include you.

Pulling the Why out of the theatre, how can one apply their Why to their personal lives? The best place to start would be establishing a **Why statement**. This one, very concise sentence can be personal, raw, and ugly – yet is rooted in promoting fierce decision-making and proactive thinking.

The cleaner the Why, the more effective it is.

When beginning, it's important to remember this work is merely a simple extension of an artist's essence. There is nothing egotistical about it because it's used to find a wider, more specific audience, yet the first step seems contradictory. To begin, one must talk about themselves. Seems simple enough, yes? As "me–me–me" as American culture is, sharing with a purpose has not yet been embraced fully.

When prompted to speak about themselves, an artist can easily go into *look-at-these-things-around-me* land, which distracts from having a genuine conversation about the topic at hand: themselves. In this context, talking about oneself is not about their pet, or their awards, it's about how these things make them feel and *why*. We may learn that they are collectors of stamps and that they have fun with friends, but how does it make them feel? What are their opinions on the matter? What are the interests, points of view, and aspects of one's life that, when tied together, inform a unique and deeply personal artistry?

These efforts are simply about finding the basic, core intentions of an artist. Diamonds are created by carbon atoms being subjected to high volumes of pressure and heat. Finding the Why isn't any different. In elementary school, students will learn that the key elements that make up basic information gathering is asking who, what, where, when, how, and why. In this instance, asking **who, what, where, when, and how** will *unleash* the Why.

Here's an example of a Why statement. What are all the parts that make up this sentence?

What. 'What' describes the characteristics of the Why statement. It can be a word, a phrase, or a sentiment that glues together the idea. For instance, in Figure Intro.2, "non-quotidian artistry" is our "what." Non-quotidian art, or non-traditional art, seems to be the driving force of this artist's Why. Off-the-beaten-path, individualistic art is what so many seek out, ways to make a stamp on this world by creating

something new and adventurous. It seems as though this artist would want to only commit themselves to projects that are groundbreaking or foraging new paths.

Fabulous – a driving force has been established, non-quotidian artistry. But if one is following the steps of basic information gathering, that's only one element discovered. If 'non-quotidian artistry' is the "what," there's still "who," "where," "when," and "how" to explore.

Who. 'Who' is the audience one is trying to reach. By looking at the earlier Why statement, it's clear that the who is "a global environment" because that's the audience this person wants to affect. By understanding this wide perspective this artist wants to reach, they are able to make decisions that might be about the larger scale. Reviewing this artist's Why statement, folks could deduce that they might not treat theatre as a hobby or in a smaller town engaging in theatre for young audiences. If they had a passion in TYA (Theatre for Young Audiences) they might have a Why statement that reads, "I produce non-quotidian artistry that benefits a younger audience."

Where. 'Where' is not the location the artist is trying to affect, but the medium in which the art is produced. Are they specifically a theatre artist? Are they specifically in arts administration? Do they place themselves in different mediums? The more specific, the better. This artist mentions that they spend their time creating in the scope of "theatre and film artistry."

When. 'When' helps an artist decipher how immediate their actions are. Take for instance, the development of a project. Musical Theatre Factory,[16] which is committed to dismantling oppressive ideologies toward collective liberation and centering artists of excellence who exist in the intersections of underrepresented groups, develops change-making new musicals in a joyous, collaborative community free from commercial constraints. Its 'when' is *now* and *immediate*.

"To me, it's thinking about the world we live in," says Mei Ann Teo,[17] former artistic director of the Musical Theatre Factory in New York City. As a producer, Teo participates in multiple facets in the growth of a theatrical piece. On top of once being an artistic director of an organization that doesn't produce yet moves towards production – Teo is someone who independently produces and is involved with advocating for production.

"And not in a reactive way," they continue.

> But in a responsive way. And it also is about the deep understanding of the zeitgeist of the moment, and

I produce current, non-quotidian theatre and film artistry that benefits a global environment.

Figure Intro.2 Example of Why Statement. Michael Kushner Photography

the zeitgeist of this time in history. And what is most important to actually heal right now. To me, it's about understanding context. There are so many incredible stories that need to be told, and there's so much need for those stories to be told. It's not like there are too many stories – *my God* – we need so much more medicine. I think about how lives are saved.

How. 'How' is the call to action. How is what makes the Why statement active. When looking at the example artists' Why statement, the how seems to be 'benefits.' Benefiting a global environment, as the artist says, seems to deliver a positive, proactive sense of artistry – one that tries to evoke change and forward thinking. Perhaps this artist connects nonprofits and charities to the work they create.

Kaisha Huguley[18] started her career working in the U.S. Department of State in Washington, D.C. Shortly after her wedding day, Huguley and her husband found themselves moving to New York. For Huguley, her Why focuses on dismantling the archaic idea of the starving artist. She ignites her 'how' by inspiring thousands by documenting her artistic journey on social media, as well as a faculty member and the director of Diversity & Cultural Creative Initiatives in the Office of Equity, Diversity, & Inclusion at AMDA.[19]

> My 'Why' statement is 'no artist should have to starve,' says Huguley. 'I think the starving artist narrative is absolute trash. I don't think any artist should have to starve and compromise a meal in order to do what they love. Artists need to eat too. We literally would not be able to survive doing the rigors of our work if we are not nourished; nourished in every sense – financially, nutritionally, all the things! I really just want every artist to have every possible resource to them so they can have the most successful career they can possibly have. Other fields are compensated well for what they do – why should a creative be any different?

Shakina Nayfack,[20] who made history starring in NBC's *Connecting*[21] as the first transgender person to be cast as a series regular in a network sitcom, is no stranger to building theatrical experiences and garnering an audience to view them. She is the founding artistic director of Musical Theatre Factory, where she helped develop hundreds of new musicals, including Michael R. Jackson's[22] Pulitzer Prize–winning *A Strange Loop*[23] and her own autobiographical glam-rock odyssey, *Manifest Pussy*.[24]

> I revisit my 'Why' from time to time because I think it helps to recalibrate and reframe it and put it in language that even if it's thematically consistent, feels fresh and relevant to whatever it is that you're doing,

says Nayfack. "But I think my 'Why' is pretty consistently embedded in making the world a better place through a sharing of the heart that liberates me and others from oppression."

As an example of just one of Nayfack's incredible artistic efforts, in April 2022, Nayfack organized a performance in Times Square where members of the Broadway community came together to lend their voices of support to Ukraine by performing a moving musical vigil and sang "Do You Hear the People Sing?"[25] from Boublil and Schönberg's *Les Misérables*.[26]

As much as discovering one's Why can be terrifying, most importantly it's *liberating* – and both cerebral *and* spiritual artists can use one. That being said, it doesn't matter how long it takes one to find a working Why statement – usually just as a Why statement is established, it can change.

"It's okay that the 'Why' changes because people evolve," Henderson says.

> What's something you used to hate but now you like? If your "Why" no longer works for you, there is nothing wrong with your process – you just have to have room to evolve as you discover who this person is.

Life happens – and these moments change an artist daily. As one grows and experiences new perspectives, relationships ebb and flow – so, too, do the stories that one is interested in telling. A Why statement one established in college may not suit someone as they turn 30. There may be similarities, but the audiences and/or type of art one produces might change. Why statements simply grow and fluctuate as a human being does.

It doesn't matter what type of artistry a human being engages in – understanding why an artist is doing something will never go out of style. By committing oneself to this understanding, it allows for agency. An artist can decide to do what they like – show up for the auditions only they want to, produce the projects that befit them, or write the plays that interest them. They no longer have to rely on anyone else to guide them and anything else that doesn't align with their Why can be disregarded. Why commit oneself to art that doesn't feel connected? It's only when one begins to act on this agency can they begin to tap into the complex, yet free artistry of the multi-hyphenate.

EPISODE EXCERPT

CYNTHIA HENDERSON

Professor at Ithaca College, Fulbright Scholar, actor, producer, director, writer, and founder and artistic director of Performing Arts for Social Change

THE WHY OF IT ALL (A MASTERCLASS IN ACTING) • **EPISODE 11**

Cynthia: We make specific choices every single day, but for some reason the minute you get a script, life becomes non specific and therefore not engaging.

Michael: I also experience that as photographer. I get that with actors that come in the space and one word that literally makes me twitch is the word "quirky"... when an actor describes themselves as "quirky". And I go, "What makes you quirky?"

Cynthia: Get specific.

Michael: Get specific. I'm asking you all these questions about who's careers do you want to steal? What stories do you want to tell? What is being produced right now that you see yourself going into? I want all these specific stories because then I'm going to match that. Because that's what a headshot is... 99.9% of the time your headshot is not going to get you the job, but it will get you in the room.

Cynthia: Because it is the first thing they see.

Michael: Yes. It's the first experience to you. That's why I say, "Ere on the side of positivity" because you don't want a casting director's first experience with you to be a photo of you being all negative.

Cynthia: Exactly. And let's talk about negative choices in acting. Because again, you make a negative choice... but I would tell people your Super Objective doesn't have to be rational... you could want the Earth to open up and swallow that person whole, but why? There is a proactive, there is a positive behind that because you don't want them to hurt someone else like they've hurt you. Because you want them to be a better version of themselves because you want them to face what they have done... so behind that negative, there must always be a positive proactive intent. I just saw Jagged Little Pill last night and I was screaming ... it's my favorite break up album. I love that album so much. Every break up I've had in my life, I have put that CD on and I'm driving down the road crying... but the character Jo sings You Oughta Know and the audience is screaming by the end because that actor (Lauren Patton) has made a very specific proactive choice... yes, eat crap and die because you broke my heart -- but I need you to know what you did because underneath it all, as angry as I am, I still love you.

Notes

1 www.cdc.gov/coronavirus/2019-ncov/index.html
2 https://zoom.us/
3 www.statista.com/statistics/193006/broadway-shows-gross-revenue-since-2006/
4 https://news.gallup.com/opinion/chairman/212045/world-broken-workplace.aspx
5 www.ithaca.edu/faculty/chenderson
6 https://books.google.com/books/about/The_Actor_s_Landscape.html?id=LAgFQgAACAAJ
7 https://broadwaypodcastnetwork.com/dear-multi-hyphenate/11-cynthia-henderson-the-why-of-it-all-or-a-masterclass-in-acting/
8 https://en.wikipedia.org/wiki/Konstantin_Stanislavski
9 https://en.wikipedia.org/wiki/Leigh_Silverman
10 www.ibdb.com/broadway-production/violet-495831
11 www.manhattantheatreclub.com/shows/2007-08-season/from-up-here/
12 www.lilytomlin.com/jane-wagner/
13 https://theshed.org/program/226-the-search-for-signs-of-intelligent-life-in-the-universe
14 www.imdb.com/name/nm5198446/
15 https://podcasts.apple.com/us/podcast/leigh-silverman-what-is-essential/id1432770164?i=1000548193442
16 www.mtf.nyc
17 www.meiannteo.com/
18 www.kaishahuguley.com/
19 www.amda.edu/
20 www.shakina.nyc
21 www.nbc.com/connecting
22 www.thelivingmichaeljackson.com/
23 www.playwrightshorizons.org/shows/plays/strange-loop/
24 www.shakina.nyc/manifest-pussy
25 www.cbsnews.com/newyork/news/broadway-stars-show-solidarity-with-ukraine-in-times-square-performance/
26 www.lesmis.com/

Reference List

1. Published by Statista Research Department, and Mar 2. "Gross Revenue of New York Broadway SHOWS 2006–2019." *Statista*, 2 Mar. 2021, www.statista.com/statistics/193006/broadway-shows-gross-revenue-since-2006/.
2. Clifton, Jim. "The World's Broken Workplace." *Gallup.com*, Gallup, 22 May 2021, news.gallup.com/opinion/chairman/212045/world-broken-workplace.aspx.

EXERCISE 1 DM-H

THE PRESSURE COOKER

Start to look past the comfortable and into the foreign. Dig deep into the depths of your soul and brain and answer this question. Pay attention to the hints you are given from yourself. Who you socialize with, what you eat, organizations you donate to . . . these are all clues to finding the common denominator that ties in all your artistic efforts.

This is a fun game called **THE PRESSURE COOKER**.

The rules are simple.

1. Have a partner set a timer for 2 minutes.
2. Now begin to stream-of-consciously talk about yourself.
3. After the 2 minutes, reset the timer for 2 minutes again.
4. Have your partner repeat what they heard you say.
5. Pay attention to the who, what, where, when, and how. What sticks out? What seemed emotional? What information wasn't relevant?
6. Then, have the partner set the timer for 1 minute.
7. Repeat your stream-of-consciously speaking.
8. The partner should begin to investigate. If they feel so inclined, while you are speaking, they can ask, "Why do you feel this way?" or "Why is that important to you?"
9. Begin to add emotion. Talk about why you've said these things. If your partner asks a question, follow it up with, "I think I feel this way because . . ."
10. Repeat steps 1 through 8 decreasing the time to 30 seconds, then 15 seconds, then 5 seconds.
11. What you say in 5 seconds should reflect your first glimmer into your Why. Are you able to put this thought into one cohesive sentence that answers the who, what, where, when, and how?

In doing this exercise, don't judge yourself. Be prepared for honest emotion, total confusion, and a journey to a path you didn't expect. Marinate as to what it means. Is there a word you said that is eye-opening? Is the sentence empowering? Or is it self-deprecating? Again, don't judge – *and let it sit*.

Keep an open mind and heart. It may be scary and totally opposite to how you've been approaching art or work. That's okay – now you can begin to add this to how you search for projects, work, schools, and so on.

Once you marinate on what you discovered in this exercise, try to put it in a sentence that you can use when someone asks you to tell them about yourself. This question is found in auditions, college auditions, press interviews, job interviews, and more. It's an important question to answer and you have to answer it the right way.

Here are a few examples as to what your "Why statement" can look like:

"I am an artist who includes ____ and ____ by looking for ____."

"I produce ____ artistry that ____."

"I am a ____ who applies ____ by ____."

A reminder, this is an ever-evolving sentence that changes based on life experiences and growth! Revisit it from time to time. Have fun with it, get creative, and get empowered!

PART I
PREPARATION

"The chips fall where they may. The work speaks for itself."
PennyWild, Episode 41, "An Artist's Guilt"

"a completely non-
moralistic assessment
of existence. Of being
in touch of something
that you want and
need, that is gentle
and comforting, and
kind and
compassionate to
yourself and to others–
and just going with it
and not judging it as
something worthy or
unworthy or productive
or unproductive."

Alexandra Silber

Chapter 1
What is a Multi-Hyphenate?

DOI: 10.4324/9781003254744-3

Ashley Kate Adams, founder of AKA Studio Productions

Career Connection

The Producers

The Producers

Who are **producers**? The answer is simple: anyone can become a producer. In terms of producing, it's up to the individual artist to decide their level of commitment and what space they want to work in. The overall purpose is to find a way to bring an artistic endeavor from the page to the stage. Or the page to the screen. The producer is then responsible to grow the piece from an idea to a three-dimensional entity. The theatrical experience can be crafted by a table read, a casual event where friends get together to read a play or musical aloud. Or it can be crafted by a workshop or 29 Hour reading,[1] which requires more structure.

A '**reading**' is a paired-down theatrical experience where a writer, and usually a producer, shares their piece so they can get a better understanding of what they've created. Sometimes it's the whole play or musical, sometimes it's one-act, and sometimes just the book or songs and lyrics. Workshops usually are more thorough presentations of a musical, even including choreography and staging. The process is long, convoluted, and a tangled ball of networking and netweaving steps involving money, which ultimately artists learn to love or hate. Either way, when one is taking it upon themselves to bring forward art, one is producing. Even if an artist doesn't wish to become a producer, they still will be engaging with them – so it's best to understand who they are and what they do. A producer is like a CEO, or the chairperson of the board, or the president of any company.

Ken Davenport[2] of Davenport Theatrical Enterprises is responsible for Broadway productions such as the Tony Award–winning *Once on This Island*,[3] *Gettin' the Band Back Together*,[4] *Deaf West's Spring Awakening*,[5] *It's Only a Play*,[6] *Kinky Boots* (Tony Award),[7] and *The Play That Goes Wrong*, among others. "Producers do the same thing as any head of a business," Davenport says.

> We find a product – that product is a play or a musical – we develop that product, we launch that product, we advertise the product, we market that product, we fix it when it's broken, and hopefully that business moves on to big success. My quick answer lately is that a producer's job is to get people in a room. I get writers and directors with an idea and let them go. I'm constantly pulling people in like putting puppies into a box – just getting them in the room at the same time so they can create something wonderful.

The producer is responsible for any number of these responsibilities:

- Producers hire and maintain a creative team, just as Ken Davenport said.
  - A **creative team** is a group of people that make up the artistic decisions of the vehicle. In the team, one would find a director, designers, choreographer, musical director, stage manager, casting director, and any other creative decision-makers.
- They bear the financial weight of the show.
  - While producers don't normally put in money into the shows themselves, it's their responsibility to raise the capital required to sustain the show.
  - Producers reach out to their band of family, friends, and/or business partners for financial involvement in a show. The person one would reach out to is known as an investor.
  - Once the show opens, the goal is to sell as many tickets as possible to sustain the show and begin to pay back investors. Once a show has made enough ticketing revenue to fully pay back its investors, the show will have reached "recoupment," or the moment at which investors are now made whole and the show can go into profit, which is split between investors and producers.
- Producers maintain the overall experience of the show.
  - Understanding and developing a strategy to market, promote, and advertise the show are critical to keeping a show afloat.
- They sustain the overall experience of the show.
  - Understanding how to market the show is critical to keeping a show afloat.

While the producer has one goal, and that's to open and sustain a show, they find a group of people who make up a team focused on cultivating a show. In a producing team, one would find the following:

- Lead producers (in the industry, we all call them "general partners")
  - The decision-makers who are fiscally responsible for the show
  - May also invest their own money or raise it from others
  - Typically between 1 and 4 people on the show
  - Notable names: Hal Prince,[8] Mel Brooks,[9] Daryl Roth,[10] Ken Davenport, David Merrick,[11] Kevin McCollum,[12]

Dori Berinstein,[13] and Cameron Mackintosh,[14] to name a few

- Coproducer
  - Agrees to help the lead producer raise money in exchange for "perks"
  - Some of those perks include billing (making them award eligible) and a financial kicker if the show reaches recoupment.
  - The lead producer will decide the threshold for a coproducer, but typically they will help to raise somewhere between $250,000 to $1 million.
  - Little to no creative involvement in the production.
- Investor.
  - Invests money in the show through either a lead producer or coproducer
  - Investment units are typically $25,000 to $50,000 (think of them as shares in a company)
  - Does not have to be a person involved in the theatre.
  - Provides an educational experience for those who may want to begin producing.
  - No creative involvement
  - Usually invited to final dress rehearsal and opening night. Producers want investors to feel special and included as a part of making the show happen!

As Davenport says, it's about getting people in the room, so they create something wonderful. Producers are active in finding the right place and right time for a story. They do so by scouring the industry for new stories and new talent regularly. Producers can be found at readings and performances or easily accessible through their social media presence. Just as producers are responsible for creating wonderful art, they are also responsible for building teams of other producers to help achieve the common goal.

Adam Hyndman[15] is an actor and producer on Broadway, having been in *Aladdin*,[16] *Once on the Island*, and *Hadestown*[17] and on the producing team for *The Inheritance*,[18] earning him a Tony nomination. He also serves on the board of directors for both Pipeline Theatre Company[19] and Broadway For Racial Justice.[20] In addition, he is a co-founder of The Industry Standard Group[21] (a community fund designed for BIPOC folx to invest and produce in a commercial theater). As a producer, Hyndman has found an artistic home by taking initiative and making himself aware of producing teams that charged him, like Octopus Theatricals,[22] who is responsible for *Hadestown* on Broadway.

> Mara Isaacs's[23] independent producing office, Octopus Theatricals, was on my sights for a while before I started working there because it is such an example and precedent for producers supporting and incubating diverse and daring work in bespoke and nimble ways (in and out of different genres, as well as in and out of commercial and non-profit sectors). I came into the fold at Octopus in a perfect moment of synergy when I was active in pursuing freelance opportunities to produce, and Mara Isaacs was looking to expand on a few projects and bring in support for her bandwidth. What is remarkable about her practice (of both producing and mentoring) is that she empowers folks with radical trust. In my first project under her, I was given such runway that allowed me to bring all my skills. Her trust has continued to be profound because her non-traditional and non-hierarchical structure of facilitation affirms and makes space for me to be a multi-hyphenate in so many areas and not have to pick my allegiance. The partnership has continued to grow and develop in exciting ways.

Hyndman found himself working in an environment based on trust, a rare and refreshing experience, and in a space that allowed him explore his many talents. He was then able to continue his work as a producer authentically, building on relationships and in search of creating art that has impact, a useful tool when reaching out to investors . . . and something he does not take lightly.

"As a producer there is a great deal of importance on investor relationships," continues Hyndman.

> My philosophy in building authentic connections and experiences with my network of supporters is actually grounded in my philosophy of producing as a whole. I endeavor to build community by sharing the belief I have in the arts; that these genres hold potential for real impact, and that they can be structured with mission and purpose for the field and within society. Even though I work in the world of commercial theatre, I treat our craft and the narratives we share as public goods. In that the value and influence of our work can, and should, have reverberating potential to touch, move, inspire, reflect, or challenge our collective zeitgeist forward. In a way, you can think about my philosophy of connecting to investors much like how you build support around a political or social justice movement. As a producer, I am a representative of a collective that stands for something that is larger than the self, and investing in one of my projects is the opportunity to support something that is mission

aligned or creates a future vision of the world one hopes to see.

E. Clayton Cornelius[24] experienced his first venture into producing with the Broadway play *Chicken and Biscuits*,[25] written by Douglas Lyons and produced on Broadway after the shutdown.[26] As the world took a blow financially and many individuals are beginning to rebuild themselves, Cornelius has found finding investors to be trickier but not impossible. Still, Cornelius reinforces that the producer–investor relationship is a special bond. "It's definitely been a challenge to find investors willing to financially give post-pandemic," says Cornelius. "Relationships are your most valuable resource when it comes to any type of fundraising. People want to invest in *you* and the success or the positivity you bring to the table." If there's any way to look at producing, no matter what level, Ashley Kate Adams,[27] who graced Broadway audiences in the 2010 revival of *La Cage Aux Folles*[28] does it wholeheartedly and efficiently. Adams is the creator of AKA Studio Productions[29] and recently released a book dedicated to producing that is entitled *#BYOP: Be Your Own Producer*.[30] Adams summarizes producing as an opportunity to tell a story.

"We all have our own individual stories and we are qualified to be the ones to tell them," says Adams.

Our stories are valid and we are qualified to speak with our experience. I think because we aren't always aware of "how things get made" we sometimes think that we don't have the true experience to execute a project or idea in our own way. But I am here to encourage you that if you take action, your greatest dreams *and projects* truly can move forward and come true.

Although Adams has performed on Broadway, Adams chooses to produce in other mediums that fit her best, like films and record production; therefore she can commit to projects that feel manageable to her and reflective of her artistic perspective. One does not have to produce on Broadway or in Hollywood to find success as a producer. Adams seemed to find her Goldilocks in terms of producing – projects that feel *just right*.

There is no rhyme or reason for when a show goes to Broadway and when or when a web series gets greenlit to be produced or when an album of one's music is produced. Yet, with a producer mentality and skillset – an artist does not have to wait on anyone else for permission. Through technology, accessibility, and a point of view – artists are choosing to wait less and less for their next job, producing it themselves. Not only are artists taking it upon themselves to create work opportunities, but they are establishing environments that promote **advocacy** and safety.

After the COVID-19 pandemic, many theater industry artists are becoming aware that shows cannot be produced in the ways they had been, rooted in the systemic racism ingrained in the fabric of American society. Douglas Lyons, who has appeared on Broadway in *Beautiful: The Carole King Musical*[31] and *The Book of Mormon*,[32] returned to Broadway as a writer with his new play *Chicken and Biscuits*, which was one of the first productions to reopen post-shutdown on October 10, 2021. He is hopeful that changes will occur in a post-pandemic Broadway. Lyons points out the progress being made while keeping his reservations by looking at the situation from a producorial point of view.

"I think I understand business," Lyons says.

So, if any of these shows are extremely successful, the other White theatre owners will want the next thing. That's just how it works. I can't speak to the future of the culture because I think that is a huge question mark . . . but I will say, coming back after the year of George Floyd[33] and this pandemic, I think there is an overwhelming sense of intolerance for racism in these spaces. Even if all these shows are not written by folks of color, non-binary, and trans folks, I think the culture itself will always be sensitive to this new movement; and that I think is a win for all.

Multi-hyphenate: an artist who has multiple proficiencies that cross-pollinate to help flourish professional capabilities

The goal of auditioning, taking meetings, and writing a new show, for example, is to get a "gig." But eventually, that gig ends. So, what's next? What happens in between the gigs? But, what could happen if one eliminated the space between gigs, and solely by creating art – could establish a steady income? Before one begins to explore this, it's imperative to understand the types of jobs an artist can experience outside of booking their Broadway show, writing their next musical, or producing a web series. Aside from a gig, an artist might experience a survival job, a side gig, and eventually a multi-hyphenated artistry.

Survival Jobs/For Now Jobs

Mary Testa[34] is a Tony-nominated legend in the Broadway community. Her credits include, but are not limited to, the 2019 revival of *Oklahoma!*[35] *Xanadu*,[36] and *She Loves Me*,[37] as well as *Eat, Pray, Love*,[38] and *Sex and the City*.[39]

I quit college after my first semester junior year and worked three jobs in Rhode Island. I was a hotel chambermaid from 7 a.m. until 1 p.m., waitress from 4 p.m. on, and teacher at the arts council on the weekends. Then I moved to New York City in 1976,

says Testa. "Because I had saved $1000, I gave myself 6 months without working to get used to the city." Oftentimes, when a young artist has dreams of show business, they are met with a relative or two who might share discouraging points of views such as

"Get used to waiting tables!"
"That's not a real career!"
"So, we have a starving artist in the family!"

While these sentiments are more than likely coming from a place of fear, or even jealousy, the 'starving artist' doesn't necessarily look like what they used to. In some folk's minds, the starving artist is barely making rent, probably dressed in black, chain-smoking down in the East Village of Manhattan, brooding about life and engaging in overtly existential thoughts. While that *can* be true, sometimes it's a future Tony

Figure 1.4 Mary Testa. Michael Kushner Photography

nominee working as a hotel chambermaid to fulfill a lifelong dream.

"After I did William Finn's[40] *In Trousers*,[41] I was lucky and received my Equity card doing *The Rose Tattoo*[42] at Long Wharf Theatre,[43]" continues Testa,

> I was working a lunch shift at the U.S. Steakhouse when I booked a revue, which were big back then, and the misogynistic owners hated me and wouldn't give me leave to do the show. A friend said, "[Y]ou didn't come here to be a waitress, you came here to be an actress." So I quit and I haven't needed that job since.

The stereotype of the starving artist certainly did exist and still does. The *Just Kids*[44] type of struggle was real, and although it seemed very unattractive to some, others coveted it. The pilgrimage to New York City, the survival, the search for love, for art – it only stimulated a growth of incoming young artists. And with television, YouTube, film, and theatre glorifying the New York experience, it prompted even more young artists to find their Manhattan story – stories like *Pose*,[45] *Friends*,[46] *Rent*,[47] and *Sex and the City*. Each experience is vastly different, but there is one common denominator: New York City.

According to the U.S. Census[48] released on August 12, 2021, New York City's population grew by more than 600,000 people in the past decade (census.gov). While that is a large number of people, for many, moving to a city like New York, becomes about survival. Moving to a prominent place like New York, Los Angeles, or London requires figuring out access to resources, paying dues, setting aside pride, and figuring out how to live simply. So, without something like a *survival job*, how long do these pilgrimages to New York City last? According to the U.S. Census Bureau, 216,000 people moved *from* the New York metro area in 2020 – a year where because of a global pandemic, these resources had vanished.

The old saying goes "The audition is the job, and booking the gig is the raise." This idea applies to many artists; just switch the audition for the internship, the meeting, or the interview. A **survival job** helps artists provide for themselves while committing themselves to an art form that might lack steady income. The survival job provides an income so that the artist can pay rent, buy food, and engage in any of the fundamental steps that allow for a healthy day-to-day life. While survival jobs can be tedious, society is progressing, and the advancements of social media and virtual engagement are lending less rigidity, promoting time flexibility, and allowing more creativity.

Why is there such a negative connotation with the survival job? Having a survival job insinuates failure. Yet surviving and staying afloat is *not* negative; it's brave. Perhaps one could find a little more creative freedom in their survival job if there wasn't shame attached to having one; it starts with how such a job is perceived. Why is "survival" only connected to art? Why is there no negative connotation to starting in a corporate setting, but artists are looked down upon when following a dream? Colleen Cook[49] served as vice president at JP Morgan Chase[50] in the Interest Rate Derivatives group from 1992 to 2006. She attributes the negative connotation of survival in the arts to the unstable flow of finances.

"I think the main difference between a starving artist and a lower corporate level job is that the corporate job is a livable wage and consistent," Cook says.

It is not gig work so even if the income is not enormous it is *steady*. You do not have to worry about booking the next gig to pay your bills each month. The ladder in the corporate world is much more reliable. If you come to work each day and perform, you will normally have your job for years to come with a career path for growth within that company. You are not looking for a new job and new ways to pay the bills after each show/project like young artists have to do.

What if the term *survival job* is switched into something a little more positive . . . like *for-now job*? Doing so relieves one of the stresses of the word *survival*. Yet, even the choice of a survival job, or **for-now job**, directly correlates to accessibility and privilege, as many artist-friendly jobs are found by being 'in the know.' Great for-now jobs can be private tutoring and personal assisting – but those high-paying and flexible jobs mostly come through some connection.

There are many ways one can find a for-now jobs – such as through a family member, a skill honed from a hometown job, answering a job posting, or a temp agency, for example. It shouldn't matter the type of job one takes to ensure they can follow their dreams – isn't everyone collectively surviving, especially after a global pandemic? If a young person with the dream of being an executive director of a company is making their way up the corporate ladder, the word *survival* is *not* attached to their identity. If there wasn't so much weight or heaviness attached to the word, might this allow someone to find these momentary jobs with more joy? It's almost as if the word *survival* is a constant reminder that an artist may be struggling.

Waiting tables is the typical stereotype of the starving artist. While, yes, many artists wait tables, it doesn't mean they are unhappy – or *starving*. On the contrary, waiting tables require great skills, and many find joy in waiting tables during the interim moments between gigs. But if one can open up their mind to finding something else, something that includes their artistic discipline – would they? For-now jobs have the potential to become a total part of one's identity but should remain at a distance where an artist can completely pull the plug at a moment's notice. They should sustain an income and, hopefully, a healthy working environment. Still, if the artist must leave at a moment's notice to work on Broadway or go on a national tour, the company would usually exist at full steam without blinking an eye. Some For Now Jobs include food service, retail, real estate, and personal assisting, just to name a few.

Yet, what if one's relationship with their for-now job is changing? How can one tell if they have found themselves in a position where their for-now job no longer seems like it's only for now and may want to begin to separate themselves? On the flip side, what if they are having a positive experience and want to continue to grow in that company? What are some things to keep in check?

- The job may be energy draining or cause discomfort or unhappiness.
- The job may take up all the time in their schedule, not leaving time to be in the studio, take creative meetings, write their play, or audition for shows.
- It's becoming a part of a person's identity in an overwhelming way.
- The stakes have elevated if the company was to lose the employee.
- Positively, the artist is finding joy in exploring their relationship to the job.
- Positively, the income is strong and attractive.
- Positively, they are forming goals of moving up in the company or have goals to form their own company.

But some for-now jobs are created with the intention of keeping the employee even when a performance, designing, or directing gig has been booked. Some for-now jobs are perfectly harmonious – born from scratch, with a creative twinkle in one's eye. In such instances, they become more than *for now* and become *in addition to*. Some call these opportunities 'side hustles' or 'side gigs' and can exist side by side with what was considered the 'main' art form.

Side Gigs

As a performer, Tim Dolan[51] served as dance captain/ensemble in the Transport Group's[52] off-Broadway revival of *Once Upon*

A Mattress[53] starring Jackie Hoffman[54] and John "Lypsinka" Epperson.[55] He was also in the off-Broadway and national touring companies of *Altar Boyz*.[56] In 2010, Tim Dolan established Broadway Up Close Walking Tours,[57] the popular walking tour company that provides a "behind-the-scenes" look at Broadway theatre, led by working actors.

"I'm not a fan of the term 'survival job,'" Dolan says.

> I never wanted any part of my life to be just survival. I seek out joy and passion whenever possible. I made a conscious effort when I started performing to try and enjoy every aspect of my life. My side hustles were always in service of the performing side of my life. While Broadway Up Close started out as much more part-time, the idea was always to grow it so that it could run parallel to my performance career with both halves of my life, business and performing, playing off of each other harmoniously.

In the 2015 report *Creative New York*,[58] from the Center for an Urban Future,[59] Adam Forman states:

> Overall, New York City's creative sector – which by our definition includes ten industries: advertising, film and television, broadcasting, publishing, architecture, design, music, visual arts, performing arts and independent artists – employed 295,755 people in 2013, seven percent of all jobs in the city. Employment in the sector is up from 260,770 in 2003, a 13 percent jump. Meanwhile, the city is now home to 14,145 creative businesses and nonprofits, up from 11,955 a decade ago (18 percent increase).
> (Creative New York, Forman, 3)

With more artists like Dolan, are these numbers in this report from *Creative New York* because more artists are creating artistic and lucrative work for themselves? Every day, more artists are becoming entrepreneurs – or **artrepreneurs** – and establishing **side gigs**, which allow for extra income and creativity parallel to other experiences. These artrepreneurial efforts are usually more artistic than *For Now Jobs*, as they rely on one's artistic skillset and find purpose within the theatre, television, and film industries. They also differ from for-now jobs because they can exist alongside any job. So even if one was to book a Broadway or television show, they would still be able to manage this side gig if they chose to. Because of the explosion of social media combined with the boom of young creatives moving to larger cities like New York, Los Angeles, and London, many more jobs have been created. These jobs are signs of the industry shifting to accommodate change: change of image, change of opportunity, and change of accessibility.

These self-created opportunities have allowed artists to find more freedom in schedule and commitment. An explosion of new businesses has arrived on the scene since so many adapted to virtual life during the COVID-19 pandemic. A personal drive, learned skills, organizational competence, and keen social media navigation all lead up to a rise in self-employment such as website design, podcasting, social media management, coaching businesses, and more. In the same spirit as Broadway Up Close, many businesses can exist while the owner might commit to a month-long gig at a regional theatre, doubling their income *and* staying connected to the industry in their home location.

Sara Kapner's[60] contract in the national tour of *The Band's Visit*[61] was interrupted by COVID-19. Overnight, she established VO Workshop NYC[62] along with Emilea Wilson[63] and Mike Cefalo.[64] Virtually, they were able to coach and produce reels for actors who began to explore the voice-over sector of the industry, a brilliant move, as voice-over was the one safe way the industry could move forward in the time of the shutdown.

Figure 1.5 Sara Kapner, owner and cofounder of VO Workshop NYC. Michael Kushner Photography

In voice-over, an actor can book and complete a job right from their own home – and they don't even have to get out of their pajamas!

"I was doing this anyway," says Kapner.

> It was the only available creative work at the time. You make yourself shift to mold whatever work is available. Why isn't *everybody* doing this right now? And so I came up with the idea because I felt there was a missing link in this arena. There are plenty of amazing coaches out there but nobody was making it accessible in a real way that felt attainable for people. It still felt like this far-off thing that people couldn't do.

Not only were Kapner, Cefalo, and Wilson able to form a lucrative and creative business to keep them afloat during the pandemic, but they were also inspiring others to do the same with the accessibility Voice-over work provides.

"If people are being taught to go for the gold," continues Kapner,

> be a lead on Broadway, be a lead on Broadway, why aren't we people how to make a living in the interim between those jobs? Voiceover is using all of those skills. We should be putting that at high priority.

Like Kapner, Stephen Mark Lukas[65] has found a way for his artreprenuerial efforts to directly help people's skills and confidence. Lukas is known for his performance career as well as his personal training career, which he's melded together. Lukas still works with his clients during his run in the recent revival of *Funny Girl* on Broadway.[66]

"What gets me out of bed in the morning is helping performers get better," Lukas says.

> I had the benefit of having a personal trainer being hired for me when I was working on *Book of Mormon* on Broadway. I saw firsthand how it affected my stamina on stage and became obsessed with figuring out how to do that for other people. I think any profession where you're focused on someone else creates empathy, much like reading good novels with vivid characters stimulate your brain. You are building empathy bridges and understanding someone else.

What happens when these artreprenurial efforts are no longer about survival but a way for an artist to stay creative and widen their audience? What happens when these

Figure 1.6 Stephen Mark Lukas preparing for Gaston backstage in Papermill Playhouse's production of *Beauty and the Beast*. Michael Kushner Photography

artreprenuerial ventures become the very thing that doesn't just help pay the bills but supports creativity fully, paired with the freedom to make whatever choices they want? What happens when the *For Now Job* or the artrepreneurial experience grows into a leading quality and extension of one's artistic identity? Thus begins the exploration of the **multi-hyphenate**; to be more specific, the showbusiness multi-hyphenate. Of course, there are different kinds of multi-hyphenates, like the corporate multi-hyphenate, or the start-up multi-hyphenate. But what goes into the showbusiness multi-hyphenate, and how does one know if they are one?

Let's break it down.

A Multi-Hyphenate Is an Artist Who Has Multiple Proficiencies That Cross-Pollinate to Help Flourish Professional Capabilities

In this case, the multiple hyphens one has act as the proficiency one is known for as an artist. So, for instance, if an artist has the hyphens (proficiencies) of actor-photographer-producer-writer-podcaster, they are, in fact, a multi-hyphenate. In layman's terms, it means that an artist can act on each of

these areas of expertise at any moment, usually calling upon multiple hyphens to inform and support artistic endeavors. Please note that the terms *hyphen* and *proficiency* are interchangeable when covering multi-hyphenate identity. The term *skill* is not. This distinction will come in handy when beginning the exploration process.

Looking at the artist who is an actor-photographer-producer-writer-podcaster, one may wonder how they would apply themselves to the definition of a multi-hyphenate? Since they are a photographer, the income of photography could then fund their producer endeavors. And since they are an actor, could those producing endeavors include them as a performer? Quite possibly! And look at the last two hyphens – writer and podcaster. If this person is a writer, could they write their own material? Or do they write about their experiences as a multi-hyphenate? The same question can be asked about podcasting. How do they tie in the other hyphens to color their podcasting experience? They are tapping into their producer hyphen to schedule guests, purchase equipment, and advertise the show. That's *one* example of how artreprenuerial efforts become an artistic identity. Each choice one makes for each of their hyphens is going to affect the other hyphens directly. As an artist starts to explore all the possibilities of their artistic persona, they will find the common denominators that bring together their hyphens, establishing a more truthful multi-hyphenate experience. The possibilities are endless – and a cycle such as this is explored at length in Chapter 4, "Access: Approach, Location, and Cycle."

Let's look at the showbusiness multi-hyphenate like an atom. There are four essential parts: the protons, the neutrons, the electrons, and the nucleus. The nucleus is one's core, soul, or, more specifically – the **Why**. As discussed, the Why is the reasoning behind what we do as artists. Looking at the remaining components, one can find the neutrons, the protons, and the electrons – parts of our cells buzzing around, doing the thankless job of keeping humans alive.

Protons are responsible for chemical and physical properties. In comparison, the proton would mirror one's proficiencies, or the hyphens, which act as an artist's properties. So, protons equal hyphens. **Neutrons** are responsible for putting space in between protons so protons can accomplish their job. Congruently, the neutron balances out the repulsion of protons, which every artist needs, as well. Artists are constantly discovering their boundaries with pace and energy. That being said, neutrons equal workflow and boundaries. And speaking of energy, the **electron** is responsible for the reactivity of the atom. Comparing this to the multi-hyphenate artist, we'd see a connection to the energy and intention needed to deliver our hyphens on a day-to-day basis successfully. Therefore, electrons equal energy and intention.

The multi-hyphenate artist is *just* like an atom. Different, moving parts make up the everyday functions required to exist. Multi-hyphenates require energy, balance, speed – all things found in the very DNA of the human being. In fact, while multi-hyphenating may seem like a fairly new lifestyle, it's been in our core waiting to be experienced. According to *The Outline*,[67] the term *multi-hyphenate* started in the 1970s. This term applied almost directly and solely to celebrities. For example, Mel Brooks is a comedic genius who made a career for himself as a writer, director, producer, and actor. Around the time this word was introduced, Brooks had released (or was about to release) quite a few projects for which he was writing, directing, and starring in: *Blazing Saddles*,[68] *Young Frankenstein*,[69] *The Twelve Chairs*,[70] and *History of the World*[71] (also produced). Since then, the word has reflected celebrities' careers like Lin Manuel Miranda,[72] Issa Rae,[73] Rachel Brosnahan,[74] Reese Witherspoon,[75] and more. The idea is swiftly showing up in popular culture – even Jeopardy made a category based around the idea called 'They're Multi-Talented' during the National College Championship Quarter Final #12.[76]

But what happens when a developmental artist identifies as a multi-hyphenate? Many times younger artists are told to find a path and stick to it. This binary view of art hinders the potential one carries within themselves. What is one's

potential if they could share their own story by being the writer, director, actor, and designer? What historic tales have we lost because someone didn't know they could call upon multiple proficiencies at once? It doesn't matter when one starts exploring their hyphens, it's just a matter of starting. In Mel Brooks' career, it's extremely noticeable that he had always balanced his proficiencies beginning as early as 1949 – no one gave him permission. There is no countdown or graduation or induction to becoming a multi-hyphenate, but there are guidelines to follow if one was to begin this lifestyle. A question often asked by younger artists and budding multi-hyphenates is, How does one know when to add a hyphen to a professional multi-hyphenate identity?

While multi-hyphenating is just being adapted into an accessible and universal way of approaching art, one should approach the multi-hyphenate identity delicately. If everyone identifies as a multi-hyphenate but doesn't act as such, wouldn't the word lose power? The following four questions will help guide an artist through the start of their multi-hyphenate identity. When wondering if one should add a hyphen to their identity, one should take into account four aspects:

1. Am I garnering an income?
2. Do I have a paper trail?
3. Am I passionate?
4. How do my hyphens support and affect each other?

Am I Garnering an Income?

Being hired for a job and receiving pay is an experience that many professional artists strive for. Yet, what if one begins to be paid for a proficiency they are just starting to explore? Work is work. If an actor-director-new photographer puts their photography work on Instagram and an individual sees their work, approaches the photographer, and asks, "What's your rate?" What does that mean? The client isn't hiring them for their other proficiencies – they are hiring them for their photography. Whether or not they have years of experience or other hyphens, at this moment, this artist is a photographer. Whether or not it's a tried-and-true proficiency like directing or a new, uncharted territory, like photography – if that artist is being hired to provide a service, it's not a fluke.

Kirsten Wrinkle[77] is a creator and theatre patron based in Charlotte, North Carolina. She is the creator of *EnTrance Theatre Talk*[78] podcast and is known to commission artists and organizations for the sake of creating art – which is an extension of her Why as an artist and supporter. As a paying customer who believes in the growth of artists, she is simply paying a songwriter to write a song or a painter to paint a picture.

"I believe we need to pay artists for their time and skill," says Wrinkle.

> I believe we build a more compassionate and connected world through the arts. Perhaps a friend or someone I admire is recording their own music after a career performing *other* people's music. I hear about a nonprofit changing people's lives because children are finally exposed to the arts or people with disabilities are getting access to the arts. I will research the organization to ensure that gifts are well stewarded.

Do I Have a Paper Trail?

In the 21st century, it's easy to request information. With Google, Facebook, Instagram, and TikTok, an abundance of information is at our fingertips. From 30-minute meals to audition tips to history lessons, social media has been proving to inspire the masses – and isn't slowing down. In an article published in January 2021, according to Elisa Shearer for Pew Research, "more than eight-in-ten U.S. adults (86%) say they get news from a smartphone."[79] That being said, what

information comes up as a search result if an artist was to Google themselves? "Googling" oneself is an incredibly helpful way to see how the world is viewing them. What are noticeable patterns? What are keywords or proficiencies that show up alongside an artist's name? If a source like the *New York Times* lists an artist by excelling in a specific proficiency, chances are it's because they are noted for being one. Just through listing proficiencies alone, in what ways is the artist making an impact on the world around them?

Hollis Duggans, an Equity stage manager who has toured the U.S. in shows such as the first national tour of *To Kill a Mockingbird*,[80] makeup artist, and now influencer, has found her efforts on TikTok have made her go viral – even beginning a paper trail for one of her hyphens. Because of her video creations, she has been picked up by sources like *Popsugar*.[81]

"Tiktok has been helpful when it comes to building a community and reaching out to brands for brand deals," says Duggans. "It's easier to grow and get recognized on Tiktok. Tiktok has become a part of my personal branding."

While Duggan's social media presence adds to her paper trail, having an article on *Popsugar* adds legitimacy. Her talents in stage makeup are now getting world recognition, therefore showing an example that Duggans is seen as a makeup artist by a wider audience.

Figure 1.7 Stage manager and makeup artist Hollis Duggans touches up Katie Collins, a client, during a headshot session taking place outside in New York City. Michael Kushner Photography

Am I Passionate?

Passion can open the doors to endless possibilities – it's the one quality that *can* outweigh prerequisites. Julie James[82] is the voice and spirit behind *On Broadway* on Sirius XM Radio.[83] She hosts *Broadway Names With Julie James*, which takes you on the town, behind the scenes, and into the studio for lively conversations with stars of stage and screen. James attributes her passion for music as being the sole reason for her hiring at Sirius XM Radio.

"Passion *was* the avenue to Sirius XM radio, because I wouldn't have gotten a foot in the door any other way," says James.

> At the time, it was very much a prerequisite that you have some sort of radio background, because it was a new and fledgling company, and a new, untested business. The notion of satellite radio predated the iPod – it was a newfangled thing. No one knew if paying for radio would work, so they were bringing in the heavy hitters who were career radio folks. But it just so happened that they were looking for someone who specialized in the classical music realm, which was something I studied and performed before focusing on musical theatre. It was dusting off the passion, in a certain way! Because they were looking for some who had that specifically in their background, it *was* the passion that got my foot in the door, that then got me hired there, that then turned into so many other things that are beyond my wildest dreams.

Ultimately, passion is the most important when it comes to multi-hyphenate identity. It's a spark within us which contributes to hours, weeks, months, and years of commitment, ultimately making hopes and dreams come true. When becoming a multi-hyphenate, the artist risks rejection for each proficiency they identify with. If one has four hyphens, for instance, actor-designer-producer-writer, that's four times the risk of rejection. If one's other hyphens are bringing joy, why be bogged down by the runt of the litter? One should spend energy on the hyphens that are fulfilling. The whole purpose of multi-hyphenation is to ensure joy and allow agency in what one creates so that one doesn't have to adhere to laborious, tedious, and heartless tasks one might find in a *For Now Job*.

How Do My Hyphens Support and Affect Each Other?

The fourth trait of becoming a multi-hyphenate is to ensure that each hyphen directly affects the others, a common quality of the multi-hyphenate that is often overlooked. If one has multiple proficiencies, they must cross-pollinate – otherwise, it's just various jobs or disconnected operations. By bridging one's hyphens, it allows a more focused and connected artistry. By taking the knowledge, the talent, the resources, the communities, and the drive of one hyphen and applying them to the other, it creates a thriving nerve center. Plus, by adding one's 'Why' statement to the overall picture, an artist is subject to impenetrable, specific, and holistic creativity.

When uniting these hyphens, it helps the artist develop a tighter artistic identity and helps determine the things in their life that serve separate purposes, like **hobbies**. Hobbies are a lovely way to relieve stress or connect with something simple, but hobbies aren't included as one's hyphens. Hobbies purposely don't become job opportunities so they can remain as pleasurable pastimes, not requiring deadlines or budgets. They can be extremely important to the mental health of an artist as they can bring joy and respite during particularly stressful times. By reviewing the questions to ask oneself when discovering if a certain art form can be considered a proficiency, an artist might be passionate about a hobby, but they usually don't garner an income, provide a paper trail, or cross-pollinate one's hyphens. Yet that doesn't mean a hobby can't become a proficiency. Many times that's how proficiencies begin. Yet when a hobby becomes a proficiency, it is no longer a hobby. By practicing or going to a college or training center is how many hobbies grow into proficiencies. How else can someone learn to fail – failure being a key element to the multi-hyphenate discovery process. In this instance, committing to failure is committing to a sense of *play*.

Alexandra Silber[84] has been on Broadway in *Fiddler on the Roof*[85] and *Master Class*[86] and in the West End in *Indecent*[87] at the Menier Chocolate Factory[88] (the run was split in half due to the COVID-19 pandemic with performances resuming in November 2021). She is also a two-time novel writer of *White Hot Grief Parade*[89] and *After Anatevka*.[90] Silber is also an active educator and attributes playfulness, similar to that of her cat Tati, as an integral part of the human experience.

"I am a human being, not a human doing," Silber says on Episode 20 of *Dear Multi-Hyphenate*.[91]

> And trying to . . . I say this a little glibly and with a little humor obviously . . . trying to learn from my cat. My cat Tatiana Angela Lansbury Romanov . . . in all seriousness . . . I look at Tati and I go, 'Do I have a snack? Do I take a fifth nap?' and she looks at me and goes, 'Of course you do! That's what I would do!' You laugh, right? But what is that? Really, what it is – is a completely non-moralistic assessment of existence.

Of being in touch with something that you want and need, that is gentle and comforting, and kind and compassionate to yourself and to others – and just going with it and not judging it as something worthy or unworthy or productive or unproductive. That is what Tati would do."

Be like Silber's cat Tati and engage in an utterly non-moralistic assessment of existence. When building hyphens, remove judgment and find a sense of play. Engage in a hobby, and if it grows into professional development, fabulous! Add it to the list of hyphens. But if one is not moved to develop that hobby into a professional endeavor, that's *just* as important.

Engaging in play provokes an artist to respond genuinely to what is attractive to their soul. What brings a human joy is cellular and impulsive, and the jobs accepted or created should be a reflection of that. During the pandemic of 2020, the act of play served a greater purpose than ever before. Does one continue to create art in the ways in which they knew before? How are we continuing to stay creative and innovative when centering social justice movements? What has society learned about themselves, and what space does one choose to take up when creating? How can play help create stories which promote joy as well as awareness and education?

The *How* is for the individual to decide. A multi-hyphenate doesn't have to wait on anyone else for them to be able to affect the world in a positive way – multi-hyphenates brave the storm and do it themselves. As multi-hyphenates find their groove, they will discover themselves taking space in a myriad of ways. On paper, the multi-hyphenate can look like a selfish endeavor – one artist alone is acting as the producer, *and* the actor, *and* the designer, *and* the writer. But taking up such space should be treated delicately, constantly negating self-focused behaviors and focusing on positively affecting *the other*, whether that be a co-creator, the audience, or a specific demographic. Self-focused-ness is an American epidemic that is shrinking attention spans, disintegrating empathy, and cheapening art. A multi-hyphenate must simply shy away from any self-centered behavior by using the self as a tool to solve problems, ask questions, and produce art that is effective, powerful, and purposeful. To do that, an artist must know how to avoid narcissistic behavior, lead with empathy, and remember: *it's not about you!*

EPISODE EXCERPT

SOPHIE THOMPSON

Olivier Award Winning British star of television, stage, and screen

ODDITIES & SHENANIGANS • *EPISODE 29*

Michael: Would you consider yourself an activist?

Sophie: Well that's another thing you said I was. I thought, "Golly, I wish I was." I'd like to think I was that more than I think I am. And I have been pondering more of what I could do to be of use. Again, we've all had lots of times to ponder and a lot of ghastly things have been unwrapped and unpeeled and revealed in very poignant ways during this time. You know it, you think crikey what can I do more? And that's something I have to percolate as time goes on, I'd love to think of myself in that way, but in all honesty, Michael, I don't think I deserve that title at all (laughs). My sis is an extraordinary activist, and I'm full of pride, but I'm afraid I don't think I come up trumps, so actually that's another thing I need to address. You're throwing a lot of things my way that I'm going to have to work on.

Michael: How does it feel though, that someone that admires your work, and has admired you since 2012, since seeing you on stage -- how does it feel that someone sees you in that light? I don't know, as I was catching up on all things Sophie Thompson and making sure I didn't miss anything -- I saw you did something My Guide and I was like... it is activism to me! That anti-fracking protest -- that's activism. Your My Guide... that's activism. You're being a voice for a marginalized group of people. I see you as an activist and that inspires me to be a better part of society. So, how do you feel if I see you as an activist?

Sophie: (laughs) Oh, Michael, well I'm glad. I'm going to have to write it in my diary and go, "Michael sees me as an activist!" and I'll make a list and I'll have a think about that...

A six-time Olivier Award nominee, Thompson won the 1999 Olivier Award for Best Actress in a Musical for the London revival of Into the Woods.

Notes

1 www.actorsequity.org/resources/contracts/Staged-Reading/
2 www.davenporttheatrical.com/
3 www.ibdb.com/broadway-production/once-on-this-island-514926
4 https://en.wikipedia.org/wiki/Gettin%27_the_Band_Back_Together
5 www.playbill.com/article/celebrate-deaf-west-theatres-2015-spring-awakening-broadway-revival
6 https://en.wikipedia.org/wiki/It%27s_Only_a_Play
7 https://kinkybootsthemusical.com/
8 https://en.wikipedia.org/wiki/Harold_Prince
9 https://en.wikipedia.org/wiki/Mel_Brooks
10 www.darylrothproductions.com/
11 https://en.wikipedia.org/wiki/David_Merrick
12 https://en.wikipedia.org/wiki/Kevin_McCollum
13 www.dramaticforces.com/about/
14 https://en.wikipedia.org/wiki/Cameron_Mackintosh
15 www.adamhyndman.com/
16 www.aladdinthemusical.com/
17 www.hadestown.com/
18 https://theinheritanceplay.com/
19 https://pipelinetheatre.org/
20 www.bfrj.org/
21 www.theindustrystandardgroup.com/
22 http://octopustheatricals.com/
23 https://theater.calarts.edu/faculty-and-staff/mara-isaacs
24 www.broadwayworld.com/people/E-Clayton-Cornelius/
25 https://chickenandbiscuitsbway.com/
26 www.douglaslyons.net/
27 www.ashleykateadams.com/about
28 www.ibdb.com/broadway-production/la-cage-aux-folles-484929
29 www.imdb.com/name/nm4017306/?ref_=nv_sr_srsg_0#producer
30 www.ashleykateadams.com/byop
31 www.ibdb.com/broadway-production/beautiful-the-carole-king-musical-495178
32 www.ibdb.com/broadway-production/the-book-of-mormon-488721
33 https://en.wikipedia.org/wiki/Murder_of_George_Floyd
34 www.playbill.com/person/mary-testa-vault-0000043053
35 https://oklahomabroadway.com/
36 https://en.wikipedia.org/wiki/Xanadu_(musical)
37 https://en.wikipedia.org/wiki/She_Loves_Me
38 https://en.wikipedia.org/wiki/Eat_Pray_Love
39 www.imdb.com/title/tt0698627/?ref_=nm_flmg_act_42
40 https://en.wikipedia.org/wiki/William_Finn
41 https://en.wikipedia.org/wiki/In_Trousers
42 https://en.wikipedia.org/wiki/The_Rose_Tattoo
43 https://longwharf.org/
44 https://en.wikipedia.org/wiki/Just_Kids
45 www.fxnetworks.com/shows/pose
46 www.imdb.com/title/tt0108778/
47 https://en.wikipedia.org/wiki/Rent_(musical)
48 www.census.gov/newsroom/press-releases/2021/population-changes-nations-diversity.html
49 www.holmdeltheatrecompany.org/post/bww-interview-executive-director-colleen-cook-reflects-on-the-past-present-and-future-of-holmdel
50 www.jpmorganchase.com/
51 www.broadwayupclose.com/timdolan
52 http://transportgroup.org/
53 www.playbill.com/article/once-upon-a-mattress-revival-starring-jackie-hoffman-begins-performances-tonight-com-372887
54 https://en.wikipedia.org/wiki/Jackie_Hoffman
55 www.lypsinka.com/
56 https://en.wikipedia.org/wiki/Altar_Boyz
57 www.broadwayupclose.com/
58 https://nycfuture.org/pdf/Creative-New-York-2015.pdf
59 https://nycfuture.org/research/creative-new-york-2015
60 www.sarakapner.com/
61 https://thebandsvisitmusical.com/
62 www.voworkshopnyc.com/
63 www.imdb.com/name/nm2305893/
64 www.mikecefalo.com/
65 https://funnygirlonbroadway.com/?gclid=CjOKCQjw3v6SBhCsARIsACyrRAkJR8YOaq92uZkygxR9Kw2717y8SSWMjeoW29GWv-1rxvOTGMdZeOMaAr46EALw_wcB&gclsrc=aw.ds
66 www.stephenmarklukas.com/
67 https://theoutline.com/post/8301/everyone-you-know-is-a-multi-hyphenate
68 www.imdb.com/title/tt0071230/?ref_=nv_sr_srsg_0
69 www.imdb.com/title/tt0072431/?ref_=nv_sr_srsg_0
70 www.imdb.com/title/tt0066495/?ref_=nv_sr_srsg_0
71 www.imdb.com/title/tt0082517/?ref_=nv_sr_srsg_0
72 www.linmanuel.com/
73 www.issarae.com/
74 www.imdb.com/name/nm3014031/
75 www.imdb.com/name/nm0000702/
76 www.jeopardy.com/jbuzz/news-events/jeopardy-national-college-championship-starts-february-8
77 http://entranceproductions.org/about/
78 https://entranceproductions.org/
79 www.pewresearch.org/fact-tank/2021/01/12/more-than-eight-in-ten-americans-get-news-from-digital-devices/
80 https://tokillamockingbirdbroadway.com/tour/
81 www.popsugar.com/beauty/farrah-fawcett-flip-hairstyle-trend-tiktok-48264637
82 https://juliejamesonline.com/
83 www.siriusxm.com/channels/on-broadway

84 http://alexandrasilber.squarespace.com/

85 https://en.wikipedia.org/wiki/Fiddler_on_the_Roof

86 www.playbill.com/article/revisit-the-broadway-revival-of-master-class-starring-tyne-daly-sierra-boggess-and-alexandra-silber

87 www.playbill.com/article/londons-menier-chocolate-factory-sets-reopening-season-including-return-of-indecent

88 www.menierchocolatefactory.com/Online/default.asp

89 http://alexandrasilber.squarespace.com/praise

90 http://alexandrasilber.squarespace.com/after-anatevka

91 https://broadwaypodcastnetwork.com/dear-multi-hyphenate/20-al-silber-human-being-not-a-human-doing/

Reference List

1. Bureau, US Census. "Local Population Changes and Nation's Racial and Ethnic Diversity." *The United States Census Bureau*, 17 Aug. 2021, www.census.gov/newsroom/press-releases/2021/population-changes-nations-diversity.html.
2. Forman, Adam. "Center for Urban Future." *Creative New York*, 2015, pp. 3–3.
3. Shearer, Elisa. "86% Of Americans Get News Online from Smartphone, Computer or Tablet." *Pew Research Center*, Pew Research Center, 12 Jan. 2021, www.pewresearch.org/fact-tank/2021/01/12/more-than-eight-in-ten-americans-get-news-from-digital-devices/.

EXERCISE 2

GOOGLE YOURSELF

DM-H

Ever wonder how the theatre industry sees you? It's simple! A quick check on a search engine will do the trick. Why is this important? Remember, one of the principles to multi-hyphenate identity is having a paper trail – or articles, facts, and content attached to one's name documenting press associated with the projects they've been a part of. Just head to a search engine like Google or Yahoo! and type in your name and a word associated with you like 'writer' or 'designer.' Once you hit 'enter,' take stock of the information shown to you by asking questions such as these:

1. **What is your 'featured snippet'?**
   - On Google, the 'featured snippet' is a showcased link at the top of the page that makes one find what they are seeking more easily. Is this snippet the first thing you want a searcher to find about you?
2. **What is the first search result that shows up?**
   - Is it your website? Is it someone else with your same name? Is it a press article? If you are a business owner, is your business being featured?
   - If your business is not being featured and you'd like to fix that – all one needs to do is go through Google Support for an easy step-by-step guide on how to fix that.
3. **What is the narrative that the first page of results tells?**
   - Are all your hyphens showing up? If you are a costume designer, teaching artist, and podcaster, are all those different hyphens clear? If not, what's missing?

- If something is missing, perhaps it's time to reach out to a news source and inquire about an interview or make a blog post on your website or ask to be on someone's podcast to talk about that hyphen.
- Is a proficiency you weren't identifying with showing up on the Google search? Perhaps you identify as a costume designer, teaching artist, and podcaster – but a few search results showed up mentioning you as a makeup artist because of one project you helped out with. How do you feel about this?

One can also do the same for their social media presence. Unsure of what type of content is associated with your name or brand? On Instagram, search hashtags that might be associated with you. For instance, if you're Sara Kapner, who is featured in this chapter, she might search #thebandsvisit #bandsvisitnationaltour #voiceover #voiceoverworkshop #voworkshop #sarakapner or any other hashtag and see what comes up. You can also check your tagged photos on Instagram. For someone like a photographer or videographer, this is helpful because it informs one of the content their clients are posting.

Google searches change based on website traffic, and if you feel you aren't getting enough clicks, that's fixable! Did you know getting a press release out for a project helps sell tickets *and* creates more Google search results?

Unsure of how to get a press release? If you don't have a press rep – emailing newsdesk@broadwayworld.com with the information for your show, podcast, or feature is a way to go. BroadwayWorld is extremely supportive to the theatre community and often publishes press releases for those creating in the theatre community.

Keep building your online presence, and you'll begin to see more search results. Remember, you have the power to shape the narrative or your online presence. For example, if you join a podcast for an interview, perhaps you request to talk about the hyphen for which you have fewer search results for, therefore building more of a presence representing that discipline. So have fun and make your online presence personal and authentic!

"...even at auditions, I can cheer for other people; people who maybe could get a job that I could've gotten. I think that's a helpful thing for mental health but also realizing what's meant for you is going to be for you."

DeAnne Stewart

Chapter 2
It's Not About You

DOI: 10.4324/9781003254744-4

Founding Artistic Director Shakina Nayfack at a Musical Theatre Factory event
at Playwrights Downtown in NYC

Career Connection
Incubators

When a play is a little further along in development and is ready to hear how an audience may respond, the writer may begin to submit to incubators and workshop their piece. Notable incubators in the theatre industry are Musical Theatre Factory,[1] PlayGround,[2] New York Theatre Barn,[3] and DNA: Oxygen.[4]

An **incubator** is a type of group or collective that focuses on growth, process, and collaboration. While incubators might not produce the musical itself, they will commit themselves to the growth of a piece until the next step of production. Incubators invest in their own types of agendas, often seeking out plays and musicals which speak to their mission or vision – or their 'Why.'

Musical Theatre Factory, based in New York City, was founded by Shakina Nayfack,[5] a trans-activist-performer-director-writer-producer. The idea came to her in the back of a van and eventually was established four floors above the original Drama Book Shop,[6] located on 40th and 8th in Manhattan. By day, the space was a gay adult film studio, and by night, it served as a theatrical incubator.

"I started MTF by looking outside myself and asking who else had the same needs and struggles and desires as I did," says Nayfack.

> I started MTF in the back of a van on the way to check out some potential recording space, just having a conversation with a friend saying, 'Wouldn't it be great to have a space where all these things are devoted to developing new musicals through peer evaluation and collaborative feedback? This sounds so cliche, but I started MTF in my mind's eye – I saw it *first* and then I made it.

The original structure of MTF was ragtag and messy. Actors, writers, directors, producers, artists of all shapes, sizes, genders, and colors – from every different level and type of career – came together, drinking whiskey, creating, and cultivating new musicals. It was a hot, new experience that allowed trans and nonbinary artists, artists of color, and allies to work together in a space that de-centered art dominated by whiteness. It was radical; it was safe for so many, and it was growing rapidly.

"If you look around," continues Nayfack, "you will find people who want to be on your team, or want you to be on theirs."

After a rise in rent, Musical Theatre Factory was forced to relocate. However, they are still in existence, now in a long-term residency with Playwrights Horizons.[7] Most notably, Musical Theatre Factory incubated the Pulitzer Prize–winning *A Strange Loop*,[8] written by Michael R. Jackson[9] which opened on Broadway on April 26, 2022.

Incubators like MTF serve a very specific purpose, and each incubator has programming that may be attractive to different writers for different reasons. MTF acts as a theatre conveyer belt, starting projects from the ground up in their POC Roundtable, Women/Trans Roundtable, or MTF Makers Cohort, which according to their website,

> is an 18-month residency that supports six teams of groundbreaking musical theater artists in the creation of new work. Through this inclusive community, Makers™ gather together at regular meetings to share work and support each other through feedback, collaboration, and discourse. In addition to meetings, Makers™ are given mentorship, education, and advocacy, and priority access to MTF's Assembly Line™ suite of activities – each team is offered two slots in our 4×15™ series and a fully-supported AEA developmental residency, plus access to other opportunities to show work in front of an audience. (www.mtf.nyc)

Incubators are not just for the writer but for new directors, new stage managers, new choreographers, new producers – anyone who wants to begin to learn if a new artistic proficiency is worth exploring. For many, incubators help serve a greater purpose when it comes to creating theatre. For example, resident director of the national tour of *Hamilton*, Zi Alikhan,[10] recently named one of the Theatre Communications Group Rising Leaders of Color of 2021,[11] has been working diligently on the creation of DNA: Oxygen at Artist Repertory Theatre[12] in Portland, Oregon.

> DNA: Oxygen is a new program out at Artists Repertory Theatre and it's essentially somewhere between a creative hub and an affinity space that is dedicated to the creation of work that is generated by, led by, and featuring artists of color. DNA: Oxygen came out of an immediate understanding and need in this particular theatre's ecosystem to not only support artists of color, but to support people of color within the institution, and from outside the institution when they

come in as contributors to every conversation that is happening within that theatre.

Alikhan is inspired by an Adrienne Maree Brown[13] quote from her book, *We Will Not Cancel Us*.[14]

"She says, 'I feel we're losing our capacity to generate belonging,'" continues Alikhan.

> I think about that all the time how theatres are these weird spaces where people come together and stories are being told . . . but I often wonder, especially as somebody who grew up as a Queer, brown kid in a lot of these spaces, how unconsciously the theatre actually revolves around structures that keep people out.

While some incubators remove themselves from future producing efforts, some can eventually provide full productions of a work in progress. For example, according to their website, Ars Nova[15] is a theatre hub that "exists to discover, develop, and launch singular theater, music, and comedy artists who are in the early stages of their professional careers" (arsnova.com).

"Ars Nova is somewhat unique in the constellation of New York not-for-profit theaters, in that we are both a dedicated new work development hub, and a producing organization," says Emily Shooltz, who served as Ars Nova's associate artistic director.

> In any given year, we support and develop far more work in our various programs than we could ever fully produce. That is by design – we see Ars Nova as a springboard and point of entry for artists, a place where they can work out ideas, meet collaborators, hone their voices, and then in a very healthy way, move on from us. Because we invest so much in our development activity, our two off-Broadway

productions each year are homegrown work – pieces that originate either as commissions or in one of our residency programs. So we aren't out there looking for finished projects to produce; rather we are lucky that a couple of times a year, we get to fully produce some of the amazing work that has gestated under our roof.

So, how does one find themselves to be a part of an incubator? Incubators are strong reflectors of the efforts of accessibility and inclusion in 21st-century theatre-making, and each incubator has its own form of outreach.

"We curate several of our core programs through open submissions," continues Shooltz,

> including ANT Fest[16] (our annual Festival of All New Talent); Play Group[17] (our early career playwrights group) and CAMP[18] (our newest program, created during the pandemic and designed to support comedy artists developing new work). It is important to us that our doors always remain open to the next wave of emerging artists, and that beyond the outreach and scouting our small team can do, we have ongoing ways for artists to find us. For each of these programs, we include a range of people outside our full-time artistic staff in the selection process, in order to bring more voices and perspectives to the table. In 2020, we also launched our Vision Residency program, wherein a group of artist-curators were given the platform and resources to each curate 4 to 6 shows of their choosing on Ars Nova Supra with the support of the full Ars Nova staff. This gave the residents a forum to uplift and spotlight new work and creators they admired, and widened the circle of new artists finding a home at Ars Nova.

Ars Nova is responsible for incubating certain Broadway productions like *Natasha, Pierre & The Great Comet of 1812*,[19] and *KPOP*.[20]

Fifteen minutes of fame can lead into a lifelong career – and with social media growing in importance daily – it seems as though principles of hard work and investment are going out the window in exchange for immediate and self-focused attention. For many, they'll do what they can to become a star – Roxie in Kander and Ebb's[21] *Chicago*[22] even *killed* because of it. The measures one will take to achieve stardom can be bewildering as show business is an easily self-focused experience. So what does it mean to be self-focused?

Self-focusedness is the surfaced attention one puts on themselves in search of immediate praise. It is in the family of narcissism, can be born out of narcissism, and can even grow into narcissism, but it is mainly *misplaced intention*. A self-focused act might be an influencer constantly posting to increase their following or an actor having little to no regard for their scene partner. Self-focused efforts are not necessarily a thing of evil, but the multi-hyphenate should err on the side of caution. The whole idea of a multi-hyphenate is to produce self-managed artistry that reflects *another* in a positive, productive, and influential way.

Success is measured in a myriad of ways. Whether or not that's income, or completing a project, or a pat on the back – success means different things for different people. Multi-hyphenating perpetuates the artist to build and control their own success. Success can lead to clout, which leads to notoriety – which goes for artists of any proficiency; camerapeople, CEOs, and directors alike. When one builds clout, they have a responsibility to set an example. Unfortunately, many beloved artists use their power for good or intend to do so but wind up failing at the prospect. When artists engage in the multi-hyphenate approach, it's usually because they aren't seeing themselves or a specific community represented in mainstream media, so they are taking it upon themselves to fix that.

When one gets notoriety for their creativity, it's easy to get wrapped up in the attention that comes with it. Multi-hyphenates aren't preventable from getting swelled egos and enjoying being in the spotlight isn't a bad thing, but because multi-hyphenating is about creating art for a greater good, being in the spotlight *shouldn't* affect the process. Hopefully, art based on responsibility for another will prevent that.

Dr. Alisa Hurwitz[23] earned her Bachelor of Science in Psychology from Brandeis University,[24] and her Master of Science and Doctor of Psychology in Clinical Psychology from Long Island University.[25] Her clinical areas of interest include diversity and identity, spirituality, trauma, and LGBT+. During the COVID-19 pandemic, Dr. Hurwitz took to social media, used her passion for theatre, and transformed it into a way to connect with the industry where she usually finds herself in the audience. According to her website on April 11, 2020, she wrote:

> In response to dealing with the anxiety, uncertainty and isolation, I am launching a Mental Health Series: Instagram Live. Each episode will feature discussion of coping skills and emotional survival between myself, Alisa Hurwitz, PsyD and a Broadway star, with an opportunity for questions from viewers. (drdrama.com)

Some of the notable names Dr. Hurwitz has had on her Instagram Live conversations include Tony winner Ali Stroker,[26] Drama Desk nominee Rebecca Naomi Jones,[27] Olivier Award winner Lesli Margherita,[28] and more.

"There's the vernacular use of the term ego, and then there's the technical use of the term ego, and there's the sociological technical term, and there's the psychological term," Hurwitz says.

Traditionally ego refers to the Freudian concept of Id, Ego, Superego, with the Ego being the midpoint of the negotiation between the expectations of the Superego and the barenaked need drive of sex, safety – anything that the self needs. I find it more useful to use the sociological construct where Ego is the concept of self that is separate from the soul and separate from the being. We all have Ego in that sense. That doesn't mean we're conceited, we just have a need to feel seen, have meaning for our life, feel like people like us.

To further Dr. Hurwitz's point, self-focusedness isn't meant to be eradicated completely. For a human to exist, one must have a sense of being able to take care of themselves and find their place in the world. Hungry? Get food. Is it raining? Use an umbrella. Self-focused behavior promotes survival but there is certainly a fine line for when it becomes self-centered. Is there a way to turn self-focused energy into something active and not self-centered?

Shakina Nayfack is no stranger to one-woman performances. Her show, *Manifest Pussy*,[29] a rock concert/standup special/ritual sacrifice that follows Shakina's pilgrimage to Thailand for gender confirmation, has played numerous theatres and spaces such as A.R.T.,[30] Joe's Pub,[31] and even traveling to North Carolina in protest of their new law, HB2, which removes LGBT people from the statewide nondiscrimination policy and forces transgender people to use public restrooms that correspond to the gender marker on their birth certificate.

Figure 2.3 Social media graphic used to promote Shakina Nayfack's one woman show, *Manifest Pussy*. Graphic by Michelle Dimuzio. Photo by Michael Kushner Photography

"A truthful, honest, unashamed, unafraid type of self-focus is probably the healthiest investment an artist can make in themselves," she says.

> But, at the end of the day, you're creating something to share. So, you always have to care for your audience, and care about your audience, as much as you care about yourself. That's the difference between being a self-focused Yoga practitioner, for example, and then a self-focused artistic creator. You can have wellness practice you are fully devoted to and be in line with your own aspirations for self-betterment, but as an artist you've made a commitment to produce works for others; and so there needs to be an attention to the bridges that you're building through your work to bring other folks to you and make yourself accessible to others.

One's relationship with self-focused energy starts young. In the toxic hierarchies of high school theatre, it's easy for a young artist to get lost in dramatic environments. As these students attend colleges, it's there where the ego and one's relationship to self are examined. Just before the COVID-19 shutdown, DeAnne Stewart[32] made her Broadway debut in *Jagged Little Pill*[33] by understudying the role of Frankie. After the production reopened, unbeknownst to her, she would also play the last performance of *Jagged Little Pill* in her understudy track as the show would then abruptly close due to COVID-19 complications. Stewart harkens back to a time when her relationship with self-focused energy shifted while studying for her BFA in musical theatre at Ithaca College.[34]

> I'd say earlier in school, it felt like there was such an intense feeling of, "Oh, me. I need to succeed," which is probably what I came into school with as an artist, but I feel like that kind of shifted from the intimacy of our classes and working in those spaces, becoming more focused on the growth and success of my peers.

Theatre programs can be any sort of combination of supportive, toxic, competitive – the list goes on. Most students begin their journeys in undergraduate programs at the age of 18, a sensitive period to be thrown into a competitive environment far away from home. Scientifically, the brain is still developing up to 4 years *after* one would graduate from an undergraduate program, largely in part because of the prefrontal cortex still forming in the brain, which ultimately influences planning and personality development. In other words, it's easy for an artist at this age to subject themselves to the negative patterns of comparison, judgment, and self-sabotage. Dr. Hurwitz continues:

Prefrontal cortex development happens up until the mid-twenties. We talk about the risk of drug use on the prefrontal cortex development prior to full development of the prefrontal cortex. That has a physiological negative impact on functions such as decision making, integrating logical thinking and emotional thought, and executive functioning. I think studying acting prior to age 25 is really healthy for that because in the context of a play, the lines are predetermined so you can try things out. It's *play* – that's how we learn to be adults, through play. I think it's really healthy, especially when understanding that we are social beings, counteracting the American value of individualism, that its nature the art form is collaborative, which is really healthy to experience.

While Dr. Hurwitz supports the theory that theatre is healthy to study from a young age, what about young adults being thrown into environments that perpetuate comparison by competition? Many theatre programs, no matter how highly rated, commit themselves to a climate that is stuck in a cycle of their own rules and culture – and while the brain is still forming, how does an environment such as this affect an artist?

"Hierarchical structures like schools can be wonderful," continues Dr. Hurwitz.

> But there can be abuse in that structure. The power differences can be taken advantage of, and so it's absolutely harmful to people. When you're in a toxic relationship with your environment, you're just trying to emotionally survive the situation. The emotional bandwidth is taken out just by trying to make it through and keep yourself safe. There's no additional emotional bandwidth for the development that is supposed to be happening at that time.

But luckily, Stewart found herself in a supportive college environment, which helped her overcome the initial self-focused energy she was experiencing during her freshman year. She quickly learned that worrying only about herself would hurt her in the long run:

> I would be emotional by seeing the growth of people in my class. Recognizing that, and being invested in that, has helped me in the professional world with realizing that, even at auditions, I can cheer for other people; people who maybe could get a job that I could've gotten. I think that's a helpful thing for mental health but also realizing what's meant for you is going to be for you. Just because you can do the same thing as someone else, if

they get it . . . it's for them. It helps calm so much of the anxiety that's built in the infrastructure of our world.

Having a self-focused perspective is only good in moderation. Too much of it and it becomes narcissistic. Too little and one loses confidence and tenacity.

Danielle Hope[35] quite literally won the hearts of millions across the United Kingdom. On May 22, 2010, Hope won the coveted role of Dorothy in the Andrew Lloyd Webber[36] production of *The Wizard of Oz*,[37] which was to play the West End at the historic London Palladium.[38] At only 18 years old, Hope became an overnight star, going on to play various UK tours and other West End productions such as the Narrator in *Joseph and the Amazing Technicolor Dreamcoat*,[39] Eponine in *Les Miserables*,[40] and Betty Haynes in *White Christmas*,[41] to name a few.

"Being on the show live on television, every weekend, there were over 17 million viewers," says Hope.

> I was 17 years old when I started. Going from school to being immediately in the public eye was a huge change and a huge challenge, of course. I will say that we were so busy on the show with rehearsals and the filming and everything that comes with being a part of a reality show because you don't go home at the end of the day. If you're rehearsing for a West End show you rehearse 9 a.m. to 6 p.m. and then you go home. Our home was all together so we lived this experience and this atmosphere for months. There wasn't time to get into your head. I have been really fortunate in the way my family has brought me up in the way I have experienced life was to really stay grounded and remember[] the whole journey to get from where you were to where you are and onward. I will say there never was a part of me that felt, "Ah yes I've made it."
>
> For me, interestingly enough, I actually kind of wish I had a little bit more Ego in a sense of celebration of what I've accomplished in what I was doing. I just really wanted to get it right and I didn't want to let anyone down. I was young. It was my first job. A lot of people had voted on the show. A lot of people had stood in my corner and said, "Yeah – she's great, she can do it." And I was just really, really focused on just not messing it up. And I wish a part of me had been able to stand and celebrate a little more and say, "Wow! This is awesome! I did a great job!" Because I don't actually think I said those words to myself once. And then of course moving into the West End with the show, so from moving from the television show to the West End show, and having some of my theatre

heroes around me such as Hannah Waddingham,[42] Michael Crawford,[43] you know being in the same show as me, standing on the same stage, and sitting in the dressing room with me. The summer before, I had seen Hannah Waddingham as The Witch in *Into the Woods*[44] at Regents Park, Open Air Theatre,[45] and I remember being, like, so fan-girling when I found out she was going to be a part of the show, I just couldn't believe it. There are moments like that when I just couldn't believe what was happening. So my reflection now, eleven years later, is one of gratitude and one of like, I'm really glad I was never lost in Ego – if Ego is being represented as a state of being perceived as me saying, "I'm wonderful, I'm amazing." and in the same breath I wish I could have been able to say that to myself a little bit more so I can say you know, it's okay to say you did a great job. My balancing of ego throughout birthing into the professional theatre world and into people's homes via television was balancing self-doubt and imposter syndrome.

The enjoyment of applause and high praise is not a negative thing. If anything, it's informative. Understanding how an audience responds to what is being produced is key to perpetuating a more informed product. Yet how can one keep themselves in check to make sure the art they are producing is not a self-focused occurrence? Here are some questions one might be able to ruminate on:

- Am I still actively and positively influencing an audience?
- Am I providing access to artists by contributing job opportunities like hiring a director, a designer, and so on?
- Am I providing access to the audience to understand a story they might not yet have been educated on?
- Am I providing a call to action with my audience so they are able to be a part of my vision?
- Am I finding that my overall presence (social media, pitch meetings, etc.) have become more about me than the task at hand?

"Serving others is such a healthy thing for all of us; thinking outside of ourselves and separate from the sense of self that is connected to ego because we get the sense that there is something more important than me and my needs," Dr. Hurwitz says.

According to a 2020 report in the *New York Times*,[46] the FBI stated that "hate crimes in the United States rose to their highest level in more than a decade last year, while more murders motivated by hate were recorded than ever before" (Arango, *New York Times*, 2020). During the political unrest of

2020 in response to the rise in hate crimes, many artists found a voice, which was especially hard during a time when the world was quarantined to their homes. People took to social media and news sources, marching in the streets to make their voice heard.

Marla Louissaint,[47] a Haitian-born performer, published model, and activist, cofounded Claim Our Space Now,[48] which according to their website,

> is a resource and multimedia one-stop-shop for information and inspiration that will educate, motivate, unionize, and mobilize us in the task of dismantling an intricately woven system that was built to keep Black and brown bodies under the foot of white supremacy.
>
> (claimourspacenow.org)

She is a 2015 Jimmy Award[49] winner who appeared on stage (*Beautiful: The Carole King Musical*[50]) and television (Netflix's

Seven Seconds[51]). While finishing her degree, she has continued to push her creative voice in several disciplines and has made it her mission to make art that claims ownership of her Blackness and her Black experience unapologetically and is committed to encourage all people to do the same.

Louissaint reared her head back, charged forward with these incredible efforts, and worked as an actress and model, all while studying for her computer science degree at Fordham University.[52] During this time of incredibly high stakes, Louissaint was able to fight for her identity and community – all while exploring her art, which she helmed, and leading a team of brilliant thinkers.

"If we continue to just put our heads down and think about ourselves," Louissaint says, "it's a cycle we will never come out of. I'm here to disrupt those cycles. I've found that through my art, through my voice and speaking loudly, using my channels on socials and conversations allow me to do that."

To move mountains in their work, one must always remember their 'Why' statement. *Why* is an artist creating a podcast? *Why* is one writing the play? The objective gets the Ego out of the path of the multi-hyphenate and helps them focus on the larger picture. By looking at Louissaint's Claim Our Space Now, their Why is very clear: emboldening urgent action to dismantle white supremacy and save Black lives. These Why statements are meant to ignite alignment, or a common cause or viewpoint, to ensure that while the artist does not stray from what's true to themselves and the vision they have for a more global perspective, they are also able to affect *the other*. They help to organize thoughts and actions, keep in check the emotional capacity for other individuals, and help one stay aware of personal boundaries.

Cynthia Henderson,[53] who discussed 'The Why of it All' in the Introduction, is not only a professor and actor but also a Fulbright scholar and the founder of Performing Arts for Social Change,[54] a program whose mission is to raise awareness and educate by giving a voice to important societal issues that are often overlooked. As a professor, Henderson is no stranger to the idea of self-focused energy in one's art, guiding students out of a self-focused mindset. Henderson's personal Why is a reflection of her teachings and how she helps the world around her.

"It makes me pay more attention to the needs of the people and what has occurred in their community, to make my work and presence necessary," Henderson says. "I have to figure out not only what they need from me, but what in my skillset is the most useful for them? And part of that is understanding why I'm here with them in the first place."

Figure 2.4 Marla Louissaint, cofounder of Claim Our Space Now, during Rally For Freedom in Times Square, New York City. Michael Kushner Photography

K.O.,[55] Tony Award winner for their turn as Anita in the 2008 revival of *West Side Story*[56] and star of the 2019 production of *Moulin Rouge*[57] on Broadway, is also a founder of AFECT,[58] or Artists for Economic Transparency. AFECT aims to empower and support the underserved, marginalized, and underrepresented communities in the arts. According to its website, its goal is to "educate the global community on multiple systems of oppression, economic violence and engage in restructuring and dismantling foundational white supremacy" (afectchange. org).

> We want to have people who actually would benefit from the things we're trying to create, which is financial acuity and a little more information about economic violence. One of the things we're working on right now is what the organizational structure is. We're looking at developing an intergenerational organization that lacks hierarchy, almost like we're at a roundtable so that people have more buy-in,

they say.

> Also, to not center experience as much, specifically education, because we know that people with degrees and a specific amount of time in a certain field usually equates privilege and accessibility. And so how can we invite people to be a part of a conversation about helping other people?

While Henderson and Olivo are able to act on their Why within the theatre community, or at least by using theatre, another artist might find that their efforts extend completely past the theatre, leaving the industry completely. Ultimately, when one leaves the industry completely – they break away from being a theatre multi-hyphenate. Yet, that's how strong one's connection can be to a Why, where it shakes everything up and points them to a new direction.

Zachary Durand[59] grew up musical theatre obsessed. In his childhood bedroom there were posters of *The Phantom of the Opera*,[60] Patti LuPone,[61] and his memorabilia from his days at the popular theatre camp, Stagedoor Manor.[62] While attending Shenandoah Conservatory[63] for musical theatre, he realized he no longer wanted to perform, but become an agent in New York. He created his own major, graduated, and joined Talent House,[64] an agency run out of both Canada and New York City. After years of acting as a junior agent at Talent House, Durand became sickened by the politics dominating American life after the 2016 election. By 2018, he fully removed himself from industry; moved to his hometown of Coral Springs, Florida; and began to infiltrate the local political atmosphere. According to Durand:

> By day I was a 9 to 5 talent agent but then after work I'd be in Staten Island coordinating volunteers for the Max Rose[65] campaign, which was the first election post-Trump[66] in 2016. His election was a big wake up call for the whole world. Once the attacks on the LGBTQIA+ community and our Black and Brown siblings started coming, I couldn't look away. I was finding it hard to turn it off, too. Over the course of two years, I was starting to make choices on how I want to spend my extracurricular time. Before the campaign, I was wondering, "Should I watch my client guest starring in this show, or should I watch *Rachel Maddow*[67]?" And having those conflicts, and choosing more often than not *Rachel Maddow*, I was understanding my interests were starting to change, my values were beginning to shift. If you're an agent or manager, or any sort of job where you have a client, there's a total give and take balance in the relationship. Any agent should be in it 100% and I really wasn't wanting to devote 100% when I was donating my time with the campaign.

Durand couldn't ignore that while at the office, he was dreaming of being at the campaign all day. His tipping point was the unfathomable tragedy at Marjory Stoneman Douglas High School,[68] just a few minutes from the house he grew up in. While celebrating Max Rose's win and simultaneously mourning the loss of 17 innocent victims and learning that Ron DeSantis[69] was elected governor of Florida, Durand chose to resign from agenting without knowing what would come next. After two years of self-reflection and considering where to better serve the community, he moved to his roots in Florida and now serves as community outreach director for the office of Fort Lauderdale mayor Dean J. Trantalis.[70] Sometimes being a true artist is simply doing the work one is spiritually called to do – even if it pulls one out of the industry that they had spent their whole life wanting to be a part of. While Durand is not a theatrical multi-hyphenate, he approaches his work in the way a multi-hyphenate should: by understanding the responsibility they hold to another.

Certainly not everyone has to leave the industry in order to make an impact. If an artist finds themselves in a show, for some, it's simply the art they create on and offstage that helps them help people. For example, Tony Yazbeck has graced the stage on Broadway in musicals such as *A Chorus Line*,[71] *Gypsy*,[72] and *On the Town*,[73] for which he received a Tony nomination for his portrayal as Gabey. While singing "Lonely Town" in the 2014 *On the Town* revival, Yazbeck used the Laban[74] principle of Open Heart – a technique he carries into his efforts of multi-hyphenating. Laban is a vocabulary of movement and exploration for the artist. Yazbeck calls on this concept to connect deeper with dance, a way he can permeate his audience:

As someone who has always enjoyed and explored being a multi-hyphenate, having this Open Heart is the key to moving forward in your career successfully. I have always looked at someone as being successful to how they have adapted or evolved to their circumstances in life. This takes an incredible amount of faith. The ability to fully trust that you are on this earth for a reason. And that reason serves the purpose of helping others in some way. When I was a kid, all I ever wanted to do was dance. I knew it made me happy and it made other people seemingly happy too. I didn't see anything else for me. When I got older, I started to want to be a storyteller in new ways. I think the whole idea of Open Heart is to open up outside of your own immediate self interest . . . to give up the plan you had to a greater purpose that will only surprise you in wonderful ways. It takes a lot of risk and that can feel scary. But the blessing is right outside the door.

Roger Q. Mason[75] is an award-winning Black and Filipinx writer, performer and educator whose work has been seen on and off-Broadway at Circle in the Square,[76] New York Theatre Workshop,[77] and The New Group,[78] to name only a few.

"We have to remember the Afrikaanist roots of Western drama," says Roger Q. Mason on Episode 51: "Wig the F*ck Out," of Dear Multi-Hyphenate.[79]

We have to remember that the first noted and Greek acknowledged ritual of theatre was the festival of Isis and Osiris in which Upper and Lower Egypt were reunited in body and spirit so that winter could become spring and the harvest would prevail. We have to remember that the reenactment of the rememberment of Osiris' dismembered body . . . that act was a civic, public, and communal event – that through performance brought unity to the people. We as multi-hyphenates were, and I think still are, spiritual leaders. We have a responsibility to the people and their connection to the stars. We tell the stories and write the tales of days gone by that remind people who they are, where they've been, and where they are going. We cast the spells that enchant nature to let the sun rise and the moon fall and the rain descend upon us and the crops to grow – that's the power we have *if* we harness and acknowledge it with humility and grace and community engagement. And so anytime I get the opportunity to write a play or work in community with people on a project of mine, I know that it is a holy act.

This holy act that Mason talks about is the power of multi-hyphenating. Multi-hyphenating is about serving others, therefore promoting access. It doesn't matter the medium in which one produces art; the art simply must be rooted in a cause that is bigger than 'me.' Whether it's from on stage, in the costume shop, or the press office – serving others only focuses the art, impacting a broader audience. But because a multi-hyphenate has many talents, the self-focused energy must be tamed for each hyphen an artist has. Once an artist begins to remove self-focused qualities, understanding how an artist engages in their proficiencies will only be more precise, more powerful, and more direct. Yet, just like any power – a witch must learn how to control it before using it in the world. So how does one start to form their hyphens and harness their potential?

A multi-hyphenate can be broken down into two key attributes: the **skill** and the **proficiency**. Learning the specific characteristics and the purpose they serve is crucial to having streamlined and focused artistry. Not understanding the similarities and differences between the two can lead to confusion and a muddled mess.

EPISODE EXCERPT

MARY JO MCCONNELL

Broadway National Tours: The Phantom of the Opera, Beauty and the Beast (Mrs. Potts), All Shook Up, Sister Act. TV: Hunters

HEALING: THE ARTIST & THE COMBAT SOLDIER • **EPISODE 45**

Michael: We're unpacking so many beautiful comparisons to the artist and the combat soldier... how they require training, they require intense circumstances of mental exhaustion, love...

MJ: And physical wear and tear.

Michael: Mm-hmm. Something that comes to mind is you're talking about the artist needing -- we're talking about the artist ensemble and camaraderie, right? But what comes to mind is that the combat soldier needs camaraderie in the moment when they're in the front lines, but really where they need the most camaraderie, I feel, is after.

MJ: Yeah -- when returning from the mission.

Michael: You brought up PTS... now, correct me if I'm wrong in saying the 'D'. You've been saying PTS, not PTSD -- is there a reason?

MJ: Yeah -- post traumatic stress and not labeling it...

Both: ... a disorder.

MJ: I use theatre as medicine tools. I use grounding, breathing, observation without judgement, personal narrative -- and then once all of that is foundationally in place and supported by community, then we can use a piece of Shakespearean text that mirrors symptoms or feelings experienced in the personal narrative and allow that artist to speak using these highly poetic words that are often written in Iambic Pentameter, which actually mimics the heartbeat. And allow them the opportunity to experience these feelings through another characters eyes and soul. And understand that after they do that, they come back to the room, they look everyone in the eye, they ground, they breathe, they observe how they are feeling -- and they take a deep breath.

MJ is the cofounder of the Veteran Arts Workshop-Online Portal (VAW-OP) and is offering free classes in arts/mindfulness to veterans and their families.

Notes

1 www.mtf.nyc
2 https://playground-la.org/
3 www.nytheatrebarn.org/
4 https://artistsrep.org/artist-development/dna-oxygen/
5 www.shakina.nyc
6 www.dramabookshop.com/
7 www.playwrightshorizons.org/
8 www.playwrightshorizons.org/shows/plays/strange-loop/
9 www.thelivingmichaeljackson.com/
10 www.zialikhan.com/
11 www.tcg.org/Default.aspx?TabID=1780
12 https://artistsrep.org/
13 https://adriennemareebrown.net/
14 www.akpress.org/we-will-not-cancel-us.html
15 https://arsnovanyc.com/
16 https://arsnovanyc.com/antfest
17 https://arsnovanyc.com/playgroup
18 https://arsnovanyc.com/CAMP
19 www.ibdb.com/broadway-production/natasha-pierre-the-great-comet-of-1812-506425
20 https://kpopbroadway.com/
21 https://en.wikipedia.org/wiki/Kander_and_Ebb
22 https://chicagothemusical.com/
23 www.drdrama.com/professional-background/
24 www.brandeis.edu/
25 www.liu.edu/
26 www.alistroker.com/
27 www.playbill.com/person/rebecca-naomi-jones-vault-0000046422
28 www.leslimargherita.com/
29 https://americanrepertorytheater.org/shows-events/shakina-nayfack-manifest-pussy/
30 https://americanrepertorytheater.org/
31 https://publictheater.org/programs/joes-pub/
32 www.deanne-stewart.com/
33 https://jaggedlittlepill.com/
34 www.ithaca.edu/academics/majors-minors/musical-theatre-bfa
35 https://en.wikipedia.org/wiki/Danielle_Hope
36 www.andrewlloydwebber.com/
37 www.andrewlloydwebber.com/show/the-wizard-of-oz/
38 https://lwtheatres.co.uk/theatres/the-london-palladium/
39 www.josephthemusical.com/
40 www.lesmis.com/london
41 www.whitechristmasthemusical.co.uk/
42 www.imdb.com/name/nm1821446/
43 https://en.wikipedia.org/wiki/Michael_Crawford
44 https://en.wikipedia.org/wiki/Into_the_Woods
45 https://openairtheatre.com/
46 www.nytimes.com/2020/11/16/us/hate-crime-rate.html
47 www.playbill.com/article/how-marla-louissaint-is-making-the-revolution-irresistible
48 www.claimourspacenow.org/
49 www.jimmyawards.com/
50 https://beautifulonbroadway.com/
51 https://en.wikipedia.org/wiki/Seven_Seconds_(TV_series)
52 www.fordham.edu/site/index.php
53 https://broadwaypodcastnetwork.com/dear-multi-hyphenate/11-cynthia-henderson-the-why-of-it-all-or-a-masterclass-in-acting/
54 www.pa4sc.com/
55 www.playbill.com/person/karen-olivo-vault-0000040641
56 www.ibdb.com/broadway-production/west-side-story-481437
57 www.ibdb.com/broadway-production/moulin-rouge-the-musical-520640
58 www.afectchange.org/
59 www.fortlauderdale.gov/government/city-commission/mayor-dean-j-trantalis/contact-the-mayor-s-office
60 www.thephantomoftheopera.com/
61 https://pattilupone.net/
62 www.stagedoormanor.com/
63 www.su.edu/conservatory/
64 www.talenthouse.ca/new-york-office
65 https://en.wikipedia.org/wiki/Max_Rose
66 https://en.wikipedia.org/wiki/Donald_Trump
67 www.msnbc.com/rachel-maddow-show
68 www.browardschools.com/stonemandouglas
69 https://en.wikipedia.org/wiki/Ron_DeSantis
70 www.fortlauderdale.gov/government/city-commission/mayor-dean-j-trantalis
71 https://en.wikipedia.org/wiki/A_Chorus_Line
72 https://en.wikipedia.org/wiki/Gypsy_(musical)
73 www.ibdb.com/broadway-production/on-the-town-497107
74 https://labaneffortsinaction.com/labans-efforts
75 www.rogerqmason.com/aboutme
76 www.playbill.com/venue/circle-in-the-square-theatre-vault-0000000092
77 www.nytw.org/
78 https://thenewgroup.org/
79 https://broadwaypodcastnetwork.com/dear-multi-hyphenate/51-roger-q-mason-wig-the-fck-out/

Reference List

1. "MTF Makers™ Cohort II–Musical Theatre Factory." *Musical Theatre Factory–NYC Theatre Development Artist Service Organzation*, 17 Nov. 2020, https://mtf.nyc/programming/makers/cohort2/.

2. "NYC'S Premier Hub for New Talent." *ARS NOVA RSS*, ars-novanyc.com/about-us/.
3. "Success Index." Gallup & Populace.
4. Hurwitz, Dr. Alisa. "Mental Health Series: Ig Live." *Dr. Drama*, 11 Apr. 2020, www.drdrama.com/2020/04/11/mental-health-series-ig-live/.
5. Arango, Tim. "Hate Crimes in U.S. Rose to Highest Level in More than a Decade in 2019." *The New York Times*, The New York Times, 16 Nov. 2020, www.nytimes.com/2020/11/16/us/hate-crime-rate.html.
6. *Home*, www.claimourspacenow.org/home.
7. "Our Mission." *Artists for Economic Transparency*, www.afectchange.org/our-mission.

EXERCISE 3

WRITE A LOVE LETTER

DM-H

There is nothing more honest than the needs and wants of a human heart. Whether it's love or ambition, hunger or thirst, the human heart wants what it wants, and there's no getting around it. This feeling should also permeate one's artistry. That's how it stays personal, organic, and original.

What does *your* heart look like? What does it say about you? How does it affect your artistry? Multi-hyphenate artistry should be about affecting *the other*, so how can one easily remember who they are trying to affect? Love letters are pure and simple forms of communicating what the human heart wants – so what if you tried writing a love letter to the audience you're trying to build and affect?

Even though most of the world is connected to their phones, a good ol' handwritten love letter never goes out of fashion. Try writing a platonic love letter connecting you to those you are trying to influence. Is it an audience? A creative team you're collaborating with? A specific writer? Complete your letter by following these instructions:

1. Date the letter.
2. Be definitive with who you are writing this letter to. If it's an audience – is it a specific group of people? Are they from a specific city? Or is it one specific person? If it's a writer – who are they? What draws you to them? The more specific, the better.
3. Fall in love. Some questions to answer can be – what is it about who you're writing to is special? What do they have to offer and what are the reasons why it's an amazing quality? Why do you want to affect them? Why do they deserve your love? Why do you want to affect them? What do they need from you? What do you see in them? How can you help them?
4. Provide a signature. As all letters have, they need a signature. How would you sign this? This is an opportunity to be creative.

Remember, it's not about you. It's about affecting the other in hopes of positively influencing them. It's always good to be reminded of the lovely, unique aspects of the people you're working with or creating for.

This letter is *not* meant to be sent. It's to be kept and reviewed whenever you need a reminder. The date is important because, remember, a Why changes – and sometimes when a Why changes, the audience you're trying to affect does as well. It's good to have a record of when one changes. All this information will continue to influence the choices an artist makes, and you never know when you'll need to tap into what was important in the past.

"I want you to make a positive choice here. One of wonder, not of worry."

Randy Graff

Chapter 3
Skills vs. Proficiencies

DOI: 10.4324/9781003254744-5

Joan Marcus

Career Connection
Photographers & Videographers

Pose. Click. Record. Edit.

In the 21st century, access to photography and videography is a necessity. With social media moving quickly, the demand for easily accessible photo and video content is at an all-time high. Even with technology advancing on our smartphones, nothing compares to the art of photography and videography with the appropriate equipment, the right eye, and art direction. Photography is meant to capture a moment in time, but in the theatre, moments in time range drastically. Different photographers and videographers serve many purposes, whether it's for production photography, headshots, portraits, social media photos, website design, reels, and so on.

Joan Marcus,[1] a legendary Broadway photographer who received a Tony Award for Excellence in the Theatre,[2] got her start in Washington, D.C. She primarily focuses on taking some of the most legendary and memorable photos of Broadway productions. When she's not in a Broadway house, she's taking beautiful portraits of her plants in her garden for fun. Marcus says of her start in the theatre:

> I wanted to be a photographer and randomly got a photography job in the theater. I loved my job and I loved theater and it became my career path in a traditional way. You work hard, your skills improve, you meet people, you're at the right place at the right time. . . . It was more organic. There was self-promotion but the process was slower. Social media did not exist. I would say that that is the biggest difference. Now there is the opportunity to shape your career rather than relying on others to shape it for you. It scares me to death but I think it's great. I have been a production photographer primarily. I believe my responsibility is to the theatre artists to interpret and celebrate their work in an honest way.

If ten theatre photographers are put in a room together, each will have a different style and responsibility. Separate from the production photographer, the headshot photographer serves another purpose altogether. A headshot is a photograph of an actor incorporating their essence, a strong point of view, and an up-to-date physical depiction of said actor. Casting directors, those hired to bring in talent to be seen by the fellow members of the show's creative team, skim through headshots to see who looks close to the image of their vision, therefore helping an actor land an audition.

Headshots used to have a lot less room to play. Only in the 2000s did headshots move from the world of black-and-white into color. Now that audition submissions are digital, it allows for many more actors and their representation to submit. These headshots go to websites such as Breakdown Express,[3] where they are minimized to a tiny thumbnail. Before the pandemic, an estimated 6,000 actors were submitting for one role – and post-pandemic, it has escalated to around 7,500 submissions for one role. Therefore, headshots have to be extremely specific. An actor must be able to describe themselves as so much more than "quirky," "edgy," or "vulnerable." What stories should be conveyed through the lens? The headshot photographer must guide the actor through a specific point of view to successfully tread the line between costume and nondescript. The way headshots hint at an emotion, a time period, or a style will help the casting director decide if they are the right for the world of the project they are casting.

Separate from a headshot photographer, certain photographers exist to help market a show or a performer. Marc J. Franklin[4] is a New York City–based photographer specializing in portrait and editorial photography and served as the photo editor and principal photographer for *Playbill*[5] from 2017 to 2022. He is currently the photo editor for NBC News[6] and MSNBC Digital.[7] His photos have been featured in the *New York Times*,[8] the *LA Times*,[9] *Vogue*,[10] *Elle*,[11] the *Paris Review*,[12] *Out Magazine*,[13] the *Boston Globe*,[14] and *Mashable*[15] and has is responsible for the production photography for Broadway productions such as *Lackawanna Blues*,[16] *A Strange Loop*,[17] and the revival of *for colored girls who have considered suicide/when the rainbow is enuf*.[18] Franklin says:

> I use photography to give audiences access to Broadway through images. I capture Broadway from rehearsal, to opening night, to the Tony Awards and everything in between. In addition to event coverage, I work to give a visual voice to the stories that make the theatre come to life by crafting editorial photo features, chronicling backstage moments, creating design retrospectives, and more. Theatre was seminal in my development as an artist, and in my role at Playbill, I am able to use my art to amplify the stories of others. A show may only be a few hours, but there are entire lives involved in a piece's creation that are just as compelling as the work onstage. I consider it a privilege to be able to shine the spotlight back on the people that make that possible while helping to

create the same sense of passion in theatre-lovers that shaped me as an artist.

The ecosystem of a photography studio is an incredible way for artists to explore high-octane, interpersonal artistry in a controlled environment. Of course, photographers are not the only ones who exist in a studio – in some shoots one will find a stylist, a creative director, and assistants, and of course, photographers would be little to nothing without a glorious hair and makeup team. Hair and makeup artists not only help convey the emotion of a photo, but they also serve as an anchor for the photographer.

"I find a headshot session is a true success when the person being photographed feels like they can see their heart and soul in the photo," says Sarah Hamaty,[19] New York City–based hair and makeup artist.

Makeup and clothes are great, but they are only accessories that help enhance the true beauty of the client. If the focus is too heavily on the external, we lose the important part. When I can connect on a deep human level with the client and help them feel the most themselves to let the confidence shine through, that's a total success.

Rebecca Michelson[20] is the creative brain and heart behind 11 O'clock Creative,[21] a full-service production and video-marketing company based in New York City. Not only is she helping theatre-based businesses grow their content, but she is also often found in the cabaret and concert circuit of Manhattan, filming artists' performances.

"You have to have an online presence," says Michelson.

So much of what you do is going to take place online before you even do it in person anymore. So if you're growing a business, you have to be posting about it – that's how you're going to get clients and sell your services. I think being an actor is a business in itself. If you're an actor, that is your brand. You need to focus on your brand online because people are going to look you up. They are going to try to see if you are who you say you are. Keeping up with it and making it authentically *you* is super important.

Oftentimes, when an artist identifies as a multi-hyphenate, they will incorporate their for-now job, or any talent or hobby as a part of their multi-hyphenate identity. This is a mistake. Why? If one was to incorporate every skill, every hobby, and ever interest – one could identify with mile-long list of "hyphens" that aren't flushed out to a professional level. Just because one loves to cook does not mean they should identify as being a chef.

One who identifies as a multi-hyphenate might say they are an actor-roller skater-knitter. Looking at a multi-hyphenate being an artist with multiple proficiencies that *cross-pollinate* to help flourish professional capabilities, how can that be justified? Are these hobbies? Are these income garnering experiences? When adding a hyphen to an identity, it actually calls for an in-depth vetting process. Let's break it down.

First, let's walk through what makes up a hyphen. As discussed, a '**hyphen**' is another word for '**proficiency**' and these two words are interchangeable. A hyphen/proficiency is often a larger, broader, and strengthened capability like performer, orchestrator, photographer, producer, writer, stage manager, electrician, designer, and more. Proficiencies are usually the broader spectrum of a skill set, and a career can be made out of just one of those art forms.

The multi-hyphenate makes a career out of *multiple* proficiencies or, in this case, hyphens. Yet, sometimes, this becomes muddled when an artist confuses a **skill** for a proficiency. While one can certainly garner income out of a skill, it doesn't always mean a proficiency. For instance, if a photographer can use Photoshop to edit headshots and *only* knows how to use Photoshop for that purpose, does that mean they will identify as a Graphic Designer? That's potentially setting up a lot of people searching for a Graphic Designer up for disappointment if the only thing they know how to do is smooth skin and brighten an image.

So how does a skill differ from a proficiency? A **skill** is a smaller, practiced effort, in service to the proficiency such as organization, Photoshop (photo editing), Final Cut Pro (video editing), social media, observational skills, sense of humor, comedic timing, self-awareness, sewing, roller blading, stage makeup, and more. They can be emotional, physical, tactical, and psychological. In terms of being a multi-hyphenate, a skill is used to connect the thoughts and actions of a proficiency and aid in the completion of the job required of the proficiency. For a film editor (proficiency) to complete a first draft, they have to use Final Cut (skill) to edit their film.

Multi-hyphenates have a responsibility to showcase their talents on the level in which it is *true*. If an artistic director hires a stage manager, they must deliver accordingly. Hopefully, one would not apply to the position just because they once stage-managed their friend's improv troupe for fun. That experience might help build a future career as a stage manager, but saying they are well experienced in that art form as a proficiency is not recommended or very professional.

Remember, many artists set a goal to turn a hobby into a proficiency – therefore, skills and hobbies *can* become a proficiency. But understanding when to professionally identify with that art form is important.

So how does a skill affect the path one goes on when finding a proficiency? Let's look at a *theatrical* photographer, as an example; the overall art and skill of photography have become an artist's proficiency, mainly because it's a broader scope of skills, and they've made a career out of performing the task.

But if a theatre photographer is called to photograph a wedding, are they eligible just because they have the skill of maneuvering a camera? Photographing a wedding and photographing in a theatre requires different skills. What skills are required of each and how do they differ?

- Both have to anticipate the drama and emotion of a moment.
- Both have to understand light, aperture, and functions of the camera.
- Wedding photographers need to have sensitivity and people skills, while if a theatre photographer is photographing the dress rehearsal of a show, they don't really have to interact with many people.
- Theatre photographers have extremely tight deadlines, while wedding photography can be more lenient and the boundaries of when photos are finished are up to the wedding photographer.
- Both must move with diligence, be able to shift focus, and problem-solve.
- Both must know how to edit using programs like Photoshop or Lightroom.
- Theatre photographers must be ready to help a producer, stage manager, or press rep problem-solve, while a wedding photographer must engage with emotional family members.
- Wedding photographers have to engage in loud, raucous environments, whereas the theatre photographer has to engage in theatre etiquette.
- Wedding photographers have their own fixed rates, while the theatre photographer might have to negotiate what the producer is offering from the show's budget.

Keep in mind that photographing weddings takes the photographer out of the theatre. In this instance, this may be a for-now job and being a theatre multi-hyphenate should be in the sphere of the theatre.

Matthew Murphy is the founder of MurphyMade Photography[22] and responsible for many iconic production photos on Broadway. When walking past the Majestic Theatre[23] on Broadway, his production photographs of *The Phantom of the Opera*[24] adorn the facade. Murphy says:

> Before I focused full-time on theater photography I took on a huge mix of other photography work: weddings, portraits, events . . . you name it I tried it. Even though I was very lucky to have some incredible opportunities come my way early on, it wasn't until I was on my fourth or fifth show that I really sensed commercial theater photography could become a long-term career. Once I set my sights on commercial theater photography, I did everything I could to get ready and stay ready for any opportunity that would come my way. From the very beginning of my career I photographed live performances and I would just continue to hone in on the exact type of work I wanted.

While Murphy calls on many technical skills to support his photography endeavors, there is one that simply cannot be taught:

> The most important skill I call on to be my best photographer is staying in tune with those around me. I always lead with kindness and I try to find the balance between being a keen observer and an active leader in the shoot. I think life is too short to not try to have fun at all times, so I draw on my sense of humor whenever I'm working with my subjects.

While Matthew's empathy, observation, and leadership are skills he calls on, they simply support the efforts of his proficiency as a "photographer." As one does not usually garner an income or a paper trail just for being a pleasant person, these would not be a part of Murphy's hyphens. Therefore, Murphy keeps certain skills as simply skills and *not* proficiencies.

Looking at the first example of the artist who is an **actor-roller skater-knitter**, it's a good opportunity to review the first three principals when finding a hyphen. Based on the principles discussed in Chapter 1, "What is a Multi-Hyphenate?" one would recall that the first three aspects in choosing a hyphen

1. is acquiring an income.
2. is a skill that is requested at a high demand.

3. which has a lengthy paper trail or numerous accolades (awards, grants, press, etc.).

Is it possible to receive an income from roller skating or knitting? Absolutely. Is it possible to be in high demand for roller skating or knitting? Sure. Is it possible to have press or a paper trail for roller skating or knitting? Absolutely! But just because they are skills which tick off one, two, or even all three requirements, it doesn't mean it's a part of their multi-hyphenate identity. Why? There is the absence of **cross-pollination**, or connectivity, between the hyphens.

Now that the difference between a skill and a proficiency has been explored, one must understand that the multi-hyphenate's proficiencies should coexist and cross-pollinate. What does that mean? Each hyphen should inform or affect the other. The ways are countless, but discovering one's hyphen relationship is critical in functionality.

Does the income of one hyphen support the other hyphen? Does an artist's podcast build a loyal audience who will then sell out their concert? Does one's creation build an ensemble through blending different artistic mediums?

The aspect of combining mediums helps add to DeAnne Stewart's[25] multi-hyphenate experience. She established her event planning company Dear September[26] during quarantine. While carrying out both gorgeous and theatrical events, she can easily find the ways in which this expands her multi-hyphenate identity – by blending two separate worlds together through the common denominators of the theatre. Stewart says:

> There are certain skills that are specific just to the event planning world, organizational things that just any artist couldn't guarantee they could do. But a lot of it is connected to artistry from the design aspect, to filling spaces, how to structure, style – it's all super theatrical.

Stewart finds the parallel between her event planning and theatrical storytelling. Dear September prides itself on curating macro memories through micro events. Not only is her artistry tied to theatrical elements, but the team she engages with are also from the theatre community.

> The connections I have to certain people in the industry are super helpful because when it comes to event production, it's a lot of the same people you need on a team when you're producing a show. Some events require lighting designers, technicians, elements of set building and carpentry.

Similar to Stewart and Dear September, if a photographer were to identify themselves as a theatre photographer, there're still mediums that differ from each other and serve a purpose in the theatre community. A theatre photographer doesn't have to be photographing the stage – they can choose to focus on headshots, press photography, backstage/dressing room photography, or press. In Stewart's instance, she simply found a different medium in which she'd like to produce, not beholden to a traditional theatrical space.

It's tempting to want to try everything when beginning as a multi-hyphenate – and artists should try to experience everything they can. Yet, with so many possibilities, it's easy to get distracted or spread oneself too thin. By clearly differentiating between skills and proficiencies, as well as making sure each hyphen supports each other, one promotes alignment. This alignment works in tandem with the artist's 'Why' statement, directing the artist's path even more specifically. The multi-hyphenate doesn't separate an artist's experiences, it combines and strengthens them.

An outsider might look at the multi-hyphenate and go, "Wow! You certainly have a lot of plates spinning!" While the plates might be spinning, at the end of the night they are properly labeled, cleaned, polished, and put away in a very specific order. Being a multi-hyphenate is not a chaotic experience contributing to an artist feeling unorganized and confused. By understanding its structure, multi-hyphenating becomes the antithesis of the phrase "***Jack of all trades, master of none.***" This phrase insinuates that an artist who has their hand in multiple tasks might be good at multiple things, but they are never *great*. Asking oneself the four questions of analyzing multi-hyphenate identity prevents that phrase from ever being true.

Take a look at Figure 3.3. The visualization is designed to help an artist decide whether it's the appropriate time to add a hyphen to their identity. To put it simply, an artist should be ready to add a hyphen to their name when they are ready to play with the big dogs. There is no shame in working to build a skill up into a proficiency – it may take time, but the investment will be worth it. Plus, fellow collaborators will be pleased with one's transparency regarding their competence. Why fake expertise in a proficiency when it will cause more harm than help?

With the understanding of how a skill relates to a proficiency, one is free to explore tangible ways to discover their official hyphens, which must be done with openness and wonder.

"The action of wonder is something I discovered organically as I got older," says Tony Winner Randy Graff,[27] who most recently played Elaine Young in *Mr. Saturday Night*[28] on Broadway.

IS MY SKILL ALSO A PROFICIENCY?

Use this to help expand your multi-hyphenate identity.

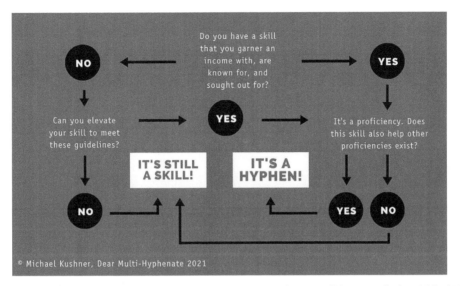

Figure 3.3 Is my skill a proficiency? An example of how to find out if a skill can be turned into a proficiency, or a hyphen. Michael Kushner Photography

The first place my students usually go to is one of worry and anxiety. Like life! Right? I ask them to open up their discovery with a choice of wonder and curiosity. With wonder you don't know how it's going to end. It's a surprise, leaving room for discovery. With worry, we assume the outcome is bad.

While worry creates anxiety, wonder creates accessibility. And that's what the multi-hyphenate experience is all about – creating opportunities for ourselves and others. Multi-hyphenating is an art and must be approached as such. If one can figure out how to cross-pollinate the example

of acting, roller skating, and (or other seemingly disparate combinations), such a mind can keep art fresh and new. It's entirely up to the real-life artist to justify if a proficiency is in fact a part of their own multi-hyphenate experience.

Thus concludes the preparation of becoming a multi-hyphenate. The thoughts and ideas that go into multi-hyphenating have been covered and now one must explore how to apply these concepts. Through application, a multi-hyphenate can begin to form access, establish a healthy workflow, embrace failure, set boundaries, and protect themselves. The functionality of multi-hyphenating can be tricky, but it's ultimately daring, exciting, and freeing.

EPISODE EXCERPT

ROGER Q. MASON

Award-winning writer, performer and educator whose work has been
seen on Broadway, Off-Broadway, and Off-Off Broadway

WIG THE F*** OUT • EPISODE 51

Michael: Regardless, we have actor, photographer, producer -- we have all of these things where it's not just black and white, it's not just boy / girl. And it's the same with gender where we're getting society to go... it's not just what you know... it's actually this.

Roger: Here's the thing you have to think about. Along the road to commercialization we lost a really key link in the chain of art making. Which is that it is interdisciplinary by nature. In fact, the very definition of art as I remember it being taught to me when I was learning oil painting comes from an Arabic word which means putting fine things together -- so it's collage like. It's interdisciplinary in nature and in etymological fact the word itself used to describe this activity which we perform is an act of putting things together. And when you start having to commodify something departmentalize something in order to put it in a box so that it could be charged for at this rate or that union rate or this or that, the fluidity of the thing gets eroded along the way. Now, there is such a thing as auteurism as well... and I want to demystify and undemonize that word because we look at the egoistic underpinnings of that -- oh someone who's a control freak or whatever. But I think I want to return to the understanding of an Auteur as somebody who sees and processes narrative information in an interdisciplinary and holistic way such that they conceive of an event -- and when they conceive of an event they are aware in the mechanisms that they are using to tell it of how different facilities, whether it's lighting - sound - directing - producing, how these all work together holistically. When I was growing up, I had many heroes. Two of them were Emily Mann and and George C. Wolfe and the reason is because they were storytellers that were able to waft between job descriptions because they understood theatre making as one harmonious whole -- one spiritual and civic event manifested by departments, but conceived of as one expression. And they possessed in their storytelling genius minds, the ability to put those fine things together. And at times they directed, or at times they wrote, or at times they did both, or at times they were producing a piece -- but the mentality, the mentality of seeing the whole thing... that is something I can never turn off.

Roger Q. Mason is a Black, Filipinx, plus-sized, gender non-conforming, queer artist of color. Their work employs the lens of history to chip away at the cultural biases that divide rather than unite us.

Notes

1 www.joanmarcusphotography.com/
2 www.tonyawards.com/news/2014-tony-honors-for-excellence-in-the-theatre-announced/
3 www.breakdownexpress.com/index.cfm
4 www.marcjfranklin.com/
5 www.playbill.com/
6 www.nbcnews.com/
7 www.msnbc.com/information/about-nbc-news-digital-n1232185
8 www.nytimes.com/
9 www.latimes.com/
10 www.vogue.com/
11 www.elle.com/
12 www.theparisreview.org/
13 www.out.com/
14 www.bostonglobe.com/
15 https://mashable.com/
16 www.ibdb.com/broadway-production/lackawanna-blues-531475
17 www.ibdb.com/broadway-production/a-strange-loop-533382
18 www.ibdb.com/broadway-production/for-colored-girls-who-have-considered-suicide–when-the-rainbow-is-enuf-532941
19 www.michaelkushnerphotography.com/my-team
20 https://rebeccajmichelson.com/
21 https://11oclockcreative.com/
22 www.murphymade.com/
23 www.ibdb.com/theatre/majestic-theatre-1252
24 https://us.thephantomoftheopera.com/
25 www.deanne-stewart.com/
26 https://dearseptemberevents.com/
27 www.randygraff.com/bio.html
28 www.ibdb.com/broadway-production/mr-saturday-night-532890

EXERCISE 4 DM-H
SKILLS IN CHECK

It's time to keep those skills in check! When completing this exercise, **do not read ahead to the end**. Take it one step at a time and surprise yourself!

You have more skills than you think – and it's time to lay them all out and see which have the most potential of becoming a part of your multi-hyphenate identity. Maybe you aren't aware you're sitting on a skill that can cause you great success! Now is the time to find out.

Make four columns. List them.

Skill. Level. Potential. Interest.

In the first column, list all the skills you have. Remember, as mentioned in this chapter, skills can be anything from organization, Photoshop (photo editing), Final Cut Pro (video editing), social media, observational skills, sense of humor, comedic timing, self-awareness, sewing, roller-blading, stage makeup, and more. Get creative here.

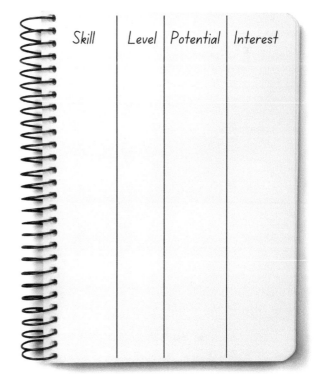

Figure 3.5 Example of column. Michael Kushner Photography

Skills vs. Proficiencies

Once you've listed all your skills, it's time to get honest. In the next column, rate what you think is your current skill level from 1 to 10, with 1 being the lowest.

When that has been completed – in the next column, from 1 to 10, rate the potential you think this skill has in growing into a proficiency, or a hyphen. If you rated a skill as a 5, you could rate it as a 0 if there is no potential in growing it into one or it doesn't belong as a hyphen. Perhaps rating it a 5 means you're unsure. Maybe a 10 means you will absolutely invest in growing this skill to a hyphen, or it already is one.

And for the final step, in the fourth column listed "Interest," rate the level of interest you have in growing this skill into a proficiency. If you want to keep it as a hobby – rate it a 1. If you're really interested in growing this skill into something professional, rate it a 10! This section helps decide what skill you might want to invest in in the near future, or leave alone for a second.

When completed, tally up the numbers for each skill.

If the skill was rated 20 to 30, this skill might be worth growing into a proficiency! Keep exploring and see if you can get an income, a paper trail, and a high demand for this skill.

If the skill was rated 10 to 19, perhaps this skill stays as a skill which helps a hyphen exist. Or, it's not yet ready to develop into a hyphen because it's still developing or the interest isn't quite there yet.

If the skill was rated 3 to 9, maybe this skill stays as a hobby. It doesn't seem like there's any use in exploring it when the interest and skill levels are rated so low.

Important: remember to make sure each proficiency will be able to effect and cross-pollinate with your current proficiencies. By completing this exercise, one should have a clearer idea of the skills which can be considered hyphens, the skills which one could invest in, and the skills which will simply help hyphens exist.

PART II
APPLICATION

"Having a coalition and having a team, a team that is open in their dialogue and communication and their delegation is completely, completely necessary in order to make it work."

Dimitri Möise, Episode 17, "Discovering Your Call to Action"

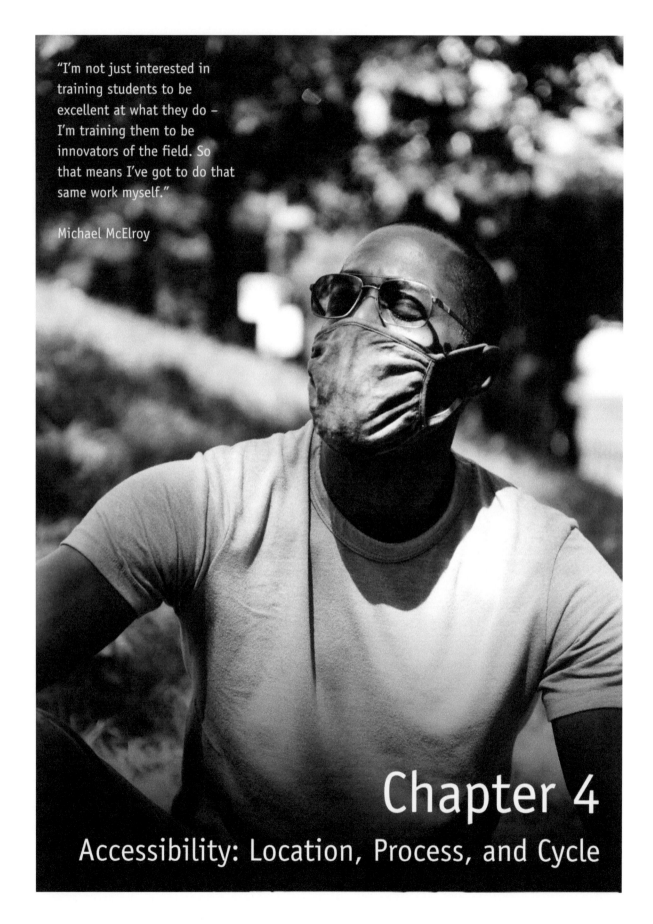

"I'm not just interested in training students to be excellent at what they do – I'm training them to be innovators of the field. So that means I've got to do that same work myself."

Michael McElroy

Chapter 4
Accessibility: Location, Process, and Cycle

DOI: 10.4324/9781003254744-7

Christine Toy Johnson

Career Connection
Grants, Fellowships, & Scholarships

How many multi-hyphenates out in the world know about grants? A **grant** is a significant monetary fund designed to support the efforts of an artist. These sums of money are not meant to be paid back – as a loan is.

Christine Toy Johnson[1] is a New York–based multi-hyphenate who has been breaking the color barrier in inclusively cast roles for over 30 years and has been featured extensively on Broadway, off-Broadway, in regional theatres across the country, and in film, television, and concerts worldwide. She is an actor-writer-director-producer-podcaster and, in 2021, was elected treasurer of the Dramatists Guild of America,[2] making her the first Asian American to be an officer of the Dramatists Guild.

"I have just received my 21st grant to support my work since I started applying for them in 2007," says Johnson on Episode 42, "Breaking the Color Barrier" of *Dear Multi-Hyphenate*.[3] "It has all come from wanting to tell my stories and finding ways to do that when some traditional ways were not available to me or open to me."

After she applied for her first grant, Christine along with her husband Bruce, was able to create *Transcending: The Wat Misaka Story*,[4] a documentary of the first Japanese American pro-basketball player from the 1947 Nicks.[5] She continues:

> [Grant writing] taught me that there was a way to make things happen. They might be different ways than you would imagine. I tell this to students all the time . . . being open to the idea that your dreams coming true often look very different from how you first imagine them is a key skill to cultivate.

Johnson isn't the only one inspiring dreams, no matter the image. Roger Q. Mason,[6] acclaimed Black and Filipinx playwright, established the New Visions Fellowship.[7] According to Episode 51, "Wig the F*ck Out," of *Dear Multi-Hyphenate*,[8] the New Visions Fellowship is an innovative and rigorous year-long professional development program created by National Queer Theater[9] and The Dramatists Guild to support emerging Black trans and gender nonconforming playwrights.

> Adam Odsess-Rubin[10] brought me into a series of conversations with the Dramatists Guild and also the Dramatists Foundation[11] to imagine how trans and gender-nonconforming playwrights could be mentored

in our changing and many times erasing business. We were very considered at that time in how to develop the aesthetics and professional awareness of young transgender, nonconforming Black playwrights because they were, and still are, one of endangered populations within the American theatre: rarely seen, often overlooked, and never truly understood.

The inaugural fellows have been awarded $5,000 to develop a play, musical, or performance experience of their design and choosing. National Queer Theater will host a professionally cast and directed reading of their play at the end of the program. They will also have the opportunity to participate in professional development sessions covering a wide range of artistic topics. In addition, they will receive a 5-year complimentary membership to The Dramatists Guild, including access to contracts, business advice, and career services, to help protect the artistic and economic integrity of their work. Mason says:

> We have a completely different way of telling story. I gave an anecdote of a theatre that gave me quite an insulting rejection of a play because there was too much white space on the page. The individual was so neurotically concerned with my ability to fulfill a certain time budget – they were worried about the play being long enough to be read or presented in a particular time frame. They were considered and suspicious of my use of white space.

While Mason provides monetary accessibility for playwrights to be better seen and understood, still, grants are not the only way an artist can benefit from financial assistance. Ron Schaefer,[12] founder of French Woods Festival for the Performing Arts,[13] established the Hancock French Woods Arts Alliance (HFWAA),[14] an organization dedicated to young people committed to a career in the arts by offering financial support in pursuing their education. The organization guides recipients financially, emotionally, and professionally. Rose Robinson, the executive director of HFWAA, has been serving in her position for the past 11 years:

> We are there to help where we can. With 50-plus years of French Woods, there are many in the industry who make themselves available to assist where they can – whether financially or sharing their craft and expertise. HFWAA also is involved in leadership training and we have collaborated with Entertainment for Change,[15]

(EFC), a 501(c)3 organization that revolves around being an Impact Artist™. The program allows young people to hold themselves accountable to intentionally making an impact on themselves, another person and/or a collective using creativity as the vehicle and the United Nations 17 Sustainable Development Goals as the blueprint to do so.

The HFWAA receives much of its donations during the summer months when French Woods is in full swing. In the summer of 2020, French Woods, like the rest of the world, dimmed their lights to dodge COVID-19. That didn't stop HFWAA from producing a virtual night of theatre to raise funds. Robinson explains:

> HFWAA primarily raises money to benefit financially in-need college students committed to a career in the arts. The majority of our funding is raised during the summer months from vendors and families associated with French Woods Festival of the Performing Arts. At that time, we were serving 22 college students. The impact of COVID-19 and cancelling camp in 2020 all but destroyed our traditional funding.

In creating *Moments in the Woods*,[16] the producing team, made up of Rose Robinson, Cameron Stefanski, and director Michael Kushner,[17] were able to include Lin Manuel Miranda,[18] Todrick Hall,[19] Jason Alexander,[20] Andréa Burns,[21] Mandy Gonzalez,[22] and many more stars in addition to the myriad of French Woods talent coming together to raise money. Not only was the event a success and watched by 20,000 people thanks to Stars in the House[23] streaming the event, but a multi-hyphenate-led team produced *Moments in the Woods*.

"The gala and telethon were exciting," continues Robinson.

> There were thousands and thousands of viewers who needed to remember how important the arts are. No one was paid for their efforts in putting this together. Many of our beneficiary students told their stories as well, putting a face on the case. We did not raise enough money to continue supporting those 22 students at 100%, but we helped some and it gave so many hope.

Rafael Jaen,[24] a multi-hyphenate who focuses on education and service, is the chair of the performing arts department of the University of Massachusetts, Boston,[25] and the vice president for communications for the United States Institute for Theatre Technology (USITT).[26] He attributes his ability to broaden accessibility because, like the team who created *Moments in the Woods*, his combined efforts with UMass and USITT result in outreach:

> One of the reasons I joined USITT is because they have regional sections and student chapters. There's USITT New England, New York Area, Southwest, Northwest, etc., and we reach out to high schools and undergrad programs to expose the students to the possibilities that they could have a higher education and pursue further an academic career. I think it's about finding models to bring those kids who are first-generation into those settings where they go, "Oh, I could get a BA where I'm not required to have a portfolio, but I do have a resume that could get me in the door." That doesn't close your doors if you want to pursue a master's later. It's about reframing the conversation and broadly understanding where they are going. They may feel that going to New York is the only answer . . . but maybe is not. Maybe they go to a program closer to home that's going to give them a scholarship and then go to the next thing. The regional section that I've been the closest with is USITT Southwest. They have good access to the high school system between Texas and some other places. They help the students get placed, get awards, and build resumes.

Location is a large proponent of one's ability to benefit from or provide accessibility. Whether or not it's through movies, musicals, or Urban legends – artists are often told that to succeed, they have to move to New York or Los Angeles. Plus, the giant leap to either coast requires finances and insight which falls under the umbrella of accessibility. Places like Massachusetts, Florida, Texas, and North Carolina, and many more offer theatrical opportunities with their abundance of regional theatres and education opportunities.

There's a science to multi-hyphenating. Like a scientist in a lab, multi-hyphenating is a trial-and-error process. In trying, one is bound to fail, but determination will prevail in the long run. Even if one becomes discouraged, one must simply persevere and try again. To revisit the steps leading up to multi-hyphenate identity, one now understands

1. the importance of having a 'Why.'
2. the factors of multi-hyphenating.
3. that it's not a self-focused endeavor.
4. the differences between a skill and a proficiency.

Once those steps are taken into consideration, applying multi-hyphenate efforts must be rooted in access. To reiterate, the multi-hyphenate must keep in mind two types of access: access for themselves and access for others. When a multi-hyphenate is creating access for others, they are creating work and collaborative opportunities so that others may succeed and benefit from an equitable and artistic environment. Doing so also creates a healthy, trustworthy, and supportive web of fellow artists. Yet, when one creates access for themselves – it's about finding stability in decision-making, trusting exploration, and asking tough questions designed to keep true and honest work at the forefront of one's mind. When providing access for oneself and others, an artist must take three things into account: **location, process, and cycle**.

Part 1: Location: Access to Environment

> The industry provides accessibility in much the way the Colonial system provides accessibility to enslaved people and immigrants. The industry "anoints" and uplifts those which it sees as reflecting its values to the highest level. Then it keeps a whole class of hopeful wannabes toiling for a chance they will never get.
> – Tony winner Tonya Pinkins[27]

It is no secret to anyone that show business lacks accessibility and is not an easy industry to break into. On top of nepotism (the favoring of one because of their relationship), it's an expensive industry that serves as a participation barrier for less privileged people. An artist can work as hard as they can to create art, but if one doesn't have the resources to get into the right rooms – such as training and networking programs – what else can they do to get seen?

Accessibility should be the concern of those in positions of power, not the people vying for it. It is their responsibility to open the doors to new voices. This includes multi-hyphenates. When creating their own work, a multi-hyphenate will find

themself in a position of power, and therefore must keep their efforts accessible to prevent more gatekeeping from happening in show business. **Gatekeeping** is what separates artists from parity and inclusion, through the idea that people at the top of the food chain control who gets what opportunity and when.

If accessibility is broadened, perhaps artists wouldn't have to commit themselves to expensive institutions or training programs, leaving artists in massive amounts of debt. Perhaps then an artist would be able to create freely and learn by doing – not having to spend thousands of dollars just to train before even searching for work. These rooms should be open wide for all, and searching for opportunities shouldn't be difficult or costly, like the college search. The college search is expensive and drawn out. For students who want to study theatre, not only are they expected to pay the application fee, but they must spend money on audition/interview materials and travel as well. Recent college musical theatre graduate Sushma Saha,[28] who is appearing in the all-female, nonbinary, and trans Roundabout[29] production of *1776*,[30] believes that accessibility can begin by ridding the audition and interview process of the travel aspect.

> I think especially with the pandemic we've seen a lot of the traveling aspects can be taken out of the audition process. A lot of filming can happen – but granted having devices to film on also is an access need. It's a certain kind of privilege. Hopefully there are high schools that are able to have those resources to help students be able to do that. I think that application fees can be a lot more affordable. I was told by my coach for every fourteen schools that a skinny, white blonde or brunette woman auditions for, she will get into two. So as somebody who was a person of color and queer – and just different in general – I was like, "Oh dear, how many colleges am I going to get into? I have to apply to a bajillion!" So students should be able to do that – raise their chances of getting into an institution.

As the industry has more conversations about access, colleges, universities, and training programs are beginning to focus much more on accessibility. Michael McElroy[31] has appeared in numerous productions, both on and off-Broadway, and in 2004 was nominated for a Tony for Best Featured Actor in a Musical for *Big River*.[32] In 1999, McElroy became the founder and director of the Broadway Inspirational Voices[33] (receiving a Tony Award for Excellence in the Theatre in 2019), a diverse, nondenominational gospel choir made up of Broadway singers. In the fall of 2021, McElroy became the new chair of the University of Michigan's Musical Theatre[34] department.

"I'm excited to engage what artistic training means in this moment," says McElroy.

> To me, artistic training is learning to be comfortable with discomfort. It means cracking open in new and exciting ways that are not always comfortable. It's about transformation of the mind, transformation of the imagination, transformation of heart as it expands with empathy, transformation in terms of technique. All of those things are difficult, uncomfortable, and requires struggling, failure, success – all of those things, so you can come on the other side and learn craft, resilience, and self-care. I find we're in a tricky space where that's being removed for comfort. That we no longer should feel uncomfortable in an artistic space, and that's not what it's about. Art in itself means stretching, discomfort, interrogating – all of that leads to a deeper understanding, empathy, and humanity.

McElroy has been working in show business for 30 years and understands what it takes to be an artist and a multi-hyphenated one at that. Yet, the access he brings to the University of Michigan is that which comes from within, connecting to a deeper artistry and understanding of the human spirit. McElroy explains:

> I'm not just interested in training students to be excellent at what they do. I'm training them to be innovators of the field. So that means I've got to do that same work myself.

Examining environments outside of the educational space, McElroy is certainly not the only artist leading by example. Sandy Gooen[35] is a queer, trans, Jewish, and neurodivergent artist who predominantly specializes in writing, music and literary department work, performance, and stage management/ production teamwork. His education and advocacy work revolves around health/disability, LGBTQ+ issues, and Judaism. Gooen says:

> In the present day, the word we need to be thinking of most is access. It applies to people who have been marginalized across the board. What I mean by that is that even the simple questions of "What do the people here need to be successful" "Who's missing, and what barriers are keeping them out?" "How can we work together best?" Those could do a lot of good. I've been working on solutions for access a lot in my music sphere regarding trans musical theatre performers because I genuinely believe there's just a gap in understanding. That's one advantage I have as a multi-hyphenate; I see and can approach that issue from both sides of the table's perspective.

Figure 4.4 Sandy Gooen, photographed in New York City. Michael Kushner Photography

"In film and TV," continues Gooen,

> it seems that there has been a more significant push for diverse representation on and off-screen. Has all of it been perfect? No. There's been an effort there, though, that theatre has stayed behind. Theatre has had a handful of moments onstage, but offstage is incredibly disheartening. Trans actors are slowly getting more recognition, especially in plays. A handful of trans writers and directors have had some success in the less commercial theaters. Still, prominent trans music directors, stage managers, choreographers, casting directors, producers, designers, professors of theatre, and more, especially those beginning their careers while out as trans, are far more uncommon. So many trans men and transmasculine people in all fields (myself included) struggle from a lack of visibility and the weird limbo that is not quite fitting in with cis men while also weirdly getting shoved into these women+ spaces that don't necessarily work for us. The intention behind those groups

is access, but umbrellas so big don't necessarily cover everyone. That said, coalitions are lovely. I also believe in the person-to-person level in asking questions and building bridges because each individual has their own specific experiences, preferences, and needs.

Accessibility is not just an idea, it's an act of ignition for genuine change or finding out ways to include marginalized communities in the same ways as folks with privilege. But careful, someone may *seem* as if they are committing to a cause or movement, also known as being performative. Something *active* must be done – changes must be made, funds must be redistributed, and programs must be instilled to ensure accessibility.

In New York, the old saying is "$20 flies right out of your pocket every time you step outside of your apartment." By observing what it might cost an artist just for the necessities of living, it's more than likely one will be spending more than $20. Solely upon moving to New York City, an artist might have to shell out:

- one month rent if one is subletting. While the numbers certainly range in terms of cost and space, an artist usually spends anywhere from $900 to $2,000 on rent with roommates. If one is signing a lease, it may require a month's rent for a security deposit, which then bumps up the cost to a range of $1,800 to $4,000 upon moving in.
- moving company fees. Price can be anywhere from a couple of hundred dollars into the thousands.
- travel. A Metrocard, New York City's subway pass, is $127 for a 30-day pass. Though with the new OMNY system, a traveler can save money if they purchase 12 rides, then the rest for that week are free.
- first food shop. Remember to include necessities that aren't taken into consideration, salt, pepper, ketchup, and so on. This run can be $300 to $500.
- first toiletry run. Toilet paper, toothpaste. Toothbrush.
- furniture. What came with the apartment? Nothing? A bed? Only a lamp? IKEA and Target certainly come in handy, but one is looking at a couple of hundred dollars, even into the thousands depending on how bare the space is.
- artist-specific requirements. Lighting for photography? Self-tape setup? Audition clothes. Audition material. Drawing board materials. Desk setup. Looking at a self-tape setup, that will run an artist $184.43. iPhone not included, one will need a mic (the cheapest Blue mic, the Snowball, is $39.99), a backdrop (Fovitec backdrops can run $55.95), and a lighting setup (a two-lightbox setup from Neewer costs $88.49). The COVID-19 pandemic

caused auditions to happen at home, therefore pushing artists to transform their living spaces into mini movie sets. It doesn't seem like the self-tape era is going to end any time soon, so these purchases have gone from luxury to almost mandatory. This is yet another reason the industry remains inaccessible for many – to simply audition costs money.

This is not to scare someone out of moving to New York or Los Angeles – it's just to put into perspective some of the finances one will have to shell out when arriving. Moving to a major city is not accessible to all, and many spend years saving for just the move. But still, many artists make waves in the industry from cities that are not New York or Los Angeles. These artists have found that these cities allow them to exist at a speed more suited to how they wish to create or infiltrate the industry.

Washington, D.C., is made up of both non-equity and equity theatres – both of which get reviewed by a staple like the *Washington Post*.[36] Actor and writer Dani Stoller[37] admires the close-knit community of actors who she can work with at any given time, although acknowledges the pitfalls that can happen when trying to find footing in the community.

"It's blessing is also it's curse," Dani Stoller says.

> It's like a rep company, and I've always loved rep companies. As of right now, I will be spending six months, plus, of next year at one theatre. That's something that's also wonderful in the sense that people then know me – I have cold-called artistic directors that I have met and been like, "Hey, can you see me for this?" You can go into a room and talk with people. When people come in, I very rarely don't know them and that's a wonderful thing.

Stoller continues:

> What's difficult is because it's a tight-knit community, shows can get cast over a year in advance. It can be hard because it's a small community to find your footing initially because people go to the theatre programs at American University,[38] George Washington University,[39] Catholic University.[40] They are working already with D.C. professionals in their colleges. So, it can be difficult to move here without knowing anyone. And for me, I've noticed that my friends in New York, the hustle that they have is insane. We don't have that here. It doesn't mean that we don't have to work as hard, but it certainly does mean that I can walk into an audition room and be like, "Hey what's up . . . dinner was fun last night." Because we are in a smaller place, we do have a little bit more room – because people know us – to sort of screw around

Figure 4.5 Dani Stoller, Washington, D.C.–based actor and writer, photographed in New York City. Michael Kushner Photography

and still take time in a room. We never get the eight bar cuts. That certainly doesn't happen here.

Only around four hours from Manhattan geographically, the D.C. theatre scene is not completely disconnected from New York. In recent years, productions like *The Visit*,[41] *Glory Days*,[42] *Next to Normal*,[43] *Come From Away*,[44] *Mean Girls*,[45] *Sweat*,[46] and *Dear Evan Hansen*[47] were either created or tried out in D.C. before moving to Broadway.

Stoller continues her conversation on Washington, D.C. accessibility on Episode 63 of *Dear Multi-Hyphenate*, titled "Jewish Representation & Washington D.C. Multi-Hyphenation."[48] Stoller explores how her next play, *The Joy That Carries You*,[49] cowritten with Awa Sal Secka,[50] came to fruition and speaks about their debut at the Olney Theatre Center for the Arts.[51]

"The thing I really admire about certain theatres in the 'DMV,'" says Stoller on *Dear Multi-Hyphenate*,

is their commitment to bringing in local talent. I think that we have a beautiful group of people there. Of course sometimes you have to bring in people from out of town. But I really do admire theatres that make a really diligent effort to utilize the people of that area to tell the stories of that area.

Similar to Washington, D.C., South Florida has a multitude of regional theatres which create many opportunities for its artists. Patti Gardner[52] is a force in the South Florida theatre community. Working in this community for over 30 years, she has received a Carbonell Award[53] as well as a Silver Palm Award.[54] She says:

South Florida has a wealth of variety within its tri-county theatre community from the premium art centers, housing large audiences with educational conservatories, to the intimate black-box spaces, committed to developing new and groundbreaking work. Opportunities are varied and plentiful, but South Florida's greatest appeal is its supportive theatrical members. We're all pulling for the local theatre and, more importantly, the artists. Support for each other is exceptional. We have each other's backs.

In a competitive industry, support is a very attractive quality for a theatre town. But just as South Florida has many theatres to choose from, there are just as many places to start. Gardner explains:

South Florida Theatre League[55] is a great way to learn about the theatrical happenings locally. Annual membership is nominal and provides information on events, workshops, festivals and auditions. Members are listed on the site for casting professionals to see. The South Florida Equity Liaison Committee is the best "first stop" for Equity members moving to the region. We can provide information and assistance and all members new to the area are acknowledged at our membership meetings. A list of all theatres and their websites are accessible for all events and audition information.

One can reach each out to the South Florida Equity Liaison Committee chairperson or any of the members for guidance. Yet, South Florida isn't the only community that focuses on support. On top of creating the *EnTrance Theatre Talk*[56] podcast, Kirsten Wrinkle[57] is a theatre artist and supporter based in Charlotte, North Carolina. She is a sought-after speaker and currently serves as a board member for Playing for Others.[58] PFO is a 501(c)3 nonprofit leadership training program that "combines personal development, service and the arts to foster leaders who are confident, compassionate and creative. To date, PFO has served more than 400 teens, 200 children with disabilities, and 150 community non-profits" (playingforothers. org). Wrinkle says:

> Charlotte is a philanthropic community and therefore willing to support the arts. We are seeing more diverse works and more diverse theater creatives making art. North Carolina has several arts schools as well. Northwest School of the Arts[59] (recent grads include Abby Corrigan,[60] Eva Noblezada,[61] and Renee Rapp[62]), UNCSA,[63] and Brevard Music College[64] are just a few of the academic institutions supporting the artists' journey.

While Wrinkle is connected to supporting the Broadway community, Wrinkle does the same in her home state and acknowledges the importance and richness of theatre found locally:

> Practically speaking, many cities with great community theater have [a] better cost of living. Until we start paying our artists better, some people find it more practical to live in an affordable city. I am a huge fan of regional theater. Many communities are creating amazing art around the country. North Carolina has great theater groups, large and small. Charlotte, North Carolina has a large arts organization that brings national tours and artists to its many venues. I have seen some of my favorite shows through our small theater groups. Few things bring me as much joy as seeing a child (or anyone) see a live performance for the first time and having their world rocked, especially as we begin to get more people in the arts that reflect ALL of us – not just straight, white, cis, able-bodied people.

In the spirit of multi-hyphenating, and thanks to Zoom, one doesn't have to choose one location to commit themselves to. Sure, Zoom lets one take meetings on the other side of the country, but what happens when a gig physically relocates someone? What happens when they have footing in New York and Los Angeles? This is known as being bicoastal. Paige Davis,[65] seen on Broadway in *Chicago*,[66] *Sweet Charity*,[67] and *Boeing-Boeing*,[68] is known for hosting the reality design challenge television show *Trading Spaces* on TLC.[69] Davis found herself living on both coasts at once for about a year:

> The hardest thing about it was being apart from my husband. I was living in Los Angeles most of the time. He was mostly in NYC. He was working on Broadway and I was working on a daytime talk show, so our time together was at the mercy of our work schedules – opportunities were far and few between. But frankly, that's a common issue for most any relationship where one or both persons are in the entertainment industry.

Figure 4.6 Paige Davis applies makeup backstage of the Broadway Cares/Equity Fights AIDS event, The Easter Bonnet Competition in 2019. Michael Kushner Photography

Even if splitting time between coasts only happens on weekends, time apart from family and friends begins to add up. There are missed birthdays, missed graduations, and missed first visits from the Tooth Fairy. Is the time traveling back and forth worth it? It's entirely up to the artist. Despite missing her husband, she was able to maintain a positive outlook. Davis joked:

> I liked that I had toiletries in two places. It made packing swift and easy when I *was* able to fly home. I did enjoy having a space that was all my own. I felt strong and confident and in control of staying healthy and focused on my job.

Even different boroughs in New York City feel like an out-of-town experience. Charles Quittner,[70] a director and a leader in the House Show circuit of Brooklyn, finds himself engaging in types of theatre that aren't found on the island of Manhattan. Quittner comes to theatre from a place of openness and hospitality, focusing on authentic queer visibility:

> Benjamin Viertel[71] and Bryce Cutler's[72] company Third Space[73] did *Stupid F***ing Bird*[74] in my living room, and moved to my kitchen, then to my upstairs, then to my backyard. I do house shows in my backyard. I am deeply inspired by Brooklyn nightlife like the drag shows I see at Rosemont that were popping up in secret warehouses and house parties, so just taking the communal aspect of a house party, serving pizzas, and offering that to the audience. Oftentimes, if I am doing an original piece in my backyard, I'll ask the writer to incorporate elements of what would be a Charles Quittner House Party into the script. In *Live! at the Boscoe Barles Backyard Center for the Performing Arts*,[75] my current house project always ends with a pizza party. I have local, queer fashion designers

do pop-ups in my windows, and the vibes are just pristine – I'm able to showcase amazing artists.

Quittner transformed his Brooklyn apartment, complete with a backyard, into a functional performance space. During his years as the artistic director, Quittner has produced noteworthy acts such as Brittain Ashford,[76] Gracie Gardner,[77] Remy Black,[78] Starr Busby,[79] Daphne Always,[80] Treya Lam,[81] and the play *Cory and Smin's Love Conquers the Earth*.[82]

> What I do isn't necessarily the most normal thing, but I create my own spaces typically in my backyard or cult bookstores. I feel like there's more of that going on in Brooklyn. I get invited to House Shows all the time in Brooklyn, where I never get invited to a Hell's Kitchen or Harlem show. In terms of Brooklyn, I'm able to come at it from a place of hospitality – there's more space. There's a spirit of irreverence in the work I do, whether it be theatre, concert production, drag shows – just a playfulness. It's just theatre.

Part 2: Process: Access to Oneself

In Chapter 3, one discovered how to name a proficiency – but how does one creatively explore others to add to their multi-hyphenate identity? After one considers location, it's time to start asking questions of the environments around them. Posing questions and deducing answers is simply part of the human condition. Although scientists have long been conducting experiments based on a structured process involving hypotheticals, Sir Francis Bacon[83] is accredited with being the first scientist to acknowledge the scientific method. The scientific method is a specific step-by-step process to conclude analysis and fits rather comfortably in the process of a multi-hyphenate. In terms of a definite process for success in the arts, there is no equation for prosperity. Yet, there *is* a step-by-step process that can allow an artist to think critically about their hyphen's relationship to the world.

The Multi-Hyphenate Process, as shown here, is loosely based on the scientific method. This process has been altered to relate more specifically to an artist adding a new hyphen and should be approached with a sense of play.

Directors lead actors through play in the rehearsal room. Technicians play with new equipment to see if it advances their abilities. Writers play with the worlds in which they are creating, establishing their own relationships and rules. Why can't multi-hyphenates? By observing, communicating, wondering, trying, sensing, and committing – *play* becomes an

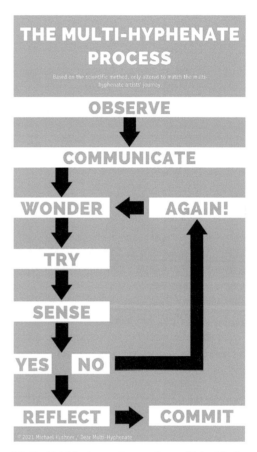

Figure 4.7 The Multi-Hyphenate Process. Insert. Michael Kushner Photography

integral process in discovering one's limitlessness. Through a sense of play, applying the Multi-Hyphenate Process can create access to oneself. This allows an artist to reflect inwards and remain open to discovering new ways to create art. This helps keep oneself in check – accessing the deepest parts of the spirit and promoting honest work.

Observe

A human's environment is key to the beginnings of development. From birth, humans are shaped based on the foods they are given, the media they are exposed to, the weather, religion, the amount of love received – *everything* shapes a vulnerable human into being into the person they become. These basic observations are what form a point of view and provide key elements to bringing one's soul into their artistry.

Communicate

It's here where an impulse can take any shape – a stomach churning out of excitement, fascination, the presence constantly on the mind – whatever the impulse, it's time to communicate within self and take stock of these discoveries.

"I think you should always listen to your impulses," says Shakina Nayfack.[84]

> I don't think you want to act on them all the time. But it's important to take stock of impulses as they arrive because it may not be the first knock at the door that gets you to open it. Art begs to be expressed because that impulse continues to arise and you can't ignore it, you can't run away from it and something in your being is like "I must do this thing." It's a calling.

Wonder

What would happen if a young person stumbled upon a thrift shop and bought a used camera? What would happen if one was watching *UNNHhhh*[85] on YouTube and thought about the type of drag queen they would be? What would happen if an established costume designer just opened their laptop and started writing a play based on the dress they designed? Wonder is all about the questioning of a moment. Wonder allows a person to take stock of where they are. It's the breath before the leap.

Try

If 'wonder' is the breath before the leap, 'trying' is the leap itself. Trying takes practice and patience and is not done in a day. Sometimes trying is an investment of years-long dedication. Sometimes trying is spending $60,000 a year at university only to realize at graduation that "this is ultimately not what I want." Sometimes trying is *very expensive*.

Pooya Mohseni[86] is no stranger to the 'try.' She is an Iranian American actor, writer, and activist who seeks stories that speak to her with rich, three-dimensional characters, good and bad, while exploring their humanity and fragility. She's fluent in Persian (Farsi) and a transgender advocate, as well as a voice for immigrants' and women's issues. She writes and cowrites original LGBT stories to shed light on an otherwise underrepresented community. As a creator of her own work, she actively calls upon her practice of patience. She's the cowriter, lead actor, and coproducer of *Transit: A NYC Fairytale*,[87] a short film about a love affair between a woman of trans experience and a cis-gendered man. Mohseni's process is a testament that trying does not lend itself to overnight discoveries:

> You need patience and focus. It may take 6 months, a year or two, but if you know what you're looking for, you won't sacrifice it just to get it out fast. Why? Getting a subpar project out, sooner than it's ready, doesn't do any favors for anyone or convey the artistry and vision that you want to the public or industry.

Figure 4.8 Pooya Mohseni. Michael Kushner Photography

Sense

When 'trying,' a person will sense if the direction they are going in is correct. It's that 'gut feeling' that has become a victim of Americans valuing material success over emotional. Sense is a key element to understanding when it's appropriate to produce a project, show up for an audition, or write a new song.

Commit

Doing anything with half the effort will only result in half the answers. Commitment is the pressing of the 'go' button, which can be any combination of raising funds, networking, launching a social media presence, or finding a writing partner to name a few options. While commitment is incredibly important when beginning a project, it's just as important when understanding to close that chapter. Jasper Grant[88] is a passionate and aligned multi-hyphenate. He is a musical director, coach, and founding artistic director of B-Side

Productions.[89] B-Side productions closed after five strong seasons in New York City.

"I learned that I am indeed capable of running a theatre company," says Grant.

> I never once thought it was too daunting or because I didn't have this skill or that connection – I would be in trouble. I also surrounded myself with fantastic artists who carried me over the finish line on multiple races. I also knew when it was time to close up shop. Following your instincts will never let you down. Many people didn't want B-Side to end. Heck, I didn't either, but running a theatre company in NYC is a full-time job and I came to the decision that ending B-Side was a gift rather than a failure.

Grant saw his theatre company through a cycle of beginning and ending a chapter. Regarding the multi-hyphenate experience, this cycle is a reflection of two forms of energy: potential and kinetic. Potential energy is the energy something requires to move or change. Kinetic energy is the energy something has acquired to move or change. If one was to stand at the top of a hill behind a ball, the ball would have potential energy before being kicked, flying down the hill garnering kinetic energy. When the movement is complete, the ball then ceases motion, restoring itself back to having potential energy.

In connection to the Multi-Hyphenate Process, Wonder → Trying → Committing. The circuit of potential and kinetic energy is the basis of the third part of accessibility, the Multi-Hyphenate Life Cycle. In this cycle, the multi-hyphenate will access the connective power between the hyphens which promotes strategy, stability, and fluidity in one's art.

Part 3: Cycle: Access to Each Hyphen

By exploring with hyphens and figuring out which ones to identify with, it's time to understand how they relate to each other. Oftentimes, a multi-hyphenate will have a **dominant proficiency** that can help the other proficiencies exist. An artist usually begins their multi-hyphenate journey with a dominant proficiency, or they will discover one along in their process. The dominant proficiency can allow a multi-hyphenate to invest time or money on other projects. Because a dominant proficiency provides one's main source of income, an artist might be able to take risks on something that may not provide an immediate income, like producing a web series.

It's rare a web series will recoup the money spent on production. Therefore, if a multi-hyphenate is new to producing and puts their money in a web series, this is an instance where they will cut their losses. For this artist, the compensation they may be receiving might be more centered on resume or ensemble building, still committing to one of the four guidelines that a multi-hyphenate should garner an income for said proficiency. The artist is not dependent on monetary income with this project because in this specific instance, this multi-hyphenate's dominant proficiency is providing the artist with a cushion to create this webseries. Ultimately, of course, the goal is for all hyphens to produce income.

Whichever way an artist chooses to invest in themselves, a project, or a specific hyphen is personal to the multi-hyphenate, yet the dominant proficiency basically serves as an investment to the other hyphens.

For a visual learner, the Multi-Hyphenate Life Cycle might help put priorities straight, helping one figure out how to organize their multi-hyphenate efforts. This cycle explores that the dominant proficiency of photography provides an income that the artist can then take to produce a project themselves if they so choose. A different artist with the same proficiencies could easily reroute their hyphens in a cycle like this, sharing how their dominant proficiency (which might be different) affects their hyphens in other ways.

Now, pay attention to the lines inside of the cycle. They are a reminder that in some way or another, each proficiency must also affect the other in some sort of way. This is to ensure a holistic identity to one's art, making sure that it's focused and connected. Yet, what happens when one loses passion when

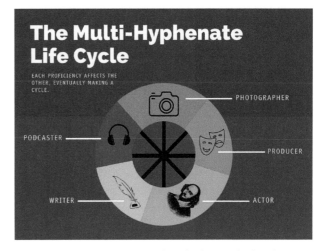

Figure 4.9 The Multi-Hyphenate Life Cycle chart. Michael Kushner Photography

it comes to a specific hyphen? Even multi-hyphenating has its own cutting room floor. Pieces of the puzzle that once fit and don't anymore might get tossed to the side – and that's encouraged. Just like one's Why, the multi-hyphenate identity is ever changing and ever evolving. Why commit to artistry and taking up space in an art form where one no longer feels connected?

As an actor and writer based in the D.C. area, Dani Stoller approaches multi-hyphenate identity just like a writer would: there is always the option to delete:

> The cool thing is you can always delete. If you have a bunch of different roads you want to go down, just go! Then you can change it. I have written pages upon pages upon pages, and they have gotten the axe because they just don't fit. But at least I know they exist. Try all roads.

Accessing the moments within oneself and within others is an attribute of the multi-hyphenate that will exist forever, even during a pandemic. During the COVID-19 quarantine, Carly Valancy,[90] creator of *The Reach Out Party*,[91] reflects on the beauty of having the agency to allow oneself the opportunity to create.

"Something that's so beautiful about this time that I would like to bottle for the future is the idea of having that impulse and having the ability and space to take action," says Valancy in Episode 34, "The Reach Out Party! of Dear Multi-Hyphenate,"[92] which was recorded during the COVID-19 pandemic.

> I think that's such an important thing when you're talking about a creative practice or habit or trying to stay creative during an isolating time; it's having that impulse and taking an action. If you can do that over and over and over again – that will be your default.

This default is what is known to be the concept of *Satz*. The concept of Satz was taught directly to Dr. Norm Johnson[92] by Anne Bogart,[93] American theatre director and founder of the SITI Company.[94] *Satz* is a Danish term that simply means to invest everything one has into one thing. Alongside Tina Landau,[95] Bogart adapted Viewpoints[96] (originally developed by Mary Overlie[97] in the 1970s), a technique of dance composition that acts as a medium for thinking about and acting upon movement, gesture, and creative space.

Bogart incorporated Satz into her Viewpoint training by asking the question, "Where is your point of focus right now?" In turn, Dr. Johnson would use this term to promote focus in his movement and scene study classes in an exercise called running circle. In a running circle, a group runs in a circle and together, must jump, stop, and/or switch directions at any given moment – promoting a cohesive ensemble. He explains:

> I remember saying, "Alright, folks, let's get on the Satz train," which means there's one thing we all want to do, we all know what it is, and it's not going to happen until every single one of us gives 100% of our attention into making it happen.

Dr. Johnson compares Satz to what the divers are experiencing in the 2021 Summer Olympics.

> They are standing on that platform and there is nothing in the world going on except what they are about to do. Everything else goes away. They're not twitching. They're not fussing. It's not about hair, the way my clothes are sitting, or the audience, or anything like that. It's about honing in. The energy is going into the funnel, and we have it and that's when we go.

Satz, or absolute focus, is the required energy of a multi-hyphenate experimenting with accessibility. Finding a location, acting on impulse, using tools, experimenting with process and cycle – it's all trial. But when trial comes, so does error – which must be met with open arms. Dr. Johnson says of his discoveries with the Satz train:

> There's the people who really, really want to be right. They tend to get ahead. But the same mentality will also cause them to slip behind because they don't want to make a mistake. They simply want to get it right. But that priority gets in the way of all the other subtle things that need to evolve. There's a lot of stuff we have to let go of – Ego being number one.

While an artist is limitless in creativity, they are limited in physicality. Mistakes are inevitable and one must learn to embrace them. By embracing the mistakes which come out of trial and error – it's only then can a multi-hyphenate artist begin to healthily acknowledge their limits, an understanding that will only help them in their *work ethic and workflow*.

EPISODE EXCERPT

TIA ALTINAY

Broadway: Aladdin, A Christmas Story, Mary Poppins

**BUILDING A PLANE
AS YOU'RE FLYING IT** • *EPISODE 28*

Michael: When we were talking about having you on the show – it's not as self deprecating as I'm about to make it seem - you were like, "I'm low hanging fruit, are you sure . . . ?"

Tia: Because when I joined Broadway for Biden, I joined in a new capacity on purpose. Like, I didn't say, "I would love to be a part of the talent and please put me in front of the camera." Although I love a photo moment, it's not like I don't love that, but I already know how to do that. So I on purpose wanted to learn something new, I on purpose wanted to be a part of a new department. So with that, of course I'm in something new, so I'm on the bottom. You know, I'm in the PR department and I'm a press coordinator which basically means I'm in the bottom. So I just figured you would want someone that is on the top something. But yes, that is part of the multi-hyphenate. I was like, "What does PR do?" So now I'm on the PR team. There's only three of us, so I'm learning a lot.

Michael: Yeah! I think that when we're multi-hyphenates and we add hyphens to our identity, we have to be able to go, "Is this something I can sell? Do I have enough experience to build another resume for this hyphen? This is a separate resume that I'm going to have because it is something that I can get a paycheck off of – or am I doing this for the time being so I can learn? What I think is really exciting and important about you, Tia, is you jumped in and you were like, "I'm going to learn!" We can always look at ourselves in the mirror and ask "Where am I right now and how can I follow an impulse to be a better and more educated artist?"

Tia: It's kind of my mantra - it's kind of the way I'm trying to live my life right now which is "just start walking towards it" and if you realize that the phantom it is, is not it – you can pivot turn girl, you could pivot turn. No one says that what you're walking towards has to be the end all be all. You need to take some steps forward.

On top of being a Broadway performer, Tia served as "Communications Fellow" for Broadway for Biden in 2020.

Notes

1 www.christinetoyjohnson.com/
2 www.dramatistsguild.com/
3 https://broadwaypodcastnetwork.com/dear-multi-hyphenate/42-christine-toy-johnson-breaking-the-color-barrier/
4 www.watmisaka.com/
5 https://en.wikipedia.org/wiki/New_York_Knicks
6 www.rogerqmason.com/aboutme
7 www.nationalqueertheater.org/new-visions-fellowship
8 https://broadwaypodcastnetwork.com/dear-multi-hyphenate/51-roger-q-mason-wig-the-fck-out/
9 www.nationalqueertheater.org/
10 www.nationalqueertheater.org/copy-of-advisory-board-and-artistic
11 https://dgf.org/
12 https://frenchwoods.com/important-staff-bios.htm
13 https://frenchwoods.com/
14 https://hfwaa.org/
15 www.entertainmentforchange.com/
16 www.playbill.com/article/stars-in-the-house-streams-moments-in-the-woods-gala-featuring-lin-manuel-miranda-todrick-hall-mandy-gonzalez-more
17 www.michaelkushneronline.com/
18 www.linmanuel.com/
19 www.todrickhall.com/
20 www.imdb.com/name/nm0004517/
21 https://andreaburns.com/bio
22 https://mandygonzalez.com/
23 www.starsinthehouse.com/
24 www.umb.edu/academics/cla/faculty/rafael_jaen
25 www.umb.edu/academics/cla/performarts
26 www.usitt.org/
27 www.tonyapinkins.com/
28 www.broadwayworld.com/people/Sushma-Saha/
29 www.roundabouttheatre.org/
30 https://playbill.com/production/1776-2022-2023
31 www.playbill.com/person/michael-mcelroy-vault-0000003383
32 www.ibdb.com/broadway-production/big-river-13526
33 https://broadwayinspirationalvoices.org/
34 https://smtd.umich.edu/departments/musical-theatre/
35 https://sandysahargooen.medium.com/
36 www.washingtonpost.com/
37 www.danistoller.com/
38 www.american.edu/cas/performing-arts/theatre/
39 https://corcoran.gwu.edu/theatre-undergraduate
40 https://drama.catholic.edu/
41 www.ibdb.com/broadway-production/the-visit-499129
42 www.playbill.com/article/new-broadway-musical-glory-days-has-closed-after-one-performance-com-149908
43 www.broadwayworld.com/washington-dc/article/Photo-Coverage-NEXT-TO-NORMAL-At-Arena-Stage-20081216
44 www.playbill.com/article/come-from-away-musical-about-travelers-stranded-on-9-11-sets-dc-tryout-cast-com-386730
45 www.playbill.com/article/tina-feys-mean-girls-musical-names-director-and-tryout-location
46 www.arenastage.org/tickets/201516-season/sweat
47 www.arenastage.org/tickets/201516-season/dear-evan-hansen/
48 https://broadwaypodcastnetwork.com/dear-multi-hyphenate/63-dani-stoller-jewish-representation-washington-d-c-multi-hyphenation/
49 www.broadwayworld.com/washington-dc/regional/The-Joy-That-Carries-You-2880684
50 www.broadwayworld.com/people/Awa-Sal-Secka/
51 www.olneytheatre.org/
52 www.palmbeachdramaworks.org/bio/patti-gardner-8
53 http://carbonellawards.org/
54 www.silverpalmawards.com/
55 https://southfloridatheatre.org/20/
56 https://entranceproductions.org/
57 http://entranceproductions.org/about/
58 https://playingforothers.org/
59 https://schools.cms.k12.nc.us/northwestHS/Pages/Default.aspx
60 www.imdb.com/name/nm2247348/
61 www.playbill.com/person/eva-noblezada
62 https://en.wikipedia.org/wiki/Rene%C3%A9_Rapp
63 www.uncsa.edu/
64 https://brevard.edu/music/
65 https://paigedavis.com/
66 https://chicagothemusical.com/
67 www.ibdb.com/broadway-production/sweet-charity-378059
68 www.ibdb.com/broadway-production/boeing-boeing-477454
69 www.tlc.com/tv-shows/trading-spaces/
70 www.charlesquittner.com/
71 www.benjaminviertel.com/
72 www.brycecutler.com/
73 www.thirdspacetheater.org/
74 https://en.wikipedia.org/wiki/Stupid_Fucking_Bird
75 https://greenpointers.com/2019/07/15/an-immersive-goodbye-party-comes-to-a-williamsburg-backyard/
76 www.brittainashford.com/
77 www.graciegardner.com/
78 https://twitter.com/remythenewblack?lang=en
79 https://arsnovanyc.com/Vision-Residency-StarrBusby
80 http://daphnealways.com/
81 www.treyamakesmusic.com/
82 www.timeout.com/newyork/theater/cory-and-smins-love-conquers-the-earth
83 www.shakina.nyc

84 www.wowpresentsplus.com/unhhhh

85 https://pooyaland.com/

86 www.gandeproductions.com/transit

87 www.jaspergrant.com/

88 www.broadwayworld.com/off-broadway/article/Photo-Flash-Andre-De-Shields-Celebrates-Opening-of-B-Side-Productions-THE-WILD-PARTY-20160907

89 https://carlyvalancy.com/

90 https://carlyvalancy.com/reach-out-party

91 https://broadwaypodcastnetwork.com/dear-multi-hyphenate/34-carly-valancy-the-reach-out-party/

92 https://www.ithaca.edu/faculty/njohnson

93 www.kennedy-center.org/artists/b/bo-bz/anne-bogart/

94 https://siti.org/

95 https://en.wikipedia.org/wiki/Tina_Landau

96 https://dramatics.org/understanding-viewpoints/

97 https://sixviewpoints.com/maryoverlie

Resource List

1. "Playing for Others." *Playing for Others*, playingforothers.org/.

EXERCISE 5

MAKE YOUR OWN CYCLE

DM-H

Every multi-hyphenate has their own cycle, and now it's time to create yours! Creating a cycle such as this helps visualize one's multi-hyphenate efforts to make sure they are as clear and concise as possible.

Materials

Paper/notebook
Pen

Step 1. Draw bubbles and arrows of a cycle similar to the one seen in this chapter. Feel free to include as many hyphens as you think you'll need. If you are an actor, designer, teaching artist, and social media manager, draw four bubbles! Keep the circles big enough to write in. *Remember: skills are different from hyphens*.

Step 2. Fill in the top bubble with your dominant proficiency. Remember, a dominant proficiency is the hyphen that allows the other proficiencies to exist. Factors like income, notoriety, and a healthy netweaving system can influence what makes the dominant proficiency the beginning of this cycle.

Step 3. Heading clockwise, fill in the next bubble with the hyphen that is directly affected by the dominant proficiency. Using the example of an actor, designer, teaching artist, and social media manager – perhaps the social media manager is the dominant proficiency, and that income allows you to exist as an actor. Keep filling in the bubbles until they are complete. Make sure to figure out how the last hyphen you fill in affects and supports the dominant proficiency. The exciting thing is that there are potentially many different combinations – mapping this out helps stay mentally organized.

Step 4. This is the final touch. Remember, each hyphen affects the other. Begin to list the ways in which each proficiency affects the other. For instance, if one is a podcaster and photographer, the podcast audience they've built also finds they hire the photographer for headshots. From monetary support, to finding collaborators, to different skills branching between the hyphens – there are many ways to connect one's proficiencies!

"I think at the end of the day, I have to make sure everything I need to do is written down in an organizer or calendar, and I have to constantly remind myself to breathe and take things one step at a time. I have to tell myself it's okay to be overwhelmed, but the trick is to be able to breathe through it and be accountable to the people you are accountable to."

Debbie Christine Tjong

Chapter 5
Workflow and Work Ethic

DOI: 10.4324/9781003254744-8

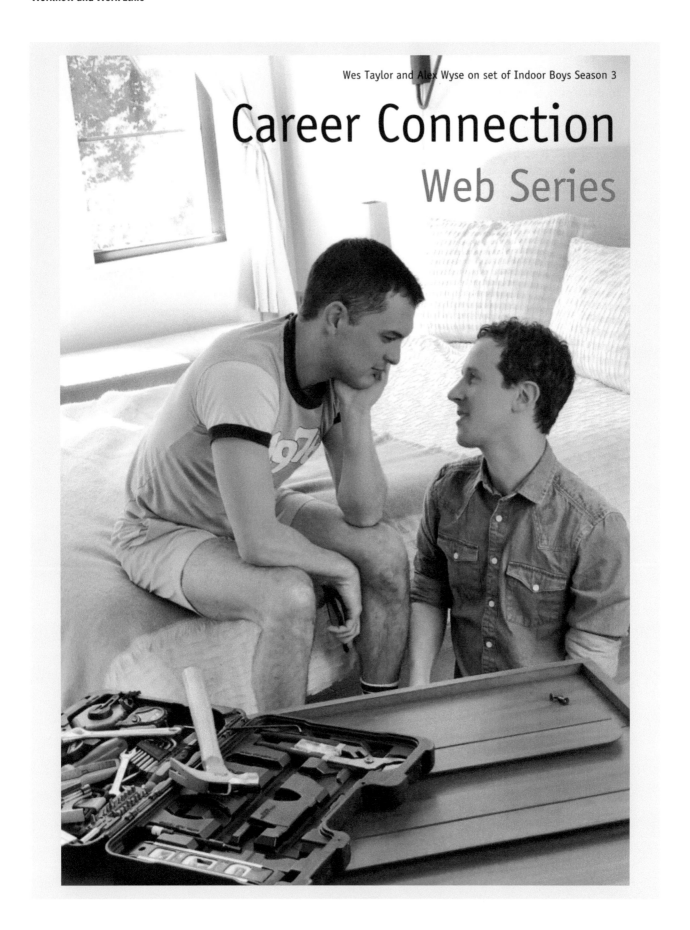

Wes Taylor and Alex Wyse on set of Indoor Boys Season 3

Career Connection

Web Series

When it comes to producing, smaller environments do not equal less powerful environments. In recent years, members of the theatre community have taken it upon themselves to write, produce, and develop their own work. By doing so, artists have more creative control over the type of art they are producing. Web series have been just as much a part of the fandom in the Broadway community as live musicals have. A web series like Indoor Boys[1] (which earned star Veanne Cox[2] an Emmy nomination), created by Wesley Taylor[3] and Alex Wyse,[4] gives its fanbase in the Broadway community more access. While it's not a commercial theatre, Indoor Boys finds similarities through raising funds, landing a producing team, and hiring a crew, but still, the differences between the mediums offer different perspectives of producing one's own art.

"My involvement with producing What the Constitution Means to Me[5] was a special experience, but I was really on the outside looking into it," says Alex Wyse of his experience producing on Broadway.

I helped provide some financial support for the show, helped to raise money, and did some things to help them connect to producers who could help bring the show to Broadway. So that was my main responsibility in co-producing Constitution. However, when I was creating Indoor Boys, that was a little more like I was the one getting people granola bars. It was really scrappy, and DIY, and I felt like I was wearing twenty different hats while I was doing it. I also just finished writing and directing a feature film, Summoning Sylvia,[6] and I had a small hand in being a producing team for that. I think film in general is a little more Wild West. I think theatre feels a little bit more regulated, like you're going to be in an air-conditioned room when you're doing theatre. When you're doing film, there are so many more elements that are at play – and I mean quite literally the weather elements – but also so many new people in the world every day, whereas in theatre there's a bit more of an established family in the room. With film every day feels like a new adventure. You show up on set and the question is, "How are we going to get this done? Are we going to be able to finish our day?" However, being in the theatre, we're re-creating what we've refined in the room, but even though we know what we're performing today, the adventure is really how it transpires to live in the moment.

Yet when it comes to web series, half the battle is one that the theatre doesn't have. In the latter, when the show is

over – the cast, crew, and audience can all go home. When a film or web series is wrapped the work is certainly not done; it then moves into post-production. It takes months, even years, of hiring a team to take care of editing, scoring, press, and so on, as well as mapping out a strategy of when, where, and how to release the product.

"Post-production involves many things and many people, especially if you have a vision that includes different people who specialize in the things you need done: editing, color correction, sound, music, etc.," Pooya Mohseni[7] says of her film Transit.[8]

Transit is that kind of project. We wanted a very dreamy look. We wanted a sound to match that. I wrote a theme song for it and asked a friend to write the melody. Then we reached out to a composer to score the film. All of that mentioned, plus the fact that the two writers, me being one of them, are also the leads of the film and we're also the producers, while trying to do auditions, act when possible and work to make money. All of that means: you need patience and focus.

Once finished, a creation in post-production can head in any direction, whether it's in the film festival circuit, released on YouTube or a website, sold to a streaming service, or sits on a shelf – never to be seen. Because these projects are the "start-ups" found within the theatre/TV/film industries, the success is not measured based on income. In fact, many of these projects don't recoup or build revenue, even if they gather accolades and awards. Yes, some do get sold to Netflix or Amazon, but even with prestigious film festivals like Frameline[9] in San Francisco, one's piece is shown at the historic Castro Theatre,[10] yet the top-voted pieces win anywhere from $500 to $1,000. That barely covers the cost of what the producer paid to fly the cast and crew out to the festival. In this case, artists have to realize that the "success" of a piece is certainly not monetary but based on what was created, the bonds made, and the experiences shared.

And that's just that – just because the creators might find their piece is getting attention through a medium like a festival, it doesn't necessarily mean it has to be shared with the world. Wesley Taylor, star of SMASH[11] and Spongebob Squarepants: The Broadway Musical,[12] feels a responsibility to tell queer stories and use his queer voice to affect others and incite change. Taylor's short film XaveMePlease,[13] starring Isaac Cole Powell[14] and Alan

Figure 5.2 Still from the short film *XaveMePlease* starring Isaac Cole Powell and written and directed by Wesley Taylor. Michael Kushner Photography

Filderman[15] and produced and filmed by Michael Kushner,[16] played the Frameline 43 Festival[17] in 2018. This short, which budget neared only $800, was up against pieces that cost hundreds of thousands of dollars to make. But ultimately, Taylor decided to keep *XaveMePlease* private after the festival's showing, with the success being the lesson learned.

"XaveMePlease was one of my short films that I directed on my own and I wanted to protect some of those training wheels and learn on my own," Taylor says. "We still played festivals with packed out screening rooms, but in terms of the internet, the internet is a scary place. Once it's out there, it's forever – and it stays forever."

Dr. Norm Johnson,[18] who incorporates Satz (part of Anne Bogart's Viewpoints) into his teachings, believes that a human being physically cannot multitask, saying:

> People who claim they are good multitaskers are actually really efficient switchers. They can switch modes with great ease. In terms of a point of concentration, there's only one thing that can be in front at a time. So I can be remembering my lines *and* remembering the blocking *and* also the choreography *and* the third instead of the tonic – but it takes a great deal of time to actually rehearse that, so it starts to become instinctive. In terms of multitasking – it's *switching*. I'm not denying the term multitask, we just have to understand that only one thing can be at the top of the pyramid at any given moment – even if it's for half a second.

The common misconception of a multi-hyphenate is that they are constantly juggling different tasks all *at once*. While that may be true depending on the situation – any human being is subject to finding themselves balancing tasks at any given moment. Multitasking is a universal idea, not just unique

to the multi-hyphenate. If one is wary of becoming a multi-hyphenate simply because their image is that of an overly stressed, manic artist trying desperately to make a deadline, it's time to revisit said image.

Just because a multi-hyphenate has multiple proficiencies or responsibilities, it does not mean they are in play at every moment. To put it simply, multi-hyphenating is not multitasking, although the two are not always separate. In the multi-hyphenate experience, there will be times when one **multitasks**, or *switches efficiently*, and times when one will delegate tasks to others. The key to success is simply understanding when.

If a multi-hyphenate is working singlehandedly on producing a web series, they might be multitasking in terms of raising money, hiring a creative team, finding a location, or directing and acting the same scene – and in this particular example situation, this all must be completed by the end of the day. This producer would be multitasking, or *switching* as Dr. Johnson pointed out, in a *hopefully* very organized manner. Even when swiftly switching between tasks, the point is do it efficiently and not in some twister of chaos.

That's just an example of how one typically would multitask, or switch. Another would be of a stage manager switching between printing out new revisions to the script while making the call sheet while answering production emails. It's simply a matter of switching between focus points. When acting, they are more likely to focus on the given circumstances of the scene as an actor would – and when cut, focus on the overall image of the piece during playback, as a director would. In a lower budget, 'we're doing it for the art' situation, this person may even find themselves as the lighting designer and costume designer as well. Hopefully, that artist has found a successful manner to switch between these responsibilities in an organized way.

A web series, for example, it is not the only time a multi-hyphenate will switch between their hyphens. During production, one might be switching at a greater speed but in one's regular day to day function a multi-hyphenate will switch as well – but at a more attainable speed. A structured schedule will help the multi-hyphenate effortlessly shift between their responsibilities throughout their work week. For example, an actor-producer-writer's schedule might look like this:

- Monday–Thursday
  - 7 a.m. – Sign up for Equity Principal Audition
  - 9 a.m. – Begin answering emails at coffee shop
  - 10 a.m.–1 p.m. – Record self-tapes for auditions.
  - 1 p.m. – Lunch
  - 2 p.m. – Zoom/in person meetings with coproducers, investors, etc.
  - 4 p.m.–7 p.m. – For-now job
  - 7 p.m. – End of day – Dedicate time to learn audition material or take class.
- Friday
  - 9 a.m.–3 p.m. – For-now job
  - 4 p.m.–8 p.m. – Dedicate time to writing.
- Saturday
  - Off! Head to a museum, hang with a friend, or have alone time.
- Sunday
  - Confirm meetings for the upcoming week.
  - Organize my schedule and prepare for auditions.
  - Make sure all deadlines are clear.

With creating comes establishing deadlines. When these deadlines are initiated, one has the duty to complete these in a timely manner so the artists involved are not negatively affected. Such responsibilities can include sending emails, scheduling Zoom calls, confirming spaces, buying materials and equipment, and lots more. Therefore, the responsibility of a multi-hyphenate is not just about tasks and delegation, it's special care and a respect to the web of artists one is engaging

with, otherwise known as a **network**. When multiple people are coming together for a common goal one must understand they hold a responsibility towards others.

Zi Alikhan[19] has a responsibility toward the artists in his network. He has found himself in New York City, Upstate New York, Oregon, California, and Washington, D.C., all at once. Thanks to modern methods of communication, committing oneself to multiple people, places, and things is possible with the click of a button. The importance of Zoom integrated itself mightily into work environments during the COVID-19 pandemic.

"It's a really strange thing that oftentimes when somebody is approaching you in conversation about the work, it is the most important part of their day," Alikhan says.

> The thing you have to constantly be doing is continuing to build trust between you and your collaborators, and so the way to do that is to respect the fact that this is the most important part of this person's day.

Multi-hyphenates often engage with people who are focused on only one project. And just because a multi-hyphenate may have committed themselves to multiple projects, it does not forgive the occurrence of dropping an important deadline or forgetting a meeting. Quality comes before quantity, so a multi-hyphenate must take on projects they have the bandwidth for. Just because one identifies as a multi-hyphenate, one is not required to commit themselves to multiple projects. They simply have the choice and the tools to do so – and even when choosing to do so, they should be able to focus on the projects they have the time, energy, and focus for.

Bandwidth is a massively important aspect of the workflow of a multi-hyphenate. **Bandwidth** is the capacity an artist has to focus on or commit to a project at a given time. Some multi-hyphenates can take on multiple projects at once, while others only commit to one at a time. It's here where personal factors come into play, as well. If one is moving, feeling exhausted, or there's a sick family member, and so on, one can check their bandwidth to see what they can accomplish safely. As artists navigated returning to work as restrictions due to the COVID-19 pandemic began to ease up, many artists discovered they could not hustle in the same way they did before the pandemic because they no longer had the bandwidth to do so. Artists with Long COVID found themselves cutting down on the number of projects, collaborations, and meetings they were committing themselves to.

Lauryn Ciardullo[20] is a multi-hyphenate performer-musician-teacher who, pre-pandemic, was a swing in *Aladdin* on

Broadway,[21] covering Jasmine. After contracting COVID-19, she noticed her quality of life begin to deteriorate – and when Broadway returned in 2021, she would not be returning with it.

"Because of Long Covid, I could not return to my position as a swing in *Aladdin* on Broadway," says Ciardullo.

> I understudied eight cast members including Jasmine and needed to be ready at any moment to jump into the show. It takes a certain amount of discipline, energy and strength to do this. When my company manager called to ask if I would be able to come back to the show in August I said that seems impossible because I can barely get through teaching three voice lessons without needing to lay down. Before getting COVID-19, I would teach a 90-minute dance masterclass, do a matinee, take yoga and then do an evening show with no problem. I am a completely different person now and have been figuring out how to manage life with my new energy level and the possibility of having a Long COVID flare-up if I do too much. I will say I feel tremendously better compared to March of 2020 because of my medicine, prescription vitamins, sleep routine and diet change. Having a low stress lifestyle has helped as well. There are times when I have to tell my parents or husband, I'm so sorry, I know we made plans, but I have to sleep now. I appreciate life and nature so much more now and I feel extremely lucky to be alive and managing my symptoms well enough to continue teaching which I love more than anything.

That being said, a streamlined and focused system of organization will only promote one's bandwidth and help prevent overexertion, dropped meetings, missed deadlines, and poor preparation. If a multi-hyphenate chooses to navigate the world constantly letting down the artist's they are collaborating with, their network of artists may shrink because people will trust them less. That's not the goal.

"Where is your focus right now?" Dr. Johnson asks. "What is your point of concentration? Even jugglers who juggle seven clubs only have one touching their hand at a given moment."

Multitasking acts as a verb, while multi-hyphenates are the noun. The act of multitasking is performing different duties at once, while a multi-hyphenate balances their art forms and applies them accordingly, also known as delegating – a useful tool to activate when one's bandwidth is full. For example, Debbie Christine Tjong[22] is a singer, multi-instrumentalist, and actress who can play instruments such as piano, guitar, bass, upright, accordion, uke, banjo, mandolin, drums, cajon,

and percussion. Her work has been at numerous off-Broadway theatres such as Second Stage,[23] MCC Theatre,[24] and ARS Nova,[25] and is on the keys for the popular band Sammy Rae & The Friends[26] An incredibly talented multi-hyphenate, Tjong likes to be able to commit herself to collaboration simply because she loves it:

> I normally feel overwhelmed when I've said yes to too many things. I love working with people from all walks of life and sometimes it's hard for me to say no to them because I so genuinely love their work and them as a person. I think at the end of the day, I have to make sure everything I need to do is written down in an organizer or calendar, and I have to constantly remind myself to breathe and take things one step at a time. I have to tell myself it's okay to be overwhelmed, but the trick is to be able to breathe through it and be accountable to the people you are accountable to.

While there's plenty of risk involved with being a multi-hyphenate, dropping a club while trying to juggle is easily avoidable. Delegation helps. **Delegation** is when one assigns tasks to an individual or group of people. Yet, there is also self-delegation, where an artist calls upon modes of organization and strategy to help better their workflow. What are some ways an artist can self-delegate?

- A clear, color-coded daily planner
- Siri/reminder app on the smartphone/Alexa
- Detailed lists; sticky notes
- A self-timer, if one is prone to not being able to keep a strict schedule
- Pairings. What treats can one pair with a task to help motivate? Editing and an iced coffee? Writing while using a foot massager?
- A break! Breaks help clear the mind and rest tired eyes.

Tim Dolan,[27] founder of Broadway Up Close Tours,[28] calls upon many different tools to support his organizational efforts, promoting more creative opportunities, saying:

> Organization skills are also key when creating a new tour that is sourced in many different places. On the business side of things, I developed a deep love for bookkeeping through QuickBooks[29] and still catalog all accounting and payroll for my staff. As a boon to our social media presence, I utilized Final Cut Pro[30] for video production and editing, and Canva[31] for graphic design, editing, and branding. There isn't a day since I started my business in 2010 that's gone by without me pulling on every aspect of my brain and skill sets to keep all the proverbial balls aloft.

So, what happens if one implements methods of self-delegation, but is still finding they are making avoidable mistakes? What if one has just taken on too much responsibility? While this may grow the budget, hiring a team of people to help may be the right move. If one is worried about budgeting, chances are the creators will spend the same amount of money fixing the mistakes made. Hiring a team of other creatives and assistants will only promote a healthier workflow.

Beowulf Boritt[32] is a Tony-winning scenic designer who has designed more than 450 shows and is the visionary behind iconic sets on Broadway such as *Come From Away*,[33] *Act One*,[34] *The 25th Annual Putnam County Spelling Bee*,[35] *POTUS*,[36] and many more. Boritt has worked with his associate for many years and together, they have built a strong relationship and workflow.

"For me, my associate Alexis Distler[37] has been with me for 13 years at this point, so we have quite a system going," says Boritt.

> She drafts the show for me – I will build a model, I'll work with the director, figure out what the design is, and then I hand that off to her and she does all the technical drawings. We've worked together so long that we don't even have to be in the same place to do that. She comes to my apartment, picks up the model, takes it home, and I say I want the drawings on July 15th and on July 14th they show up in my inbox.

For Boritt, having an associate is more than just about workflow, it's about trust:

> The other important thing that she does that is really what I look for in an assistant is she and I have similar enough visual tastes, and she's good enough at knowing what I like that if I leave her alone in a tech and something needs to change, I'm comfortable with her making that decision. If she has to make a decision on the fly, even if it may be a decision I wouldn't have made, it probably will be something I'm fine with. That's the harder thing to find . . . is someone that I'm comfortable with making those decisions and also someone who is congenial enough and friendly enough and good enough with crews, that when she's giving people notes, the work gets done. It's very important and it's not something I can tell right away. It's something with a young assistant, I will probably hire them onto a smaller project or bring them on as a second assistant on a bigger project and try to get a sense of how they deal with people and what their taste is.

Dimitri Moïse,[38] an actor who has been seen in *Beautiful*,[39] *The Book of Mormon*,[40] and *Titanique*,[41] is also a queer, HIV+ activist. On Episode 17 of *Dear Multi-Hyphenate*, "Discovering Your Call to Action,"[42] Moïse discusses delegating, an important factor in raising funds for Claim Our Space Now:[43]

> All you have to do is take one step at a time. So I would say for me, one of the things that definitely kicked into gear would be my project management skills and organization because I knew that if this was something we really wanted to do and really turn into an organization . . . and mind you, at this point we were already receiving funds. People were just like, "Where do I send money?" And we had money just sitting around and we were like okay – what should we do? And I said, alright, if this is what is happening then we gotta file this, we have to incorporate this way . . . and I kind of just talked everyone through the steps of what it takes to file and form a nonprofit, which I've already gone through.

Moïse continues:

> I would say, and this is something I'm still learning definitely how to do – delegating. I think delegating is something that is so necessary. Having a coalition and having a team . . . and a team that is open in their dialogue and their communication and their delegation is completely, completely necessary in order to make it work.

"No one does it by themselves," says *RuPaul's Drag Race*[44] Miss Congeniality Nina West[45] on Episode 50, "Drag Race ASMR," of Dear Multi-Hyphenate.[46]

> No one does it alone. I'm grateful for my support network that's like, "You're capable. You are awesome. You are

Figure 5.4 Dimitri Moïse photographed in New York City. Michael Kushner Photography

going to succeed at this." We all need cheerleaders. I need my cheerleaders. I need my support network to be the multi-hyphenate that I am.

For Colleen Cook,[47] former vice president of JPMorgan Chase[48] turned producer, she acknowledges the importance of building a team to avoid mistakes potentially brought on by multitasking. In the theatre or film set, delegation helps her run a tight ship – similar to her corporate background.

> My corporate background also gave me a lot of managerial, organizational and communication skills which are critical to producing. The key is building a team who feels seen and appreciated. Once you have that together, it is often hard to fail as everyone on your team feels as invested as you are. I recall one night when filming Betsy Wolfe's[49] Christmas concert, *A Pants Optional Holiday*,[50] I was having some doubts as to if we were in over our heads. We were all doing something we had never done before. My Director of Photography said, "Stop worrying – you have surrounded yourself with all the best people in all the different roles and none of us will let you fail." Those words righted the ship for me that night.

For Cook, her team not only delivered on expectations, but provided a supportive environment. Cook wasn't solely responsible for putting out preventable fires or subject to stretching herself too thin. Instead, the job was completed with no mistakes.

> The key to success in the corporate world, producing, and really any other area in life is surrounding yourself with quality people and then trusting and supporting them to do their jobs successfully. I also learned in the corporate

Figure 5.5 Betsy Wolfe performs in her one-woman Christmas concert *A Pants Optional Holiday*, which was produced virtually by Holmdel Theatre Company and streamed with BroadwayWorld. Michael Kushner Photography

setting that every member of your team is important and should be treated as such from the lowest rank to the highest. I think sometimes people forget that and forget to thank the people who do the less glamorous roles on a production. To me it is important to make sure everyone is felt, seen, and appreciated.

Unsure of when to start hiring a team? There is no justification needed to hire an intern or assistant . . . especially if one is working by themselves on a day-to-day schedule and needs a bit of help. If one is feeling overwhelmed or tired, extra help is a smart move. Completing a job by oneself is *not* a heroic act. Instead, it risks failure. While failure is a necessary lesson to the growth of an artist – the idea is to *try* to avoid it. There's always something to learn from a mistake, but when there's thousands, if not millions of dollars at stake – that's certainly an *expensive* lesson.

What does one think about a person who is requiring an intern? What is the image that comes to mind? A CEO? A fast-talking executive from Los Angeles? Miranda Priestly from *The Devil Wears Prada*[51]? Sure, these people have interns and assistants and teams of people keeping everything in check. But who else can have an intern? Anyone, really. And who can be an intern? Again, anyone. What purpose does the intern serve? An **intern** is an entry-level position, usually catered for someone who wants to learn about a new field or type of occupation. Internships are fabulous opportunities for college students, or recent college graduates, to find themselves in a room that is otherwise extremely difficult to get into. These opportunities provide useful insight that cannot be taught in a classroom.

A multi-hyphenate might hire an intern or assistant when needing help on a specific project, answering emails, managing social media, or when in search for support with their schedule. For whatever reason, an intern can come in handy for anyone and any given time. So how does one realize they need an intern?

The Multi-Hype Workshop,[52] created by Ashley Kate Adams,[53] Kimberly Faye Greenberg,[54] and Michael Kushner, is the first workshop dedicated to teaching and honing the multi-hyphenate experience for individual artists. The class implores artists to always be in search of an intern.

"Multi-hyphenates can get overwhelmed so easily," says Greenberg.

> Plus we need to stay focused on our long-term goals. Consequently, don't be shy to hire an assistant or intern. They can get the more basic tasks done so you stay

focused, but also so that you can get further faster! It's worth it.

And to promote access, when hiring an individual as an intern, one must make it a priority to pay the intern appropriately. While they are still getting a priceless education, they still deserve proper payment.

Delegation is a form of **investment**, which multi-hyphenates experience two aspects of: time and money. When it comes to the **investment of** *time*, one incubates a relationship by establishing integrity or trust – which can take years, yet it promotes a trustworthy team to collaborate with. As for the **investment of** *money*, mistakes can be expensive but avoidable by hiring a social media person or a schedule manager or a stylist. While all these artists deserve to be paid accordingly, their efforts will also provide a more specific image – feeding the artist with more views, downloads, ticket sales, or engagement. If one has access to funds and resources, spending money will promote money, otherwise known as an investment.

When the pitfalls of multitasking are harnessed into something focused and streamlined, it can prove extremely helpful. While the idea of multitasking (or switching) is denounced by some artists, it helps stimulate others. Wes Taylor and Alex Wyse are the brains and queer voices behind the Emmy-nominated and Indie Series Awards[55]-winning *Indoor Boys*. The web series, executive produced by Michael Kushner, Jim Kierstead,[56] and Jim Head Jr.,[57] was written, directed, and starred the two multi-hyphenates.

While they were creating the three seasons of *Indoor Boys*, the idea of multitasking was an integral part of their process to get this smaller budget venture on its feet. They would constantly

Figure 5.6 Alex Wyse (left) and Wesley Taylor (right) in a promotional photograph used for Season Three of the award-winning web series *Indoor Boys*. Michael Kushner Photography

switch positions behind the camera, directing scenes the other was not in, making changes to the script, and problem-solving all at the same time. But, because they are a smart duo who have an organized workflow, they were able to delegate different responsibilities to each other and their small team to avoid expensive mistakes. Their next collaboration, *Summoning Sylvia*, a feature film shot in 2021, proved to be momentous regarding their creative process. How? By expanding their outreach to finding a larger supportive team to carry out tasks, lessening Taylor and Wyse's workload. While still reaping the benefits from focused multitasking, they were also able to delegate tasks appropriately.

"Multitasking is a part of multi-hyphenating one hundred percent," says Taylor.

> If I'm writing a script, while simultaneously putting myself on tape as an actor for a job, while going out to dinner with investors trying to raise money, while interviewing department heads for our crew, that's multitasking as an actor, writer, producer, director, writer. It quite literally affords me the opportunity to be a multi-hyphenate artist by making sure that I am multitasking all of those responsibilities. However, I will say, something that was a really exciting development for Alex and I on this movie was that we finally have gotten to a place where we had a budget large enough that we were able to hire, like, thirty-five people to do all the various crew jobs that we've done ourselves all these years. So now we find ourselves able to focus solely on directing the movie which is really liberating and quite rewarding.

Taylor isn't the only artist who finds multitasking necessary and helpful. Elena Maria Garcia[58] cannot function on a task unless the concept of multitasking is a part of the process. She looks at multitasking and multi-hyphenating like bullets in an outline for a report, saying:

> Multi-hyphenating is the main. If we do an outline, that's number one. Multitasking is the a, b, c, d underneath it. I'm more successful multi-hyphenating when I'm multitasking. If you give me one task and I just have to do it, I'll never get it done. I'll be looking for other things to do. In a meeting, if I'm listening to *the suits*, it's like *Charlie Brown* – wah, wah, wah – I despise it, so I will bring work with me and I can tell you everything they say. If you take that away from me, I don't even know why I'm there.

The visual of three-time Carbonell Award[59] winner Elena Garcia crocheting while in a meeting with a creative team is not a rare occasion, proving every artist has their own process. But finding a process, or a streamlined way of approaching work certainly helps when delivering a product. Because multi-hyphenating has so many moving parts, finding a process that proves effective to one's vibe is extremely important.

So how does one find a process? How does one learn a good work ethic? How does one learn about the repercussions of dropping responsibilities? How does one learn about making deadlines? Fortunately, for young artists, training programs scatter the cities and states, opening up their arms to children who are drawn to the arts for whatever reason. Sleep-away camps like Interlochen,[60] Stagedoor Manor,[61] and French Woods[62] provide incredible hands-on learning opportunities that not only hone the craft of a young artist but expand one's networking web. In these vulnerable stages in a young person's life – the lessons learned in these environments only benefit a future multi-hyphenate.

French Woods, the sleep-away camp mentioned in Chapter 4, "Accessibility: Location, Process, and Cycle," is based in the Catskill Mountains of New York. The camp prides itself on offering children and teens a unique, individualized camping experience. Campers completely determine which activities they will participate in by selecting "majors" at the beginning of every session. The majors can range from the play or musical they are cast in, to movie production, to participating in the largest children's circus in the world. At the beginning of every day, the campers select "minors" that are based on the camper's inquisitiveness. One day they can take tap, and the next they can take fitness. If a camper there has been cast in multiple shows, sometimes their minors will act as majors because the shows require daily rehearsal. Children are offered a wide range of performing and visual arts in addition to programs in sports, waterfront, horseback riding, and much more.

Figure 5.7 A bunk on the grounds of French Woods Festival for the Performing Arts in Hancock, New York. Michael Kushner Photography

The most unique thing is that French Woods cultivates the multi-hyphenate experience from a very young age. If a camper wants to direct a movie while also being in a musical while also taking a playwriting course – they are not only able to; they are also encouraged to. Keeping to the idea that each hyphen exists to support the other, this camper will take what they've learned in playwriting and rehearsals into their moviemaking experience.

Beth Schaefer[63] has been a part of French Woods since she was a camper. Her father, Ron Schaefer, is the brains and heart of the camp, which was founded in 1970. Growing up watching her father influence the lives of thousands, Beth now continues to do the same as the owner of French Woods, still directing productions every summer but also committing to the camp as a whole:

> "French Woods is an individualized program that provides children with unique opportunities to participate in Music, Art, Theater, Dance, Magic, Tennis, Sports, Circus, Horseback Riding, Cooking, Film and more. Just within the theater department, kids can perform in a show, assist on a younger kids show and work in tech theater in the same day. Most kids at camp are drawn to the program for one area of specialty and discover areas that they may never have considered before. We often have kids who are musicians in addition to being star athletes and dancers who become circus performers. It would not be unreasonable to say that French Woods is, by its very nature, a multi-hyphenate experience.

The multi-hyphenate experience isn't just something she bestows on younger artists; she also experiences it herself. By using both principles of delegating tasks to others and switching between proficiencies herself, Schaefer finds multi-hyphenating *necessary* in her day-to-day life:

> For me, life is always about being a multi-hyphenate. "I handle staffing, payroll and a host of other business-related issues, but I also direct a show every session of the summer. I love the kids, but so much of what I do is administrative. It would kill me not to have both a creative outlet and a good excuse for a joyful interaction with the kids every day. One experience informs the other and I develop meaningful relationships, which better supports everything else I do.

Environments like French Woods promote healthy learning environments. As accessibility is such a driving force in the multi-hyphenate experience, French Woods remains accessible to those who might not be able to afford a sleep away camp. They believe economic privilege should not dictate arts opportunities, and all kids deserve a chance to thrive. They offer financial need-based scholarships throughout their season, in addition to work-study options. The Hancock French Woods Arts Alliance[64] also provides scholarship opportunities for their counselors to pursue education in the arts when they are not at camp. Even if a training ground like French Woods is not the trajectory for a young artist, many regional theatres offer internships or apprenticeships, which offer priceless insight into building theatre – many of which are found in a simple Google search. These are often a mix of paid and unpaid opportunities, while some offer academic credit.

While hiring an intern is important from the perspective of the working multi-hyphenate, how is becoming an intern helpful to the budding multi-hyphenate? This exposure is the chrysalis to an informed work ethic and artistic process. Sometimes a multi-hyphenate starts out as an intern or assistant, which is an incredible way to learn the fundamentals of show business.

Although internships and apprenticeships at theatres can be tricky situations, they can be extremely informative. Many are a "do as we say" sort of situation, where the intern is finding themselves doing everything from coffee runs to being thrown on stage as a last-minute replacement. By subjecting oneself to an entry-level position such as this, they are often only compensated $150 per week, *if* they are compensated at all. There are few to no days off as they serve as the solutions when it comes to problem-solving. Interns work around the clock, subjecting themselves to harsher work environments but ultimately receiving a crash course in theatre production. In the theatre/television/film industry, interns serve as unsung heros.

Is this 'pay your dues' outlook healthy? Is it humane? Is it archaic? Ultimately, it's up to an artistic director, or the artistic head of a theatre, to decide if they want to provide an opportunity such as an internship, and it's up to the artist to decide if they want to participate. Whichever the choice, it will inform an artist of the type of art they would like to commit themselves to in the future by tapping into a sense of play and participating in sandbox-like environments such as small-budget films and web series or internships and apprenticeships.

Figuring out the ways in which workflow and work ethic works best can be messy, therefore forcing an artist to face failure. These events become lessons that help dictate decision-making and promote healthy boundaries. While failure has a massive negative connotation – it proves to be a necessary step toward success. With opportunities like *Indoor Boys*, Wesley Taylor attributes failure as a massive ingredient in its legacy.

"Failure is totally part of it," Taylor reflects.

> We failed a lot on *Indoor Boys* and yet, ultimately we didn't fail. We succeeded because we failed. Because we allowed ourselves to fail, we succeeded. The end result is still really quality because we allowed ourselves to fail and learn.

Failing is a positive act. So how does one begin to embrace the positives of failure? Just because one has won a Tony Award for a certain project doesn't mean they didn't fail multiple times during the process. Artists will fail again and again – in fact, all art is just figuring out a healthier relationship with failure. It only becomes helpful when one is able to embrace this terrifying, yet misunderstood concept. It requires a great shift in perspective, understanding that one who fails must do so with great fortitude.

"I am learning that it's okay when you mess up or when you need help," says Tjong. "People are always ready to help, and they won't necessarily think less of you if you ask for help."

EPISODE EXCERPT

KIMBERLY FAYE GREENBERG

Actor, dresser, coach, and creator of her one person show, Fabulous Fanny -- which has been critically acclaimed by the New York Times, Huffington Post, and Associated Press.

MULTITASKING VS. MULTI-HYPHENATING • EPISODE 35

Kimberly: It took me a long time to give myself permission to actually ask for help where those kinds of things are concerned. We're always so fearful especially because we're balancing a lot of plates, that if we give away some of our power, something is not going to be done or a plate's going to be totally dropped and we aren't going to be able to pick it up again.

Michael: And it's your mother's nice china.

Kimberly: Exactly, exactly. Our whole life is riding on our hyphenates. This is what we live for, it's like our passion in addition to everything else. You know what I mean?

Michael: And it's also sort of hard because I don't want to say we have to prove things for people, but I think that there are people waiting to go, "The multi-hyphenate lifestyle doesn't work. You have to pick one thing," And the moment that you fail at it, the moment that you drop something, people go, "See? Your hands are in too many things." And it's not about our hands being in too many things, it's not even about multi-tasking. That's not what it's about because I actually have a theory you can't multitask. I learned this from a professor of mine at Ithaca. Dr. Norm Johnson once said this . . . multitasking is not really a thing because you can't put equal focus on multiple things at once. That's not what multi-hyphenating is . . . multi-hyphenating is not multitasking, It's not that . . . that's what I'm trying to say.

Kimberly: I totally agree, I totally agree.

Michael: I devote an hour a day, well – not an hour a day, maybe two or three – to each proficiency, figuring out my chunk of the day when I'm a photographer and that is when I have a client at 12:00 and then it ends at 3, when my shoot ends – and then I put on my producer hat and then I answer those emails and schedule my next project.

Kimberly: And I had to do a lot of those things, too, because maybe five or six years ago it definitely was me moving back and forth multitasking, which obviously does not work. So now I do a lot of time tracking and I do a lot of writing things down and set a timer – this sounds

so anal retentive – but I'll literally set a timer and be like, "For 50 minutes you're going to work on this thing, and it's for this project." And when the time is up – I move on to something else. And that works pretty good as well.

Greenberg is the first and only actress to play leading roles in two off-Broadway musicals at the same time.

Notes

1. www.indoorboys.tv
2. www.imdb.com/name/nm0185274/
3. https://en.wikipedia.org/wiki/Wesley_Taylor
4. www.playbill.com/person/alex-wyse-vault-0000120763
5. https://constitutionbroadway.com/
6. https://variety.com/2021/film/news/travis-coles-michael-urie-summoning-sylvia-lgbtq-horror-comedy-1235009164/
7. https://pooyaland.com/
8. www.gandeproductions.com/transit
9. www.frameline.org/
10. www.castrotheatre.com/
11. https://en.wikipedia.org/wiki/Smash_(TV_series)
12. https://en.wikipedia.org/wiki/SpongeBob_SquarePants_(musical)
13. www.imdb.com/title/tt9640574/
14. https://en.wikipedia.org/wiki/Isaac_Cole_Powell
15. www.imdb.com/name/nm0276859/
16. www.imdb.com/name/nm9799055/
17. www.frameline.org/year-round/audience/calendar/frameline43-calendar-listing
18. www.ithaca.edu/faculty/njohnson
19. www.zialikhan.com/
20. www.laurynciardullo.com/
21. www.ibdb.com/broadway-production/aladdin-495244
22. https://maestramusic.org/profile/debbie-tjong/
23. https://2st.com/
24. https://mcctheater.org/
25. https://arsnovanyc.com/
26. www.sammyrae.com/
27. www.broadwayupclose.com/timdolan
28. www.broadwayupclose.com/
29. https://quickbooks.intuit.com/
30. https://en.wikipedia.org/wiki/Final_Cut_Pro
31. www.canva.com
32. www.beowulfborittdesign.com/
33. https://comefromaway.com/
34. www.lct.org/shows/act-one/
35. https://en.wikipedia.org/wiki/The_25th_Annual_Putnam_County_Spelling_Bee
36. www.ibdb.com/broadway-production/potus-or-behind-every-great-dumbass-are-seven-women-trying-to-keep-him-alive-533991
37. www.alexisdistler.com/
38. www.ibdb.com/broadway-cast-staff/dimitri-joseph-mose-500488
39. www.ibdb.com/tour-production/beautiful-the-carole-king-musical-500924
40. www.ibdb.com/tour-production/the-book-of-mormon-jumamosi-499334
41. https://titaniquemusical.com/
42. https://broadwaypodcastnetwork.com/dear-multi-hyphenate/17-dimitri-moise-discovering-your-call-to-action/
43. www.claimourspacenow.org
44. https://en.wikipedia.org/wiki/RuPaul%27s_Drag_Race
45. www.ninawest.com/
46. https://broadwaypodcastnetwork.com/dear-multi-hyphenate/50-nina-west-drag-race-asmr/
47. www.holmdeltheatrecompany.org/post/bww-interview-executive-director-colleen-cook-reflects-on-the-past-present-and-future-of-holmdel
48. www.jpmorganchase.com/
49. www.betsywolfe.com/
50. www.broadwayworld.com/new-jersey/article/BWW-Review-BETSY-WOLFE-A-PANTS-OPTIONAL-HOLIDAY-Live-Stream-Featuring-Jessica-Vosk-at-Holmdel-Theatre-Company-20201211
51. www.imdb.com/title/tt0458352/
52. www.multihypeworkshop.com
53. www.ashleykateadams.com/
54. www.kimberlyfayegreenberg.com/
55. www.indieseriesawards.com/
56. https://kiersteadproductions.com/
57. www.imdb.com/name/nm1563471/
58. www.imdb.com/name/nm1470289/
59. http://carbonellawards.org/
60. www.interlochen.org/
61. www.stagedoormanor.com/
62. https://frenchwoods.com/
63. https://frenchwoods.com/important-staff-bios.htm
64. https://hfwaa.org/

Reference List

1. www.carbonellawards.org.

EXERCISE 6
MULTITASK FOR 5 MINUTES

It's been made clear that multitasking is active switching between tasks. How well can you switch? And how fast can you switch? Ask yourself what is on your list of tasks you need to get done. Have to send a few emails *and* finish writing an article *and* set up your self-tape studio all within the day? What if you tried doing that all within five minutes?

Here's what you'll need . . .

Materials

Anything you need to attempt three specific tasks.

A timer.

> **Step 1.** Set up three tasks you need to complete. Make sure they are not tasks that if you made a mistake, it would cause harm or damage. Make sure they are

easily fixable if you mess something up. If you don't have any tasks, just incorporate three things like painting your nails, brushing your teeth, and reading a page of a book.

Step 2. Set up the timer. Put 5 minutes on the clock.

Step 3. Once you start the timer, try to get all your tasks done in the time allowed.

Step 4. When the timer stops, take stock of what happened. How much did you get done? Did any of your tasks get completed? Did you complete your tasks but made a mistake? Did you complete your tasks without mistakes but not as thoroughly as you would have liked?

Step 5. Feel free to try it again with 10 or 20 minutes on the clock. Having 5 minutes on the clock is meant to promote higher stakes. Multi-hyphenates are often under pressure and deadlines. What happens if there is less pressure? Are you able to get more done? Are you stressed more or less?

There is no wrong answer!

"At first failure was a very intimidating boyfriend," Miami based, three time Carbonell Award winning Elena Maria Garcia says. "Really nasty. I always wanted to impress failure and was just terrified that failure wouldn't like me. What happened was I realized that failure is not a bad thing. Failure is a wonderful tool and I now encourage everyone to fail big."

Elena Maria Garcia, 3 time Carbonell Award winner

Chapter 6
Fortitude of Failure

DOI: 10.4324/9781003254744-9

The Growing Studio in NYC

Career Connection
Teaching & Coaching

Education does not end when one graduates from their school. Art is ever evolving, and there are opportunities in show business to hone one's craft and web of connections through studios that have grown fast and furiously – serving as hubs to start learning the ins and outs of the industry.

Danny George established The Growing Studio (TGS)[1] in 2014 and has become the largest acting studio in the world with more than 6,000 students annually in New York, London, Amsterdam, and more. TGS offers low-cost workshops and classes that help actors further their careers and grow as artists along the way, according to its website.

"Theatre is ever evolving, but its premise has consistencies that have endured since inception," says founder Danny George.

> Education alongside opportunity has long been some of the most valuable artistic training . . . from undergraduate institutions with showcases to URTA[2] programs with regional theatres, the hybrid model works. Learning in a professional environment is a game changer.

TGS not only provides opportunities for actors to connect with creatives in the industry but also allows for paid opportunities for said creatives to be able to do so. This studio encourages connection and growth, almost ensuring a safety net for artists of any age to form. This helps artists audition more comfortably, interview more effortlessly, and create their own projects with more of a support system. Still, TGS is one out of a myriad of unique education options. Ari Axelrod[3] is the founder of *Bridging the Gap*,[4] a 5-week master class focusing on how to bridge the gap between musical theatre performance and the intimate art of cabaret:

> When I was in college, I participated in The St. Louis Cabaret Conference.[5] Before this, I thought cabaret meant Joel Grey[6] and fishnets. Learning from titans of the art form completely changed my life. Shortly after that summer, I moved to NYC and started getting invites to see friends in their "cabarets." Except, what my friends were doing was not what I learned cabaret to be. What I saw was young, professional actors singing to a spot on the wall, in front of a microphone, risking very little, and hiding behind a character as if it were a musical rather than simply being themselves. I learned from my mentors that cabaret is a very generous, deeply empathetic, powerful, life-changing art form that asks something profound, meaningful, and compelling of the audience

by reflecting humanity onto them. Just because there's a singer, a microphone, a stand, and a piano in a dimly lit room does not make it a cabaret.

Axelrod took a step back and realized that the lack of awareness and education surrounding real cabaret was not the performers' fault. He then decided to act fast and create something that had never been there before.

> I realized that there was no professional studio in NYC devoted to training and educating working actors on doing this kind of work. I reached out to some of my mentors and asked for their blessing to start teaching. I taught two one-off classes for a "pay what you can" price, and it was clear to everyone in the room that magic was bubbling up to the surface. Within two months, I started my company, Bridging the Gap, the first and only true professional studio devoted to training and educating working actors in the art of cabaret, which I define as the art of being yourself on purpose.

Axelrod both teaches and coaches and finds there is a distinct difference between the two.

> Teaching is the act of teaching someone a new skill set. Coaching is the act of taking a skill set that someone already possesses and facilitating the growth

Figure 6.2 Ari Axelrod, creator of *Bridging the Gap*, photographed in New York City. Michael Kushner Photography

of that already established skill set. In my classes, I'm teaching people brand-new skills within the framework of solo performance. When I coach clients privately, I am facilitating their growth of a skill set they already possess. Coaching and teaching is my calling. It is my purpose. It gives me life. It makes me feel whole.

Axelrod's *Bridging the Gap* is not the only coaching experience based on application of skills. The Multi-Hype Workshop,[7] created by Ashley Kate Adams,[8] Kimberly Faye Greenberg,[9] and Michael Kushner, was born during quarantine to stimulate the growth of the multi-hyphenate artist. No such workshop had existed before, and its arrival into the industry during the COVID-19 pandemic was a reflection of why this workshop was needed.

"Multi-Hype is a great class geared towards all who balance many creative entities, hyphenates or endeavors," says Greenberg.

> Michael, Ashley, and I want to give power to those who do all the things and encourage them to aim big, form a fully well-rounded life in the arts, as well as be able to hopefully create some form of income to live the life of your dreams. As far as the workshop and its evolution, it's been very cool to see how our students allow themselves to embrace their own unique journey and their own projects once they finish the course to really empower both themselves and their art and even, most of the time, help others as well in the process.

The workshop is dedicated to actors who are writers, writers who are photographers, photographers who are directors, and others. Whatever combination of any artform, this class crafts an experience specifically catered to each student. But still, education through coaching continues to get even more intimate and more specific.

Amanda Quaid[10] is an actor, writer, and dialect coach who started studying speech and dialects when she was 18 and, for the past 20 years, has coached dialects without even having to advertise.

> My teacher told me I had an ability not only to make the sounds, but also to explain it. She suggested I pursue teaching and started sending me students she couldn't take on, starting when I was 19. Since then, I've run a private practice, coaching actors and others from all over the world.

Quaid attributes her love of language to be what ties her hyphens together and drives her work. Coaching always sustained her financially, which allowed her to support herself while she found work in the theatre. Quaid explains:

> I'd say it helps me live better. I really like who I am when I'm teaching. It feels like the healthiest version of myself, looking at a client and seeing the best in them and using my skills to help them reach their goals. I think the first step is to understand that the ability to do and the ability to teach are different. They're related, of course, but teaching is its own art. That's crucial. You can be great at something yet be unable to communicate effectively about it – especially to people who learn differently from the way you do. So you need a real curiosity about who's sitting in front of you and how they learn best. It takes a sense of humility, a constant desire to learn, and the ability to shift your teaching approach on the fly. You also need good boundaries, time management skills, and a high tolerance for imposter syndrome. You need the confidence and knowledge to ask for what you're worth. And of course, you need to know what you're talking about, at least some of the time!

Ari Axelrod agrees with Quaid in believing teaching is an art. The old and very archaic saying of "Those who can't do, teach" is not only completely disrespectful but is also not true. Teaching is its own art form and therefore its own hyphen. And hyphens, as it's been made well clear, can exist alongside other hyphens and undergo a very specific process before one can apply them to their identity. Axelrod says:

> Some people disagree with me, but I believe that not everyone can be a teacher. Much like being able to sing, it is a gift. Unfortunately, not everyone has that gift. Just because someone calls themselves a teacher doesn't make them a teacher. If you feel the itch to teach, get a group of friends together, and start teaching. Build from there. For those who do have the gift of teaching, talent, when cultivated, becomes skill. The only way to improve this skill is by doing it. The more you do it, the better you will become. The better you become, the more people start to notice. The more people start to notice, the more reputable you become. The more reputable you become, the more qualified you become. The more qualified you become, the more established you become. You learn and grow while you facilitate the learning and growing of others. Do. Teach. Learn. Grow.

Trigger Warning: This chapter involves information regarding suicide and frank talk of death.

"I fail constantly . . . failing is necessary," says Wes Taylor.[11]

"There is so much power that can come from the reconstruction after 'failure,'" says Ashley Kate Adams

"Failure is essential to growth," says Lindsay Warfield.[12]

"Fail . . . Fail gloriously," says Tonya Pinkins.[13]

"Accept the lessons failure teaches us," says Jasper Grant.[14]

When Sammi Cannold[15] was directing *Evita*[16] at New York City Center,[17] she and set designer Jason Sherwood[18] had the idea of beautiful floral plinths flying in and out while the ensemble was standing underneath Solea Pfeiffer,[19] playing Eva Perón.[20] During a rehearsal, one of the plinths hit a piece of scenery, causing a loud crack, and causing a nervous stir within the creative team.

Figure 6.4 Sammi Cannold, director of *Evita* at New York City Center, photographed in New York City. Michael Kushner Photography

"Even though our stage management team had been impeccably cautious, the plinths were just not cooperating," Cannold says.

> I was like, "Everybody – get off stage!" The ensemble left the stage and Solea was standing there by herself on the balcony, and I was like, "Wait a second – this is so much better!" She's singing to millions of people, historically. For us to have twenty-five people on stage waving handkerchiefs – you cannot even begin to represent the millions of people. For her to be singing to nobody, but to be singing to us, the audience, makes it feels like she is singing to millions of people because it is so vast that we can't even embody it with humans. It came about because a piece of scenery crashed. I wouldn't call that anybody's failure – maybe it's *my* failure. But it's certainly where the right artistic idea for that production came about because something went wrong.

The brilliant Cannold isn't placing blame on anyone else but herself. Her original idea failed, but it led to something much more poignant.

"At first failure was a very intimidating boyfriend," Miami-based Elena Maria Garcia says.

> Really nasty. I always wanted to impress failure and was just terrified that failure wouldn't like me. What happened was I realized that failure is not a bad thing. Failure is a wonderful tool and I now encourage everyone to fail big. Pero – *pero*, it's because you tried, not because you didn't put the work in. You failed because you just completely threw yourself full force from head to toe into the pool, not because you were like, "Uhhh – I don't want to get wet. Forget it." No. I like failure.

Garcia is a first-generation Cuban American multi-hyphenate actor-producer-writer-director-educator who dominates the South Florida theatre community with her prowess and inspirational career. Over the years, Garcia has been an educator at institutions such as New World School of the Arts,[21] Florida International University,[22] and Barry University.[23] She also has won awards for her one-woman play *Fuácata! or A Latina's Guide to Surviving the Universe*,[24] which she cowrote with Stuart Meltzer of Zoetic Stage.[25]

Elena not only lives her life as a multi-hyphenate but also creates an environment for her students to thrive as one. As a final assignment for her students, she asks her classes to write their own one-person shows. They will not only be writing and performing (their own shows) but also designing, directing, stage managing, and running them as well. She *literally* embeds the multi-hyphenate approach into her teachings. In doing so, she promotes a positive environment for her students to fail and therefore rise from the ashes. When she is engaging as an actor, she prides herself on working with directors who will allow her to fail. She sees it as an opportunity for the director to open themselves up. "Within that failure," she continues, "I think that opens their eyes to other possibilities."

Tony nominee John Cariani[26] is known for his portrayals of Nigel Bottom in *Something Rotten!*,[27] Itzik in *The Band's Visit*,[28] Julian Beck in *Law & Order*,[29] Motel in the 2004 revival of *Fiddler on the Roof*,[30] and most recently starring as Stuart Gellman in the Roundabout Theatre Company's revival of *Caroline, or Change*.[31] Also a writer, Cariani created a television show, yet after it was passed over – in a similar light to Elena Garcia – Cariani's failure would allow his director to see the future of his work – helping it transform into something quite different and even more impactful.

"Back in the late nineties," says Cariani,

> a bunch of my character actor friends and I put up these strange little evenings of sketches and short plays that I had written wherever and wherever we could afford to. These evenings were fun and silly and weird – and had a variety show vibe. And they were popular – we got ourselves a bit of a cult following. A scout from NBC happened to see one of these shows and invited us to be a part of something called "Performance Space NBC" at the Here Arts Center.[32] At the time, NBC was looking to cultivate new comedians and writers – probably to sustain it's Thursday night "must-see-TV" line-up. NBC would put up our show a certain number of times over the course of the year – and gave us free space, publicity, and tech support. In return, the network would own the material we were performing for 90 days. The hope was that NBC would option the sketches and short plays we were performing and turn them into a TV show. I obviously jumped at the opportunity NBC was giving me. And I had high hopes! Unfortunately, NBC didn't option any of my material after our first show. Or after our second show. Or after our third or fourth or fifth or sixth show. And just when I wondered what all our labor was for, director Gabe Barre[33] saw one of our shows and approached me afterwards and said, "I think you have a play here."

Cariani had set out to make a television show, not a play. "Gabe then asked me if I had more sketches and short plays like the ones he had seen," continues Cariani,

> "and I told him I did, and we met up and pored over the few dozen pieces I had written. And he helped me realize

that quite a few of them were all set in a small, northern non-town called *Basketville, Maine* . . . and they all took place on a Friday night in the middle of winter under the northern lights . . . and they were all surreal, magical love stories. As we started working together, the non-town of Basketville was renamed Almost. And the rest is history."

Almost, Maine[34] would become the most produced play in North American high schools 2009–2010 and 2011–2012.

"Funny – the story of *Almost, Maine* is a string of "positive" failures," continues Cariani.

> The off-Broadway production was short-lived and went largely unnoticed. But it slowly, steadily found its way. And now – almost 25 years after I wrote it, it's one of the most popular plays in the world. There's so much more that can happen to you (good and bad) that your little mind can dream up. The earth, the universe dwarf the mind. Well – they dwarf mine, anyway.

While it may seem terrifying, failure is a necessity, it gives the opportunity to dissect what went wrong and how it can be better next time. In an industry in which there are few mathematical or scientific approaches, it also serves as the catalyst for strategy and action. Failure, much like many aspects of show business, shows its face in a myriad of ways; an out-of-town production of a new Broadway musical might get panned by critics, or a writer might lose the rights to their own story, or an actor showed up to an audition which they botched. Failure can be any combination of hysterical, embarrassing, humbling, or devastating – but whatever the occurrence, there's always something to learn.

Because multi-hyphenates tackle so many different proficiencies and art forms, there is an even bigger chance of failing. A budding multi-hyphenate must remember that failure is inevitable, and the idea that one will *not* experience failure is a failure all in its own. The real questions are, How does one recover from it? How long does one grieve or spiral? How long does one take to plan the next step? And how does one formulate the lessons learned from it? Failure is a paradox – one must fail in order to avoid failure. An artist, especially a multi-hyphenate artist, *cannot* avoid it, but knowing how to heal from mistakes is key. Acknowledging and understanding the failure are imperative to forming a healthy relationship and learning from a false move.

"I actually think an example of my own personal failure is when I lose sight of the bigger picture," Christine Toy Johnson[35] says. "And consequently, lose faith in myself or my work and question the outcome because of that."

Christine, who always tries to consider what kind of impact her work will have, acknowledges that losing sight of the bigger picture means she's lost sight of her purpose:

> The bigger picture is always at the core of intention. I discovered several years ago that one of the best questions to ask myself is whether to work on a project – or leap into a project – you know, put my heart and soul into something . . . would the project have impact? How can I have an impact with this particular endeavor? If the answer is, "I'm not so sure that there is a way for me to have maximum impact," then I consider whether or not I should let that project go. It's always part of my intention to have a positive impact on whatever I'm looking at with my actions."

Harkening back to the first steps of multi-hyphenating, Christine uses her 'Why' statement or her personal guidelines, to help dictate her understanding of why she's experiencing a misstep. This helps make one aware of the types of work and relationships to avoid or commit to. Failure is informative, and therefore, educational. The idea must be implemented into the educational setting, but the issue is that as an American concept failure coincides with shame.

Florida State Thespians[36] is a high school–level theatre festival that encourages students to share works from published plays and musicals such as monologues, solo songs, duets, small and larger group scenes or musical numbers, school mainstage productions, one-acts, costume design, scenic design, and more. The festival is part of the Educational Theatre Association,[37] but is different from any other chapter. Averaging more than 500 Thespian troupes, its large size separates this state's Thespian festival from any other state. Lindsay Warfield is a multi-hyphenate director-producer-educator-designer-artistic director and also serves as the state director for the Florida State Thespians from Tampa, Florida. Warfield says:

> I think the great thing for the budding multi-hyphenate is that they can really try a little of everything . . . and they can find success doing a little of everything. It's also why I really like the empowerment of the term "multi-hyphenate." It's not like they have to make that decision and be a playwright or an actor or a designer. They can do all of those things when they do Thespians because they can participate in the individual events, they get feedback, and they can excel at all of those things.

The festival also requires Warfield's students to act as a multi-hyphenate when producing the event. Because of the mammoth size of Florida State Thespians, Warfield created a student leadership element while running the festival for the past decade. Warfield bestows heaps of responsibility on her high school students, trusting them as they prepare to quite literally take over the city of Tampa. From folding thousands and thousands of shirts to setting up chairs, to running individual event rooms, to hiring trolleys for transportation, Warfield's efforts ensure an educational experience unlike any other. In 2020, the festival – which was expecting 12,000 attendees – was canceled 72 hours before opening day due to the pandemic. They pivoted to a virtual experience for the next two years and moved back to in-person participation in March of 2022.

"They really have to switch hats," Warfield continues.

> The students who are in my student leadership also tend to be my top performers or technicians. So, my stage manager is often my State Representative. It's the students who are really dedicated and want to pursue theatre. If not, they want to go into business or arts administration. I have a lot of students who have graduated from my program and have gone into arts admin. We always say, "Work smarter, not harder." They are looking at schedules and always have to flip the switch, finding efficient ways to process 300 high schools' registrations at the same time. They learn clerical skills, organizational skills, problem-solving skills – that you would not otherwise get in high school. I can't think of any other opportunity in high school where you would be organizing a 12,000-person, city-wide event.

But just as much as Warfield implements a fail-proof decade-long enterprise, she still encourages her students to do just that: fail. Florida Thespians encourages young artists to work on a common goal, fight self-doubt, and overcome obstacles. For every category that exists at Florida State Thespians (solo music, duet music or scene, playwriting, etc.), a panel of three guest adjudicators who are active professionals in the industry arrive to support these participants and offer feedback. After a performance or presentation, a student will receive written feedback as well as an overall score – superior, excellent, good, fair, or poor.

"Failure is essential to grow," she continues.

> "We can't grow if we don't fail. I really believe in peer critique. I believe it was Liz Lerman[38] who created the form of feedback which is about giving feedback to a work in progress. You're looking at the thing, as presented, giving honest and authentic feedback but not imposing your own view. We take the word "failure" out of the equation so that everything is a work in progress. I think the word

failure, especially in the educational setting, has such a strong negative connotation that it feels like the end. If you fail . . . it's done. I think as creative artists, we're only done if we choose to be done. Otherwise, it's all about learning. "Why didn't it work? What could I have done differently? How can I adjust my approach for the future?"

The positive outlook on failure begins early. How as a society can we implement it as a good step in creative growth? Even in baseball, youth teams are required to line up at the end of the game and shake hands with each other saying, "Good game." Yet, failure is so terrifying to some that they enforce bodily harm on themselves. Cornell University,[39] an Ivy League school in Ithaca, New York, has experienced students committing suicides during high-pressure times. According to a *New York Times* article, "classroom demands of an Ivy League university – and new factors, like the evaporation of internships and jobs for graduates during a bleak recession, had provoked the recent deaths" (*New York Times*, Gabriel, 2010).[40]

So, how can failure be implemented into an artists' process in a constuctive way?

Los Angeles–based actor and writer Josh Johnston[41] approaches failure with humor. It allows him to connect deeper with not only his art but also his life in general – and both certainly go hand in hand:

> To fail in an audition or a role is to not try at all. That's by not committing, by not doing your research and work as an actor, by not being a scene partner or a directable actor. I failed at asking out my crush to prom because I didn't even try. I did *not* fail at being a waiter in a restaurant because I quit after two days. Because I tried it, and I learned very quickly that I would do more damage than assistance to everyone around me if I showed up for day three. I didn't fail passing on an audition for a dance-heavy musical. I don't dance. That's not a vague statement. . . . I never could have been taught to do this kind of dancing in one month of rehearsal. It would have wasted everyone's time – and I used that time to continue working on things I *am* good at. I've gone in for roles I am not right for, but even though I didn't get the part, those are humbling auditions, because they teach me it's okay to live in the world of a character where you do not know what is going to happen next, and that is a valuable lesson to understand.

Beginning to fail is a little like skydiving – one is staring out the door, looking at the earth below them at 6,000 feet. They can easily jump – or choose not to. While they might flail as they free-fall, the parachute will open catching them. As they

try more and more, they will fall more effortlessly – allowing one to do stunts and tricks. Yet, no matter what, the parachute will open. *Hopefully*.

Saying yes is an integral part of not only discovering one's hyphens but also understanding a relationship to failure. Saying yes is the jump, or the kinetic energy – allowing *something* to happen. Broadway Podcast Network (BPN)[42] had to jump headfirst into the theatre community in March 2020. With the industry shutdown, BPN was able to find themselves ferociously building momentum as they provided access to the Broadway community for so many when producing efforts elsewhere had ceased. Even though they were making headway, they still were making blunders.

"We made so many mistakes," says co-creator Alan Seales.[43]

> We still do. However, trying and failing is better than never trying at all. Part of our early success came from us saying "yes" to pretty much any new challenge. When COVID-19 shut down the entire Broadway industry, BPN was only five months old. We had to learn, adapt, try new things, and find yet another place in this brand-new unknown.

Saying 'yes' is an incredible way to learn about oneself as an artist, including the ways one handles and grows from failures. Yet, everyone's relationship with 'yes' is different. Some feel one should get into as many rooms as possible, while others feel as if saying 'yes' leads to stress. Because many think of the artist as being 'starving,' the idea of work coming one's way *seems* rare, therefore an artist must take every opportunity that comes. This is certainly not true; the multi-hyphenate approach is meant for artists to create their own work, so saying 'yes' is soul-filling, not only because one has to pay their bills. It also allows an artist to say 'no' to projects if they feel unsafe or uninterested. Saying 'no' protects oneself, and it took Ashley Kate Adams, author of *#BYOP: Be Your Own Producer*, quite some time to understand her relationship with 'no' – but she arrived there eventually:

> Saying "No" is one of the hardest lessons I have ever had to learn in my life, period. I think so much of this relates to how we value ourselves personally and subsequently, our work. It all comes down to giving ourselves permission. It's funny, when I moved to New York City I made a "deal with the devil" as I called it. I told myself I would say "yes" to everything in my first five years in the city. I would say "yes" to every audition, "yes" to every appointment and "yes" to every opportunity. I felt that by saying "yes" it was the equivalent of "working as hard as I possibly could," but it was not the case. I was living in

a perpetual state of unbalanced living that only focused on my work, and that is *not* a sustainable choice to make for a lifetime. To "always say yes" is not worth it. We must preserve some of our energy for ourselves and "yes," we must preserve some of our energy for ourselves in our *real* lives. I like to say, "Say yes so that you can learn to say no." And what is crazy about all of this is, I personally didn't feel comfortable saying no in my career until I felt I had a reason to, which was the creation of my own production company, AKA Studio Productions.[44] Because I struggled with saying "no" so much, I had to create that boundary for myself and then I was finally able to acknowledge my worth and understand my "Why."

Adams uses a very important word every multi-hyphenate must learn: *boundaries*. After years of being taken advantage of, artists in the 21st century are finally creating work opportunities themselves. Because artists put so much of their control in other people, it's as if one loses complete and total agency over their lives. By just making small changes and applying personal boundaries, an artist may find themselves navigating collaboration in a much healthier and focused way.

"For me as a multi-hyphenate I like to say 'yes,'" says *RuPaul's Drag Race's*[45] Nina West,[46]

> I had to learn to say "no" and I feel like it's a sign of failure. If I tell somebody no, I can't do that or I'm too busy, or saying that their ask isn't valuable or worthy of my time – I don't want anyone to think that. I learned that. And through my therapy I've learned how to politely and powerfully say "no." That's powerful.

EPISODE EXCERPT

ELENA MARIA GARCIA

Three-time recipient of the Carbonell Award, Assistant Professor of Theatre at Barry University in Miami, Florida.

I WILL NOT APOLOGIZE • *EPISODE 10*

Elena: Ironically. one of my former students had written his one man show about his father's . . . how he got to this country. And we starting talking back and forth and in the end we helped each other rewrite our pieces and we helped each other and directed each other in our pieces. And then it became what it became. I stepped back and I said, "What is my strength? Improv." Then Elena, improv. When the audience talks back to you, talk back to them. Whatever happens happens, you're just telling your story – and that's it. Right now, if anybody wants to see it, it's on the YouTube and that was my last performance. It was a lot of fun to do. It really was a lot of fun to do. And I wasn't worried about, "Oh my God – am I going to make these people happy? Are they really gonna like me?" No, no. You know what? I'm going to tell my story and I believe that many will connect. It's just like – remember when we did Give A Boy A Gun and I was stopped by faculty members, I was stopped by parents, "How dare you put on a show about gun prevention. How dare you? I own six rifles and blah blah blah. You are promoting killing at schools, etc." Now this was right after Columbine, so there was no Marjorie [Stoneman Douglas] obviously, or any of that, but there had been a lot of mass shootings. But you know what? I said, "No, I know y'all are so gun pro and this and you want to make all your wealthy parents happy . . . I don't care. I have something to say and this play has something to say. And you can choose. You can choose in the end. I'm not telling them to take your rights away. I'm just putting a picture up. And as artists we put the picture up with no apology. I will not apologize. Here ya go."

Michael: And there's no reason why you should apologize for something like that. It's so interesting – as we permeate certain demographics and groups of people, people say that they want to see a reflection of themselves seen. But when that actually happens in a setting like Give A Boy A Gun, that's when ultimately, you know, we're met with negativity and told no we can't do certain things. Remember the cast? The cast on that show.

Elena: Beautiful.

Michael: So into it. It was exactly what you called it. You called it Can and Stick theatre. It was ramps, boxes, and stairs.

Elena: That was it.

Michael: You got the rights to take a book by Todd Strasser, turn it into a play – and we told that story. Was it tough? Was it hard? Yeah – we had to live honestly as if we were experiencing a school shooting every single night.

Garcia: Yes, yes. Every single night. The journey that you guys took at such a young age – because really . . . you were very young. To trust each other and trust me . . . and just say, "I'm going to take this. I'm jumping on and I'm going." And there were no egos! There was none of that because everybody understood that you had something important to say.

> Garcia is the first artist to create the only Spanish speaking, short form improv troupe in the US, which was called Quien Sigue a Quien.

Notes

1 https://thegrowingstudio.com/
2 https://urta.com/
3 www.ariaxelrod.com/
4 www.bridgingthegapny.com/
5 www.stlouiscabaretconference.com/
6 https://en.wikipedia.org/wiki/Joel_Grey
7 www.multihypeworkshop.com/
8 www.ashleykateadams.com/
9 www.kimberlyfayegreenberg.com/
10 www.amandaquaid.com/
11 www.playbill.com/person/wesley-taylor-vault-0000043881
12 https://wildetheatre.org/
13 https://en.wikipedia.org/wiki/Tonya_Pinkins
14 www.jaspergrant.com/
15 www.sammicannold.com/
16 https://en.wikipedia.org/wiki/Evita_(musical)
17 www.nycitycenter.org/
18 http://jasonsherwooddesign.com/
19 https://en.wikipedia.org/wiki/Solea_Pfeiffer
20 www.britannica.com/biography/Eva-Peron
21 https://nwsa.mdc.edu/
22 www.fiu.edu/
23 www.barry.edu/en
24 www.theatermania.com/shows/miami-theater/fucata-or-a-latinas-guide-to-surviving-the-universe_337225
25 www.zoeticstage.org/
26 www.imdb.com/name/nm0137121/
27 www.ibdb.com/broadway-production/something-rotten-498917
28 www.ibdb.com/broadway-production/the-bands-visit-514964
29 www.imdb.com/title/tt0203259/
30 www.ibdb.com/broadway-production/fiddler-on-the-roof-13483
31 www.ibdb.com/broadway-production/caroline-or-change-523864
32 https://here.org/
33 www.gabrielbarre.com/
34 https://en.wikipedia.org/wiki/Almost,_Maine
35 www.christinetoyjohnson.com/
36 https://floridathespians.com/
37 https://schooltheatre.org/
38 https://lizlerman.com/
39 www.cornell.edu/
40 www.nytimes.com/2010/03/17/education/17cornell.html
41 www.broadwayworld.com/people/Joshua-Johnston/
42 https://broadwaypodcastnetwork.com/
43 https://broadwaypodcastnetwork.com/hosts/alan-seales/
44 www.imdb.com/name/nm4017306/?ref_=nv_sr_srsg_0#producer
45 www.imdb.com/title/tt1353056/?ref_=nv_sr_srsg_0
46 www.ninawest.com/

Resource List

1. Gabriel, T. "After 3 Suspected Suicides, Cornell Reaches Out." *The New York Times*, The New York Times, 17 Mar. 2010, www.nytimes.com/2010/03/17/education/17cornell.html. Accessed 10 May 2022.

EXERCISE 7

TRY SOMETHING NEW

DM-H

What is something that scares or excites you? Is it skydiving? Is it writing a play? Is it dancing recklessly at a club? Whatever it is – as long as it's safe and responsible – it's time to try something new.

Materials

Whatever you need to try something new

Something to write on and with (journal, paper, computer, etc.)

Step 1. Chances are one fails when trying something new. Remember riding a bike? As soon as you fall off, you had to get back on so the fear became less and less. Eventually, you were gliding down the street with the wind in your hair. What's something you can do today similar to riding a bike, failing, and getting back on to try it again?

Step 2. When you've completed the task, journal about your experience. What did you learn? Did you fail? How did you fail? How did it feel?

Step 3. Try it again. Now that you know basic information just from one attempt – what would you do differently? Here is your chance to apply that new information. Was it less nerve-wracking? Less scary? Scarier?

Step 4. Journal again, incorporating any new discoveries.

Trying something new promotes healthy exploration of the self. By trying something new, maybe you've discovered a new skill! Maybe you've found a new hobby. Maybe you've found a new stress reliever. Maybe it was nothing, but at least you learned something.

"Creating boundaries is really hard for me as someone who is a non confrontational person. That was something that was really hard for me to learn how to do."

Colleen Ballinger, Backstage of Waitress on Broadway

Chapter 7
Boundaries

DOI: 10.4324/9781003254744-10

Executive Director of Broadway Cares / Equity Fights AIDS, Tom Viola

Career Connection

Fundraising

The theatre industry is known to give back in many ways to its inhabitants. The Actors' Fund alone provides a myriad of resources for theatre artists, including housing. Productions like Broadway Cares/Equity Fights AIDS' *The Easter Bonnet Competition*[1] or Playbill's *Glimmer of Light*[2] each have their own goals and specific audiences they try to affect. Each requires a dedicated team to carry out those efforts. These experiences require smaller teams and because they are not-for-profit, they are often done on little to no budget, which causes more creative thinking and problem-solving. These types of experiences are 'all-hands-on deck,' and one can learn quickly.

Broadway Cares/Equity Fights AIDS[3] is a 501(c)(3) nonprofit, tax-exempt, charitable organization that helps men, women, and children – at every street across the country, receive lifesaving medications, health care, nutritious meals, counseling, and emergency financial assistance. Since 1988, Broadway Cares/Equity Fights AIDS has raised more than $300 million for those in need with HIV/AIDS and other illnesses. Broadway Cares/Equity Fights AIDS' outreach and programming span far and wide, even producing mammoth events in Broadway theatres accruing funds for their mission. These events, such as *Broadway Bares*,[4] *Red Bucket Follies*,[5] and *The Easter Bonnet Competition* entices the theatre community, its patrons, and its fans to buy a ticket to support the cause.

The Easter Bonnet Competition, produced by Broadway Cares/Equity Fights AIDS, is a competition where cast members from different shows (on and off-Broadway) put together a musical number or sketch and don their unique "Easter Bonnet" hats. A panel of celebrities votes for the winner of the prestigious tradition. These performances have been solo, in groups, sung, spoken, danced – really anything the participants come up with on their own. The competition usually finds a home in a Broadway theatre during a dark day, or a day when a Broadway show is not performing. In 2019, Broadway Cares/Equity Fights AIDS raised $6,594,778, which is the highest amount ever for a Broadway Cares/Equity Fights AIDS event. Notable names who have participated in *The Easter Bonnet Competition* are Lin Manuel Miranda,[6] Bette Midler,[7] Patti LuPone,[8] Stevie Nicks,[9] Nathan Lane,[10] and more.

What's it like to produce something like this? How is an event like this similar to producing commercially on Broadway and how is it different? How does an organization such as Broadway Cares/Equity Fights AIDS choose what to produce and what to pass on? Tom Viola[11] has been the

Figure 7.2 Tony Winner Stephanie J. Block and ensemble perform a number representing *The Cher Show* at Broadway Cares/Equity Fights AIDS' *The Easter Bonnet Competition*. Michael Kushner Photography

Executive Director of Broadway Cares/Equity Fights AIDS since 1997, and in 2010 was recognized with a special Tony Award for his Excellence in Theatre.

"You have to understand that what you're doing is fundamentally different from producing a show," Viola says.

> You can look at that both in terms of how you produce and market it and very importantly, how you sell it. When we go into a Broadway theatre to do an event, we have to follow all the union rules that everyone else does. Sometimes folks mistakenly think that either us, or another not for profit charity, get all kinds of breaks in production and cost and the answer to that is: no.

Because Broadway Cares/Equity Fights AIDS' productions are so etched in tradition and serve such an important cause, actors and stage management gleefully donate their time to be a part of the programming. On top of actors and stage management donating their time, the access to the theatre itself is also donated.

"You get to put the key in the door for nothing," Viola says.

> But after that, everything is on contract. Everything is paid with a settlement through the theatre. It's not cheap. To mistakenly think you're going to make a lot of money because a lot of costs are deferred is not the best way to go about this.

When producing something like *The Easter Bonnet Competition*, it's to fundraise – not profit off the production like in commercial theatre.

"You're not raising money to invest in a production," continues Viola.

> What you are doing is hopefully raising major donor money and sponsorship money, to cover what you anticipate what your costs will be. Let's say you're going to do a one-off, one night at The New Amsterdam,[12] and you know it's going to cost you $80–90k, really just basically to pull this off from Monday morning to Monday before midnight – you really do want to know that you have that money in the bank in sponsorship before you start thinking about selling tickets because there is nothing worse to my mind when doing one of these events that break even. It's not why everyone should be expending such creative time and talent to break even. If you're not doubling what your budget is for the not for profit or charity involved, or certainly more, you're not going into this clear eyed.

Playbill,[13] a monthly U.S. magazine for theatergoers handed out at the beginning of every performance on Broadway and select off-Broadway and national touring productions, went virtual in 1994. The shift, helmed by editor Robert Viagas,[14] made *Playbill* a database of news, job postings, features, content, and more. Bryan Campione[15] is the first ever Creative Director of the company. In June 2021, *Playbill* produced its first-ever live event, *Glimmer of Light*.[16] Campione, alongside Leonard Rodino[17] and the *Playbill* staff, created an epic concert benefiting the Born This Way Foundation.[18]

"I am the first Creative Director that Playbill has ever had," Campione says.

> What my role is to make sure that there is a creative angle on everything that we do, that is not only symbiotic with the brand of *Playbill*, but also with theatre and arts in general. I look at my role like an ever-changing chameleon because it depends upon the project what my specific tasks and goals are going to be. It could be writing a script for one of our virtual performances, such as *The Progress of Pride*.[19] I saw it through with all the artists, all the sponsors, etc. to make sure their voices were heard but also, we were able to provide access to resources or information to the communities that were watching. That might be one thing I may be doing.

As a leader, Campione's objective of bringing *Playbill* into the 21st century comes from within himself, seeing the industry around him. As creative director, he has a big responsibility to keep the magazine in forward motion, making it accessible to a swiftly shifting industry. Paying attention to trends, news, and information happening around him helps him create a viable story for the 21st century.

"For *Glimmer of Light*," he continues, keeping note of how his responsibilities change,

> it's putting on this massive event for 500 guests. [I'm] the Executive Producer of it – going up on stage welcoming people to be there, making sure everyone is situated, making sure tickets were working, marketing was working . . . it's really wearing a multitude of hats at different levels, depending on the project.

Yet with these incredible productions and fundraising opportunities, it requires respect and patience. Many are donating their time, their funds, or their resources which are precious goods. In turn, it requires respecting boundaries. Boundaries are an important tool to keep everyone's expectations on the same page when creating, providing, and collaborating.

Trigger Warning: This chapter shares a perspective from a situation involving gun abuse and violence, which may be triggering to some.

The unimaginable occurred on February 14, 2018, when 17 innocent lives were taken during a mass shooting at Marjory Stoneman Douglas High School[20] in Coral Springs, Florida. This senseless act of murder and violence not only shook up the city but the world – igniting the foundation of March for Our Lives,[21] which according to its website, "harnesses the power of young people across the country to fight for sensible gun violence prevention policies that save lives" (marchforourlives.com).

While the horrific events occurred, drama teacher Mel Herzfeld[22] hid a group of students in her classroom until it was safe to leave the building. Her heroism was noted on a global degree, and past students nominated her for the 2018 Tony Award for Educator of the Year. After the nightmarish day, she noticed her classroom energy shift into something different.

"When you're running a theatre program that's very competitive – you got the part, you didn't, get over it – there was no soft-coding rejection," says Herzfeld.

That's what kids did at the beginning of every year. They would do our season auditions, the lists would go up, and they would know where they stand for the year. After [the tragedy] there definitely was hemming and hawing of feeling overlooked, feeling like they were passed over. There was definitely animosity going on, no one wanted to take direction, kids were challenging decisions more, challenging the sanctity of what we did in the theatre. One kid would not stop chatting or texting and there's only so much anybody can take of that, and so you're chastising this person being like, 'Stop. What are you doing? You're disrupting the entire thing.' And little by little, there was so much animosity in the group – I was feeling the tension. I was losing control of what was happening on the stage.

So, I called a circle, and when you call a circle, it's going to be a long talk. It was very sensitive at that time.

I asked one of our counselors to come because people were getting really upset and thank God I did because I was not prepared for what these kids had to say to me. They were upset with me, I think. That's what it probably was on the outside but meanwhile it had nothing really to do with me. It's more about them feeling their own sense of worth and that probably the program and me was all they had to feel that way.

I had not changed one thing about who Herzfeld was. I was still teaching exactly the same. I was still directing exactly the same. So, many of them had been with me for many years. What was it that changed? That incident changed their perspective of things and that they wanted something more. It was a very difficult transition. That was one of many talks that we had in that group. We've been piled on. We had the shooting. We had COVID. We had the horrible death of George Floyd.[23] They wanted to be heard. And they needed to say something, and I became a punching bag.

I did find that I had to take a step back. I did find that personally I was neglecting everything in my family,

Figure 7.4 Matthew Morrison (left) and Kali Clougherty (right) share a moment together after rehearsing for their song during tech rehearsal of *From Broadway With Love*, a benefit concert held in Fort Lauderdale in honor of the victims of the tragedy at Marjory Stoneman Douglas High School. Michael Kushner Photography

in my house, for this program. Everything came second and it was a hard reflection of my life because my kids are all grown. What did I miss out on? Why can I remember this show or that show, but I can't remember one thing with my own children. And it was like, "What am I doing? And at what cost?" My direction changed because I needed to step back and I needed to start putting things in order in my own life, because if I'm not in control of my own classroom, what good am I? It's not a classroom. It's not a learning environment. I have to be that leader and I have to do things in a different way. And that meant being better but also being less involved. When you're so close with your students, you're the third parent and that's why they treat you that way.

Herzfeld found herself implementing strong boundaries to continue to deliver as a drama teacher and as a woman who has a life and a family outside her classroom. Boundaries exist so that the artist may exist as well. In the theatre, television, and film industries, they come in different sizes. Exerting even the smallest ones can move mountains by causing healthier working environments, stronger relationships, and streamlined workflow.

Boundaries are the act of establishing a safe distinction between oneself and another. That 'other' can be a person, a job, a habit, anything that might require an examination of distance. Boundaries can be applied in a myriad of situations such as one's personal life or, in a true multi-hyphenate sense, when providing a self-created character, act, or product – which is known as intellectual property. **Intellectual property** is a legally protected work of art like a play, a book, or a song.

Over the past decade, Colleen Ballinger[24] has become an internet, television, and stage phenomenon. The talented comedienne created a character by the name of Miranda Sings and posted a video of the character on YouTube in 2008. Since then, Ballinger has raked in more than 4 billion views on her social media platforms worldwide and has received awards such as the Teen Choice Award. In 2016, Ballinger released her Netflix series *Haters Back Off*,[25] and later in 2019, she made her Broadway debut in *Waitress the Musical*.[26] Ballinger single-handedly paved the way for celebrities and stars to be born by posting their creations and content on channels like YouTube.

Ballinger's rise to fame required her to assert boundaries between herself and the industry, especially when it came to quality time with her family.

I had to learn how to create boundaries and it's still something I'm learning because I was walked all over and taken advantage of a lot for many years in the

beginning when I was starting to do this. Creating boundaries is really hard for me as someone who is a non-confrontational person. That was something that was really hard for me to learn how to do. My agent actually was the first person to tell me, "You can say no." And I think that was the first boundary I ever learned; the power of saying no and how important it is to say no because when you're trying to create your own business and you're trying to make it in this really painful industry, you're taught to say yes to everything always which is important sometimes but also can destroy you. I was getting destroyed by saying yes to everything and just being accommodating to everyone by trying to do everything all the time. Family is my other boundary. You can't interrupt a family event, holiday, or birthday. Family time is always number one.

While asserting boundaries is certainly healthy for the individual, they often come with negative responses from outside sources. While Ballinger has learned to implement advocacy for herself and her family, she still experienced the disappointment of others and loss of work.

Figure 7.5 Colleen Ballinger on stage at The Town Hall in NYC during her show *Miranda Sings Live*. Michael Kushner Photography

"It was really hard for me to learn that I was going to disappoint people sometimes," continues Ballinger.

> That's another thing you're taught in this industry, especially being raised in musical theatre. I feel like you really do anything and everything you can to please your director, or your teacher, or anyone higher up – you just want them to approve of you, and cast you, and love you, and give you attention. To kind of erase that, when I became a business owner and trying to make it for myself, it was like, "Okay, you're going to disappoint these people you've looked up to and you're going to have to say no to these people for your own mental health and safety," was a difficult thing at first. Now that I am a mother, the industry responds terribly to my saying no because of family reasons. I have lost big deals because I've said, "My son is not here to promote your product." So setting boundaries has certainly caused some issues for me, but they are all healthy boundaries that I needed to set.

Similar to how one learns from failure – boundaries are also incredibly educational. If someone is not willing to respect a limit one puts up, is that even a person or team worth working with? Disrespect of boundaries is probably insight into how they plan on treating someone.

Boundaries are meant to be asserted in both personal and work environments. Whether or not one is on stage, in the wings, or in rehearsals – these barriers are put in place to promote healthy work settings. When applying them in a professional context, they don't start when someone books a job. They start in the interview and audition process – oftentimes even before going in for the audition. That way, when a creative hires someone, they are already in place.

Boundaries can also be flexible upon inner reflection. Taylor Misiak[27] is the female lead of *Dave* on FXX[28] and Hulu,[29] playing Ally. *Dave*, starring Lil Dicky,[30] is a comedy about a rapper's rise to stardom. Season 2 premiered on June 16, 2021. Misiak revisited her boundaries when she was offered an audition for *Dave*.

> I received an email from a casting director I had taken a workshop with about a month earlier that began "Not sure if you're familiar with the rapper Lil Dicky . . ." I was *very* familiar with Lil Dicky. His video *Lemme Freak*[31] came out the week I moved to LA, and I was responsible for most of its views on YouTube. This casting director was casting a new music video for Lil Dicky, shot in the same lip sync style, and she was curious if I'd be interested in auditioning. The catch . . . there was a decent amount of nudity and simulated sex."

> "Here's the thing, I had figured that one day, perhaps when I was in a Julia Roberts[32]/*Pretty Woman*[33] level of a situation, that I would "do nudity." Sure. However, I did not think that my first-time tackling nudity and simulated sex would be on set for one of my very first, and relatively small, acting jobs. Telling your parents you're taking your top *and* bottoms off for a video on YouTube is *not* a fun conversation.

Misiak was faced with a decision. Would she enforce a boundary between herself and this opportunity? Or would she revisit her comfort level and explore new possibilities? There is no wrong answer, but outcomes do shift when they are altered.

"Ultimately," Misiak continues,

> it came down to my belief in the project. Everything I had seen of Lil Dicky's work was funny, smart, and well executed. This video was gonna be great – I just knew it. I believed in his comedy, I believed in myself, and I felt in my gut, as scary as it was, that this was the direction I wanted my career to go in. I remember explaining to my family that while it may not have seemed like it, I believed *Pillow Talking*[34] was going to lead to more career opportunities. Little did I know it would directly lead to my biggest break. Dave went on to sell a comedy pilot to FX and I was one of the very first to audition for the series regular role of his character's girlfriend.

She landed the role. Like Misiak, how does one decide to keep, edit, or throw away a boundary or establish a new one? While there's no rhyme or reason for it, working backward certainly helps. An artist must be able to take note of what makes them uncomfortable, stressed, tired, overworked, disrespected, and *why*. Additionally, in terms of safer working environments, more and more efforts are being made to promote protection from harm. For instance, intimacy coordinators are welcomed into the rehearsal room to ensure artists' boundaries are being met.

Joey Massa[35] is a writer and a filmmaker. Their work has appeared at Symphony Space,[36] Playwrights Downtown,[37] the Providence Fringe Festival[38] and Brown University.[39] On top of writing and filmmaking – Massa also serves as an intimacy coordinator.

"Intimacy coordinators, often referred to as intimacy directors in the theatrical setting, act as advocates for performers in TV, film and theatre," says Massa.

> We choreograph scenes involving simulated sex acts, other forms of intimacy, or nudity and convey that movement to

actors in a way that is clear, desexualized, and repeatable. Intimacy professionals should have an intersectional and trauma-informed approach to their practices. In addition, we work with directors to fulfill their artistic visions while working with actors to ensure their boundaries are respected and a culture of consent is foregrounded in the process. Intimacy coordinators also monitor closed sets, manage nudity riders, and adhere to SAG-AFTRA guidelines for nudity and simulated sex.

We've always needed intimacy coordinators, but many people credit the #MeToo and Times Up movements with bringing an awareness to issues related to harassment and consent in the film industry. This paved the way for the formalized position of intimacy coordinator. Actors are in incredibly vulnerable positions. They're taught they have to be easy to work with and make directors happy or their reputations in the industry will be at stake. Intimacy coordinators are vital in advocating for actors because of the power dynamic that exists between actors, directors, and other professionals in this field.

"I would be remiss if I didn't also mention that there are professionals who've been doing many aspects of this work for decades without this title. Wardrobe and costume professionals, fight choreographers and directors, and others in production have been using many of the same tenets to help ensure actors' safety for many years. I've worked with a number of women in production who've recounted past experiences on sets in which they were tasked with making actors comfortable during scenes involving nudity, intimacy or simulated sex simply because they may have been one of the only women on set. These people are part of the lineage of intimacy work and should be recognized.

Intimacy coordination isn't the only occupation in show business that requires healthy boundaries. Rachel Buksbazen is a child wrangler who has worked with American Ballet Theatre at Lincoln Center,[40] Broadway Cares/Equity Fights AIDS' *Red Bucket Follies*, and *Trevor* at Stage 42.[41]

"You are there to take care of the kids, but you are always and most importantly the parent's first point of contact," says Buksbazen.

Relinquishing the care of a child is something that can be scary for parents, so fostering a caring and nurturing work environment and having open channels of communication is key to making them feel comfortable and quell any concerns. However, you are not their child's babysitter or their employee. Oftentimes parents will try to squeeze you for information, extra after-hours care, taking unauthorized production photos, and lots of other things that could make you uncomfortable. Setting healthy boundaries for yourself will help keep these relationships as professional and stress free as possible. Ultimately, the bonds you will make with these kids and helping them grow in their personhood is worth anything this job will throw at you.

Between Herzfeld, Ballinger, Misiak, Massa, and Buksbazen, boundaries are applicable to any experience in show business – and multi-hyphenates must instill them to function well. By claiming this personal strength, a multi-hyphenate can access agency, a trait that many artists forget they have.

Things move quickly in the theatre industry; therefore, the application of boundaries is often overlooked because of the high stakes of a situation. There are many moving parts and at any time there can be a wrench in plans. A producer might have forgotten to hire a videographer. Someone bailed on their promise of their $25,000 unit when investing in a new Broadway show. An actor unexpectedly took a different show, leaving a role open and rehearsals begin tomorrow. When these issues come about, oftentimes boundaries are looked over with an **opening night mentality**, a mentality of immediately solving a problem in just a few steps. Sometimes these issues are fixed by crossing boundaries and committing to doing something that might make an artist uncomfortable. So, in these situations in which the stakes are higher, how can a problem be solved while still acknowledging boundaries?

In the pre-Broadway tryout of *On the Town*[42] at Barrington Stage[43] in 2013, Gabey's song "Lucky to Be Me" was not receiving the right response with the audience. With time running out before the critics came for opening night, the need to fix the number was dire. During rehearsal before the second preview, Tony Yazbeck,[44] with the permission of the creative team, restaged the number in hopes of a better response from the audience. After Yazbeck reshaped the number, the audience responded more positively. How was he able to do that? What does that say of his relationship with director John Rando,[45] choreographer Josh Bergasse,[46] and music director Darren Cohen[47]? How did he advocate for himself so that he was able to take initiative and problem solve without overstepping any boundaries?

"The best kind of art will always be a collaborative one," Yazbeck says.

As an actor who in this case also sang and danced, my whole heart and soul was in this piece. I was living and breathing that Bernstein music. It was part of me. I had made relationships and built trust with the team enough so where they listened and considered ideas when I brought them up. I continually asked myself questions. What works? What doesn't work? In the end, the director is the captain of the ship. We must *always* preserve that. But, it only helps a director create a terrific product when they have a great team of artists to work with. That's why casting is half the battle in the first place. Theatre should never be "paint by number." It needs to live and breathe. A performance will never be the same as the night before so it is imperative that we as performers use our agency to collectively create the world in which the play can be brought to life every night.

After the second preview, the number was a success and therefore frozen for opening night. This collaborative effort worked.

While Yazbeck and the *On the Town* creative team experience was truly collaborative, the word *collaboration* has become a buzzword that lacks nuance, meaning, and interpersonality. The word, although it seems well intentioned, has become a weapon against boundaries. It has become a cover-up word for *free work*. While the intentions are hopefully from a respectful place, free work can be as big as performing an act for free – or something as small as going out to a cup of coffee. If someone asks one to go out for coffee to "pick their brain," that's a lot of priceless information given in exchange for iced coffee at $5.99. That's not to say taking someone out for coffee is off the table – it just must be *active*. It has to be an equal exchange of energy, not an artist sharing their insight and information for a cup of coffee.

How can **both** artists keep themselves in check when starting to understand their relationship with fellow artists, their schedule, and their newly formed boundaries? For clarity's sake, when going through this list, the artist who is reaching out will be known as the *prospective*.

- An artist can establish paid work hours or coaching services. That way, when a prospective artist who wants to 'pick your brain' reaches out, the artist has established a clear boundary that must be adhered to by the prospective *and* will be compensated for that time.
  - This allows an artist to garner an income from the situation. An artist's time is not free, so if the prospective wishes to gather information from an artist, the artist has every right to charge for that time. Why not turn it into a coaching experience and charge an appropriate hourly rate?
  - As an added plus, this can create a hyphen to one's multi-hyphenate identity. If they are known to have a coaching service, paid to have a coaching service, and there is a demand for the coaching service, an artist

could add **coach** to their hyphens, as discussed in the Career Connection (Teaching and Coaching) found in Chapter 6.

- The artist can include an intake form on their website, which cuts time out of the process. The prospective can provide all the information upfront which will help the artist choose how to move forward.
  - An artist should never have to do the work to gather information from the prospective who is trying to receive help. The prospective should come prepared, providing all the information needed to utilize the best use of the artist's time. A prospective must make it easy for the artist, since they are asking for their time.
  - Moving forward can look any sort of way – scheduling a coaching session, a coffee date, a phone call, or keeping the correspondence to an email. It depends on the boundaries the artist would like to set forth.
- The prospective can provide a clear **call to action**, or a purpose for the email. 'Picking your brain' is generic and insinuates an experience where the prospective will receive free information.
  - *What is a call to action?* It is an idea meant to create engagement. Some call to actions that might stimulate a response:
    - I'd love for you to be a part of my charity. Would you consider donating a photoshoot?
    - I'm a senior at your alma mater. I'd love to interview you for my final and I have a budget to compensate you for your time.
    - I am a producer in Los Angeles and was just offered this project. As I've always wanted to work with you, I think this would be a good opportunity for us both. Could we chat more about the project to see if it would be a good fit for you?

These smaller steps toward a clearer give and take helps an artist get more comfortable with establishing boundaries, and advocating for oneself will become second nature. That way, everyone is working toward the same goal and feeling emotionally, spiritually, and monetarily fulfilled. Advocating for oneself is fun, healthy, and respectful! It's just a matter of implementing these guidelines.

While enforcing boundaries on others may be hard, establishing boundaries with the self is going to be harder. One must be patient with themselves as they implement new boundaries, especially after years of creating in a boundaryless way. Personal time, Netflix time, running in the sunshine, dinner with a loved one . . . it's all just as important as the work itself. This is when saying no becomes personal – it protects the part of one's life that can be brought to the work.

Traveling the world, creating relationships, and investing in family are all things that will make one's art better. There must be room to breathe. Creating theatre and film is a reflection of the human experience; therefore, a human must have experiences out of the theatre to create. So when is it time to breathe and look elsewhere for fulfillment and inspiration?

- If one is finding they are skipping meals or bathroom breaks, it's time to say no.
- If one is double booking themselves and dropping responsibilities, it's time to say no.
- If one has not had down time to process, grieve, or celebrate, it's time to say no.
- If one is finding they've scheduled themselves in Battery Park at 12 p.m. and the Bronx at 12:30 p.m., it's time to say no.
- If one is being taken advantage of by a client or a supervisor, director, producer, or others, it's time to say no.
- If one is feeling the burn out or a disconnection, it's time to say no.
- And if one simply just does not want to do the task at hand, it's time to say no.

Folks must take care of themselves. If one doesn't take care of themselves, then there won't be any work to delegate, create, or protect. Establishing these boundaries helps one avoid burnout, or the total loss of drive and focus. How can one avoid that if they are totally wrapped up in the goings-on of overcommitment? Staying mentally *and* physically healthy is extremely important. Without the artist, there is no art. That being said, there is one type of work that many people remove certain boundaries for, just for the cause. Simply because it speaks so deeply to the artist, **donated work** is work without monetary compensation that might wind up being challenging and time-consuming – but it's work that feeds the soul and illuminates the spirit. While donated work is performed without pay, it is *not* free work. **Free work** is uncompensated work that insinuates the prospective client will benefit from the artist's expense, leaving the artist with nothing out of the experience – similar to the relationship explored with someone 'picking your brain.' Donated work creates an artistic partnership ensuring an enriching experience that both parties can benefit from. And of course, there are logistical positives like extending one's network, strengthening the resume and portfolio, and tax write-offs.

Donated work is often an extension of one's soul. It's so fulfilling, that it doesn't seem like one is performing duties without pay. Yet, it is a value often found in the United States that one must be monetarily compensated for any deed or task performed. Still, there are many people and organizations who commit to donating energy for good. Rafael Jaen,[48] chair of University of Massachusetts Boston's[49] Performing Arts department, comes from a tradition of service. Jaen not only shapes and encourages the careers of his students, but he even donates his time engaging with younger artists who have a goal:

> My father was a great example of that. He was always involved with the high school board and was always watching out for me. I think because he felt I was different and somewhat vulnerable. Carefully, not being too obtrusive, he was always around. I know he also did that with community. He grew up alone. He always said he was an orphan, raised by a sister. He built communities around him. He taught me to be joyful and giving – so I think I inherited that gene. As a costume designer-educator-historian-author, I'm always curious about how people in other countries tell stories, via textiles or traditions – how do we keep voices alive? And I think it's investing in the younger crowd that comes into our community. I want to replace myself; I don't want to keep repeating myself. I think because I'm always intrigued about what's next – I'm like, hey – let me open a door for you.

While Jaen is able to provide free resources for artists he comes across, he still sets boundaries within his schedule, his giving, and his personal life. By doing so, he is able to keep space for the capacity to donate his time. The same goes for an animal lover who might volunteer at *Broadway Barks*[50] or the participants of Covenant House Stage and Screen Sleep Out[51] who donate their time in service of homeless youth.

"Covenant House is an incredible, incredible organization that has been so near and dear to my heart for the past eight years," says Rachel Brosnahan on Episode 13, "Covenant House – Get Involved" of *Dear Multi-Hyphenate*.[52]

> Covenant House is an organization that helps provide vital support and services to young people overcoming homelessness in 31 cities across the U.S., Canada, and Latin America. I first got involved with them about eight years ago through an event called the then *Broadway Sleep Out* and now *Sleep Out Stage and Screen* as we expanded to include our film and television colleagues . . . and it was a night where members of the Broadway community basically looked around and realized that the young people who call Covenant House home were our Broadway neighbors. And, you know, there's something at the heart at the city of New York in particular . . . neighbors are really important and taking care of our own is, I think, something that's at the heart of this city. And

so they wanted to do more to be able to raise awareness and funds to support the brilliant work that Covenant House was doing. We spent a night sleeping on the street in front of Covenant House to raise money and awareness and we spent the evening before then learning more about the incredible work that they do, and the tireless staff who work there, and the courageous young people who reside there. It moved me so profoundly and changed my life . . . and I've been involved ever since.

With Covenant House, the ways in which a donation affects a larger cause is extremely discernible, but not every organization is as clear. While this may seem cold, when donating time, it's perfectly viable to field opportunities and requests. Sometimes an organization's search for donated work is just a company wanting to cut corners. There could be a moment where everyone else is paid, *except* the artist who donated their time. And with these types of occurrences, when word gets out that an artist will allow themselves to commit to work without compensation – it's like blood in the water, flooding one's email inbox with requests. Based on the way someone pitches their 'ask', it can be very hard to establish boundaries because artists tend to be more empathetic people.

"There is no research about artists and boundaries, per se," says Dr. Alisa Hurwitz.[53]

But there is research on actors and empathy (feeling the emotions of others) that I think can be informative and we can extrapolate from. As a group, stage actors tend to score higher on assessments of empathy. A tendency to feel empathy can easily lead to more porous boundaries because of overidentification.

Overidentification, in terms of what Dr. Hurwitz mentioned, is when an artist might feel connected to every single charitable request that comes their way. Committing to every single charity, on top of one's work and personal life, simply doesn't seem healthy or possible. It may seem ill hearted to say "no" to a charity, but one should only commit to donating time if it truly moves them *and* they have the bandwidth to do so – one artist saying no will not crumble the efforts of a million-dollar gala. The success of the gala does not rest on one artist's shoulders. Unsure of what type of donated work to commit to? Reviewing one's 'Why' is a great way to keep this in check.

Even though committing oneself to free work is the idea that one's time and talent is being used for nothing in return, that's not always the case. Free work can be another form of investment, a concept discussed in Chapter 5, "Workflow & Work Ethic." By investing time into an experience, one can only hope that they will get something useful out of it. At the

beginning of his career in 2014, director Zi Alikhan[54] took a gamble and said 'yes' to 2 weeks of free work:

A teacher of mine had written a musical that was on Broadway that was being directed by someone I had really admired. It had an incredible cast and somebody who I had briefly met through a fellowship I had just completed was the Associate on the project. Both my teacher and the Associate reached out to me and were like, "This tech process just needs another person in it. We can't pay you but it could be a great opportunity for you to just look at Broadway." It was an opportunity for me that had a limited time. It was two weeks. It would put me in the room with the director who was somebody I had long admired . . . and in a cast full of people I was completely enamored by.

Alikhan was able to review the situation and sense whether this opportunity would be worth it. He would eventually see that assessing his boundaries and following his gut in this situation would prove the right choice.

What it was going to do was essentially without pressure, I was there to do some work, I was there to do a job. I wasn't any kind of central focus in that space. What it taught me was language, it taught me processes. I got to zoom out and observe a fair amount which gave me a very rudimentary set of building blocks so the next time I went into a room that looked like that I would be at least two weeks ahead of the game, which put me in a place that was hireable and desirable. Funny enough, three months later the director was working on an Off-Broadway play and I was the first person he called to be his assistant on that project. Going to that space with the intention to learn and the intention to make relationships very quickly paid off for me in that way and I got my first Off-Broadway assisting gig where I was being paid.

Alikhan invested time into an experience. Though he would not be paid for that situation, he created a relationship with other artists who would eventually provide work experiences that were compensated.

While free work crosses the boundaries of many in the industry, it isn't completely off the table. One just needs to consider what they are giving and receiving when committing to free work. What's the experience? Will one change the lives of a specific group of people? Will one get a credit on the resume? A priceless education? An expansion of an artist circle? Whatever it is, even if the artist is not compensated monetarily, they should be able to walk away with a tangible lesson, relationship, or perspective. If one's body, mind, and soul is not going to be richer from the experience, one can simply act on their boundaries and simply say 'no.'

As one does this work to implement boundaries, one should also remember to respect others' boundaries. If they are setting rules in place, it should be heard and respected. They act as a precursor in achieving protection – paired with having active strategy, legal perspective, and teams to help root preservation.

While saying 'no' is certainly asserting a boundary, that's not the only way one can defend themselves from harm. What if a bully tries to take away one's creation? What if one tries to take advantage of another artist? What if one creates a legal firestorm? Protecting one's art is a crucial step in sharing inventiveness. Without it, one risks everything, therefore creating a shield of protection is imperative to a functional multi-hyphenate.

EPISODE EXCERPT

ALET TAYLOR

Producer, writer & star of one person show Punk A** B****, The Hunters on Amazon Prime, and The Producers (National Tour)

PUNK A** B**** • EPISODE 24

Michael: You were so aware of the task at hand. You gave me beautiful energy but it's amazing to see where our relationship unfolded.

Alet: What was it, Michael? Was it Studio Sessions?

Michael: Yea, it was Studio Sessions with Stage Network and you had your producer hat on. It was impressive. It was like, "Ooh... when I produce something, I want to be her."

Alet: I was putting out fires. It was whack-a-mole. I was hyper focused – you're right.

Michael: You were aware, though, of everything. People were clawing at your hems to get your attention and you gave everyone the attention that they deserved . . . and it was so beautifully done. But you bring that, what I'm trying to say is that you bring that into every aspect of your life . . . being a mom, being a writer, being a performer, when you train me – your awareness is just so beautiful.

Alet: Yeah, I didn't know I was that kind of a person until – I guess I'll just drop it on your podcast -- until I got sober. So I've had an enormous amount of therapy in my life, but also during that time when I was newly sober in my first two years I had a concentrated daily amount of therapy. I remember my therapist saying, "If you can do this Alet, if you can stay sober – the amount of energy that you took to maintain your alcoholism and perform at the same time, the amount of energy that you took to make sure that no one found out that you were an alcoholic. If you took all of the energy and put it into your creative self and the things that you want to accomplish in life and you put it into your ambition without a putting a lid on it, then there's no telling what you will be capable of doing," And I looked at her like she had three heads because at that point, no one was speaking to me and I had burned so many bridges and my family was rolling their eyes every time I said I wasn't going to drink anymore. It was really awful. But she had such faith in me and she said,

"You're going to be extraordinarily productive with the way your brain works." And I had no idea what she was talking about. I figured it out. I couldn't just perform. I couldn't just be a mom. I couldn't just teach aerobics. I couldn't just write with the combination of all four of those things with a little sprinkling of producing – then my brain was on fire. Then I felt alive and electric.

Notes

1 https://broadwaycares.org/category/post-event/easter-bonnet-competition/
2 https://playbill.com/glimmer-of-light
3 https://broadwaycares.org/
4 https://broadwaycares.org/category/post-event/broadway-bares/
5 https://broadwaycares.org/category/post-event/red-bucket-follies/
6 www.linmanuel.com/
7 https://en.wikipedia.org/wiki/Bette_Midler
8 https://pattilupone.net/
9 https://en.wikipedia.org/wiki/Stevie_Nicks
10 https://en.wikipedia.org/wiki/Nathan_Lane
11 https://broadwaycares.org/from-executive-director-tom-viola/
12 https://newamsterdamtheatre.com/
13 https://playbill.com/
14 https://encoremonthly.com/about-us/
15 www.linkedin.com/in/bryan-campione-3968944
16 www.playbill.com/article/playbill-to-celebrate-pride-with-glimmer-of-light-its-first-ever-live-concert-event
17 http://lenrodino.com/about
18 https://bornthisway.foundation/
19 https://playbill.com/the-progress-of-pride
20 https://en.wikipedia.org/wiki/Stoneman_Douglas_High_School_shooting
21 https://marchforourlives.com/
22 www.npr.org/2018/06/08/618163002/parkland-drama-teacher-to-receive-tonys-education-award
23 https://en.wikipedia.org/wiki/Murder_of_George_Floyd
24 https://en.wikipedia.org/wiki/Colleen_Ballinger
25 www.netflix.com/title/80095900
26 www.ibdb.com/broadway-production/waitress-502861
27 www.imdb.com/name/nm5357286/
28 www.fxnetworks.com/shows/dave
29 www.hulu.com/series/dave-ac3a96f0-9614-46af-b524-f59c7d281946
30 www.lildicky.com/
31 www.youtube.com/watch?v=zbmH7iX9sJE
32 www.imdb.com/name/nm0000210/
33 www.imdb.com/title/tt0100405/?ref_=nv_sr_srsg_0
34 www.youtube.com/watch?v=NWWeQlXfSa0
35 www.joeymassa.com/
36 www.symphonyspace.org/
37 www.playwrightshorizons.org/about/programs/playwrights-downtown/
38 http://fringepvd.org/index.html
39 www.brown.edu/
40 www.abt.org/
41 www.trevorthemusical.com/
42 www.ibdb.com/broadway-production/on-the-town-497107
43 https://barringtonstageco.org/
44 https://en.wikipedia.org/wiki/Tony_Yazbeck
45 www.playbill.com/person/john-rando-vault-0000020456
46 https://en.wikipedia.org/wiki/Joshua_Bergasse
47 http://darrenrcohen.com/
48 www.umb.edu/academics/cla/faculty/rafael_jaen
49 www.umb.edu/academics/cla/performarts
50 https://broadwaycares.org/category/post-event/broadway-barks/
51 www.covenanthouse.org/charity-blog/over-180-broadway-and-hollywood-stars-joining-together-august-24-first-ever-virtual
52 https://broadwaypodcastnetwork.com/dear-multi-hyphenate/13-rachel-brosnahan-covenant-house-get-involved/
53 https://counselingcenter.com/provider/alisa-hurwitz/
54 www.zialikhan.com/

Reference List

1. "Mission & Story." *March for Our Lives*, 17 Sept. 2020, march-forourlives.com/mission-story/.

EXERCISE 8
YOUR COACHING BUSINESS

To avoid time spent on giving away precious insight over cheap cups of coffee, coming up with a structured coaching business or class will help promote healthier boundaries – between you and another artist in search of free advice. Plus, it's always great to potentially garner some extra income!

What is a hyphen you have that you could do in your sleep? What is a hyphen you have that you could teach to 5-year-olds? Coaching can be offered whenever, and it's always good to have a class or two in your back pocket – a class that can be taught at a school, a training facility, or a festival. This helped so many during the pandemic as the world went virtual!

Materials

A   journal or computer
A   pen

Step 1. Think about a hyphen that comes extremely naturally. Perhaps this is your dominant proficiency. Or maybe it's the one you're most known for so it will be easier to advertise. Or maybe it's one that you enjoy talking about the most.

Step 2. Figure out your audience. Who is it that you would want to teach? Teaching younger children is much different from teaching high school students, which is much different than the collegiate level. Which demographic are you the most drawn to?

Step 3. Create a lesson plan. Make sure there is a beginning, middle, and end to your class. How would you open your coaching session? What is the lesson? How would you end it? What exercises are involved?

Step 4. Come up with different versions of your workshop. Could you turn it into an hour-long class? A 2- to 3-hour class? What about a week-long version? Make sure you come up with different price points for each version. Pro tip: A good place to start would be $50 to $75 an hour, per person, for a new class.

Step 5. How would prospective clients find you? Through your website? Through your social media? For easy access, make sure all advertisements and social media posts direct everyone to one place.

Having a class, workshop, or coaching service will prove lucrative and convenient. Educational programs, high schools, colleges, and camps are always in search of guest artists – why not stay ahead of the game and have one prepared. Plus, you can pitch it to these different educational groups. You may be the very thing these schools are looking for!

Chapter 8
Get a GRIP

(Methods of Protection)

"I'm learning that the older I get that less is more. Keep it more mysterious. Keep them wanting more, rather than giving it all out for free – not playing all your cards, showing all your hands. Keep stuff at bay so that people actually want what's out there and what else you have to say."

Wes Taylor, Backstage of Spongebob Squarepants on Broadway

DOI: 10.4324/9781003254744-11

Tina Scariano prepares for Feels Like Home at Holmdel Theatre Company

Career Connection
Representation

Entertainment lawyers, managers, and agents form a trifecta of protection and awareness for their client: the artist. Agents tend to focus more on the negotiations, while managers focus on brand and image. Agents and managers are not just for performers; artists of all kinds can find representation. Entertainment lawyers dissect a contract, making sure everything is crystal clear and in favor of the artist who is signing it.

Many artists are searching for representation, and while it is hard to find an agent or a manager, it is certainly not impossible. After years of searching, if an actor finds a manager who wants to represent them, does that mean they should sign with them immediately? No. Managers usually take 15%, 5% more than agents who the union regulates. The union does not regulate managers, and their agreements can be tailored much more to their intentions, which may not be the best for the actor – especially if they are multi-hyphenates. Does the manager take 15% off all income? Or just from performances? It's in the fine print – and if that's not paid attention to, it can prove devastating to a multi-hyphenate's income.

While receiving attention and a potential partnership may seem incredibly exciting, it doesn't mean it's the correct one. If an agent or manager wants to sign an individual, that individual does not have to do so, although sometimes the industry certainly makes it feel that way. Somehow having an agent or manager became a level of success or clout in a social setting, yet no representation is better than having poor representation. If one person or team is excited about a prospective client, partner, or artist – chances are more people will be excited about that prospective client, partner, or artist. It may take another year to find them, but it will be worth it, especially if all the correct precautions are taken. Yet, while there are some scams and agents/managers who don't have their clients' best interest, there are teams that certainly lead by example.

"A manager's job is to guide and nurture a client's career," says Rochel Saks of SAKS&.[1] "We are very hands-on and it's a highly personal relationship. A good manager always has their client's back and does everything they can to further the careers of their clients."

Figure 8.2 Beowulf Boritt, Tony Award Winning Scenic Designer and author of *Transforming Space Over Time*, photographed in New York City for Broadway for Biden just before the 2020 election. Michael Kushner Photography

As covered in Chapter 5, "Workflow and Work Ethic," sometimes a multi-hyphenate will begin to build a team to delegate tasks. While teams can be assistants and interns, teams also take the form of agents, managers, and entertainment lawyers. These teams make decisions for the multi-hyphenate artist in hopes of protecting and serving them. If an artist and their team agree on committing to a project, these moments of 'yes' become 'yes *and . . .*' with stipulations in a contract set forth by the agent, manager, or entertainment lawyer. These stipulations usually involve pay increase, first right of refusal, vacation time – incentives that make the job opportunity more appealing.

Tina Scariano,[2] podcast cohost of *Obsessed with the Best*,[3] is also a multi-hyphenate singer-actor-makeup artist. Over the pandemic, she has cultivated a solo music show called *Feels Like Home*,[4] which is taken care of by her music manager, whom she has a close relationship with.

"I met my manager Kristen Ernst of KMEntertainment[5] while working on another show that she managed," says Scariano.

> The first time we met after one of the concerts we instantly hit it off and knew we wanted to continue to work together. Over the years we stayed in close touch and became good friends. We would get together over margaritas and brainstorm possible show ideas and how we could keep working together. I'm very lucky in that I have an incredibly close and candid relationship with my manager. She in particular has been very hands-on in the creation of my show because the genre of music is something we are both so passionate about. I can't speak to how my manager differs from a traditional theatrical manager because I've never had one! My manager of course does all of the negotiations, the administrative stuff, the drawing up of contracts – but she also deals with her artists and their shows with attention and care. She really takes the time to know the artists on her roster so when she is pitching their show she is speaking from the heart! Her hashtag is #KMEFam and it really does feel like a family!

Yet agents are not limited to actors and singers. Other artists, like set designers, find the need for representation.

"What I say to young designers often is you will know when you need an agent," says set designer Beowulf Boritt.[6]

> In most cases, an agent doesn't get a set designer work. Basically, I get work from directors, and it's not

to say I've never gotten a job from my agent; I've gotten some quite important work from my agents once or twice.

Jen Namoff is the producer/partner/manager of Soffer/Namoff Entertainment.[7] For an artist, a manager is more geared towards the overall image of one's career, while an agent is more specific with a proficiency. For example, a multi-hyphenate Broadway and concert performer and writer might have a manager, as well as a concert agent, an acting agent, and a literary agent. They all have been delegated different responsibilities by the multi-hyphenate artist.

"Knowing your clients helps you make the best decisions on their behalf," says Namoff. "Anticipating something before it happens is how you protect your client."

Rochel Saks furthers the point that building teams helps slim down the chance of failure, especially for clients that identify as multi-hyphenates.

Figure 8.3 Rochel Saks, founder of SAKS&. Michael Kushner Photography

"A manager's job is to further a client's career across the board and to look at all of the ways in which a client can be successful," says Saks. "This is going to be specific to each client, but in this creative climate most people do more than one thing and a good manager will strategize with their clients to maximize potential success in all areas."

In the 21st century, both the agent and manager are starting to meld together, although they still have specific responsibilities, strengths, and weaknesses.

"There certainly is crossover, both the agent and manager are working to get clients auditions but the manager is the one that a client will text when there's something they need," continues Saks.

> A manager is the one who will look at 2,000 headshot proofs and choose the ones they like the most. And a manager is usually the rep who is working to further a career across the board, not just from an audition perspective.

But sometimes an artist still has to stay alert when bringing on a team of people. On paper, the agent and manager work for the actor – yet with a large supply of actors and a smaller demand to represent them, agents and managers have power by receiving the privilege of being selective of who they decide to sign. Many young college graduates are keen to find representation, but the relationship isn't supportive, establishing an unhealthy situation.

"Earlier in my career, I ran into resistance with reps who didn't want me to be out regarding my sexuality," Stephen Mark Lukas[8] says of his relationship with his old representatives.

> They wanted ambiguity as to whether or not I was gay or straight. It was under the guise of maintaining mystery. I still do receive pushback from the industry in terms of my sexuality; I think it is more disguised now. I've heard things said about me after I leave an audition.

On the opposite of Lukas's experience, Carole Dibo,[9] of Carole Dibo Talent Management based in Chicago, is an extremely supportive and hands-on manager who likes to develop young talent by bringing them onto her roster earlier than most other managers do.

"A manager is your guide," says Dibo.

> They are the first person up to discuss and disseminate what projects work to build your journey and your career and which ones don't. For instance, is it better to pass on a very low-budget indie film and stay available for something else or is it better to take because it is going to enhance your reel? We also work with the actor's agent to negotiate contracts. I am very particular about creature comforts. Does the actor need a quiet place to study if they are in school? When the client is ready I help interview publicists and lawyers to add to the team.

In terms of protecting her clients, Dibo does not miss a second to come to bat for her client.

> I have had female actors arrive on set to find that a scene has been rewritten and suddenly they are asked to do something that hadn't been agreed on. That is a legal issue, but I usually solve it by speaking to the showrunner or producer. If I can't defuse it, it's time to call in a lawyer.

Dibo mentions a crucial aspect of what a manager contributes to: protection. While an artist asserts boundaries, boundaries are only worth the amount one instills them into their daily practice. One can say they have limits, but are they actually implementing them? If an artist has trouble doing so, teams like agents, managers, and entertainment lawyers step in to help solidify the boundaries, creating a shield of protection around the artist – an imperative cog in the wheel of a multi-hyphenate journey.

While the agent and manager experiences seem like they can't fit into the multi-hyphenate identity, artists of the 21st century are finding a way to bridge that gap. Jason Rodriguez[10] is the unequivocal face of voguing for an entirely new generation of dancers and dance enthusiasts. He starred for three seasons as Lemar in Ryan Murphy's[11] Emmy- and Golden Globe Award–nominated television series "POSE,"[12] where he also shared his expertise with the cast as Movement Coach and Choreographer. He and his business partner, Ricardo Sebastian,[13] are trying to change the game with their new agency Arraygency[14] – with the singular mission of bringing Black, Indigenous, people of color (BIPOC); trans; and queer people to the forefront of all creative industries.

"We're trying to build a support system for talent when they walk into set," says Rodriguez in Episode 52, "Agencies in the Theatre Industry" of *Dear Multi-Hyphenate*.[15]

> When they go to their jobs, when they do their gigs . . . their projects . . . create their production . . . and they know they have a team behind them that they can relate to . . . that see them . . . that understand them and then it just becomes the work between the talent and the work. Nothing else is in the way.

Just like many multi-hyphenates, Arrangency was born out of the need for something – and in Rodriguez's case, he simply didn't want other queer artists to battle the same issues he did.

I come from a place of . . . I am grateful for everything I have received, now how can I give back to the place, the streets, the neighborhoods that have raised me. So in 2019, I'd also let them know I wanted to make an agency, like specifically because of my prior experience with an agency – I was part of a talent agency, part of a management agency and I just did not feel like I was being propelled 100%. If it's around the timeframe of World Pride and you gay and you don't feel propelled on World Pride with the work that you have lined up – you gotta ask some questions . . . so I'ma leave that on that. And so, I don't think any other talent should receive that experience that I have. I'm a stickler for the experiences I've received. You need to hear about it, but you don't have to experience it.

Integrity: Noun. The Quality of Being Honest and Having Strong Moral Principles; Moral Uprightness

John McGinty,[16] an actor who happens to be deaf and has appeared on Broadway in *Children of a Lesser God*[17] and *King Lear*[18] starring Glenda Jackson,[19] uses his gut instinct in an environment where many feel they have no control: the audition room.

"Follow your instincts," McGinty says.

> If you know that something goes awry, protect yourself. I have had an audition in the past where [the creative team] would bring someone to "sign" (not interpret) for me and I lost the job because I could not understand what the signer was asking me to do. Before you walk in the casting room, make sure you have the accommodations you need that will help you strive. Do not work for them. Make them work for you.

By McGinty assuring the right steps are put in place for him to succeed, he is finding a way to protect himself and his art. An artist has every right to assert specific boundaries that help them deliver fully in a professional element. Creating art calls for alignment, and there are many tools, methods of communication, and strategies that can help an artist properly advocate for themselves. This alignment is a **shield of protection**. Artistic integrity, intellectual property, heart, brain, impulse, nondisclosure agreements, and contracts are just some tools of empowerment that make up an artist's shield of protection. It can span from the ethereal and spiritual all the way

to the concrete and formal. Yet, one cannot activate it without understanding the two elements included: heart and brain.

"You have to have those connected," Bryan Campione[20] of Playbill[21] says.

> There has to be that visceral flow of not only thought, but passion. Passion can come from a thought. Blood flows from the heart and throughout the body, if it's not

Figure 8.5 Portrait of actor John McGinty taken in New York City. Michael Kushner Photography

going to flow through – where is that passion going to? There has to be an end result. That is either artistically, or creatively, or both.

Here is an example in which both the heart and brain are activated. Say a producer commissions a playwright to write a new play. The playwright had an overall *positive* experience with this producer before. Yet, to work together again, the playwright has minor adjustments to make in the working agreement, the process, and the creative environment. Spiritually, the playwright felt nourished by this experience making them want to work with this producer again. Concretely, the artist would find it in their best interest to seek counsel from a lawyer or agent to put these stipulations on paper. Let's raise the stakes with another example. What if two writers working on a musical disagree on the creative process, and the lyricist removes themself from writing any further because their artistic spirit is not being fulfilled and the environment is toxic? Legally, who has the rights to this piece? What is the composer to do now?

As discussed in Chapter 6, Fortitude of Failure, the concept of failure is a necessary part of one's artistic process. After experiencing both the successes and failures of engaging in a project, the multi-hyphenate will begin to see a symbiotic relationship between the heart and brain. It allows multi-hyphenates to react in a more informed manner when committing to a project. While an artist should always be in touch with what excites or deters them, impulsively deciding to 'sign on the dotted line' without seeking counsel isn't always the way to go. One must breathe, take stock, and touch on their shield of protection.

So then, what are the tactical, legal, and practical ways an artist can protect themselves? Who does an artist trust? And how can one use their brain to stay protective of their brand or voice, while their heart remains vulnerable to the world around them?

The multi-hyphenate artist is a business that combines both the brain and the heart. But because it's an art form managed as a business, there are juxtapositions that come with it. Because it's a single-handedly owned and run business, one must treat it as being the CEO of their own company while maintaining approachability with boundaries. One must stay open to accumulating creative opportunities and be able to cut the fat. One must build a team that has the client's best interest rather than just out to profit off the artists' creativity.

"We have to teach these folks how to make it in the business," says Roger Q. Mason[22] on Episode 51, "Wig the F*ck Out," of *Dear Multi-Hyphenate*.[23] "At the end of the day, we are the CEO's

of our own S-corps, and we are small businesses, and we have to learn not only how to build art but how to talk about it."

So, where to begin? One must understand when and how to activate their shield of protection. The artist is a superhero – and all superheroes need a way to defend themselves. Activating this shield is possible by getting **GRIP**, the four different approaches that blend the heart and the brain:

- Gut Instinct
- Regulation
- Incorporation
- Protection

Gut Instinct

The gut instinct is usually an artist's 'Why' statement before it's formulated into words. It's the most vulnerable form of an artist's desire to do something. It's often a spiritual feeling that may not be able to be explained. When listening to their gut, one might say:

> "I don't know what it was, but I just have to get accepted to that college. I really see myself going there!"
>
> "I know we only met for a minute, but we clicked and I can just tell that we're going to write something great."
>
> "They were telling me about this new show happening in Brooklyn, and I don't know what it is but I have to be involved somehow."

While gut instinct is an informative feeling, it's not always an educated answer. Oftentimes, some people will say, "My gut is never wrong," while others will base their decisions solely on impulse. In both cases, it might interest them to do a little more vetting. **Vetting** is the act of downloading more information to help make a decision.

Reputation is certainly a factor in deciding when to work with someone, yet many things get misconstrued and dramatized over time. While one might have a strong gut response to a person or an idea, it still might behoove them to do a little more investigating. When researching, one could look for

- clear and concise information.
- respect for boundaries.
- an energy or presence about them that is attractive or stimulating.
- common denominators in their backgrounds or histories that make them seem more human and approachable.
- a Google-able online presence.

When revisiting John McGinty's unfortunate audition experience, one might believe he lost the role because of a poor setup, but really, maybe it was a win. If the producers couldn't even set up the audition room to help John, maybe rehearsing and performing in this environment would have proven harmful to him. Perhaps he completely dodged a bullet. Possibly, but an artist should never lose out on a job opportunity because of the uneducated efforts of the people they're auditioning for.

While one shouldn't just rely on gut instinct, it contributes to one's positive reaction to a person or project. Yet, since multi-hyphenating is born out of access and taking control of a situation to avoid abusive or negative experiences, an artist should make efforts to establish a safe space for themselves and others right from the beginning. How can one ensure it? Take ongoing inclusion efforts; they must be handled with care, and artists in power can

* acknowledge one's gathering is held on stolen land due to colonization and make known the group of people whose land it belonged to.
* hiring an intimacy coordinator to ensure healthy physical boundaries while engaging in occurrences when personal space is in question.
* assuring spaces are safe for BIPOC artists of all proficiencies and avoiding tokenism and "diversity hires."
* presenting pronouns when introducing oneself.

"Sharing pronouns in any space is important," says Marti Gould Cummings,[24] activist and drag artist. "Cultivating a space that is safe for people to be themselves is crucial. We have to expand our horizons and allow people to be who they are."

While many artists across the world are doing their part to provide safer spaces for all involved, Garrett Zuercher[25] has had some experiences which proves how much more work the industry must commit themselves to before being known as 'inclusive' as it's thought to be. Zuercher is one of the founders of *Deaf Broadway*,[26] a groundbreaking series that provides full and complete American Sign Language (ASL) access to beloved selections from the Broadway catalog.

"I feel like I am constantly fighting to do this – to protect the integrity of my vision and my art, which comes squarely from my experience as a Deaf person in a hearing world," Zuercher says.

> Unfortunately, hearing people don't like to be confronted with how oppressive they are to Deaf people. Ignorance is bliss. In addition, the industry is still overwhelmingly hearing, audist, and largely ignorant of the intricacies of Deaf Culture and American Sign Language, so I am

Figure 8.6 Activist and drag artist Marti Gould Cummings in New York City. Michael Kushner Photography

> often expected to force my square Deaf art into a round hearing establishment. It's all about compromise, though. I won't win every battle, so I choose the elements that are more important to me and sacrifice others. It's like the studio battles with the Hays Code in the early days of Hollywood. They would include overtly scandalous material, with the full intention of removing them later, in order to trick the censors into overlooking other, lesser things that might not have slipped past otherwise. I push the envelope further in order to scale back to the bare minimum of what I really want and need to protect the integrity of my art and my identity. It's a delicate balance of trying to trick hearing people into swallowing more than they are often willing to. In a perfect world, I would like to be able to focus solely on my art and create plays without constantly having to worry about dual forms of access – how Deaf *and* hearing audiences follow the whole play at the same time in two different languages with polar modalities (auditory *vs.* visual).

While Zuercher is making incredible efforts to create art, he still runs into the same issues that prevent inclusivity and equitability in show business. The purpose of the multi-hyphenate is to create access for oneself and others, which is exactly what Zuercher has found to be missing for himself and his Deaf siblings. Unfairly, Zuercher has to work extra hard to help hearing people understand his art, solely because he depends on them for support, saying:

> For me, this process starts at the very beginning. Access is number one. The play and the art are second. For once, I would honestly love to be able to focus on the story first and not have to worry about access until later, but that's a form of privilege that I sadly don't have as a minority Deaf artist. My art is created for Deaf people like me, but I depend on hearing people for financial support, so I have to play the game. And that's what this is: a game between creating art that reflects my identity and making it accessible and appealing to people who often don't know the first thing about that identity. The past year in grad school (MFA in playwriting at Hunter College[27]) has been interesting because I've received a great deal of feedback on my plays from the other students in my cohort and my teachers, all of whom are hearing. Their feedback is great and very profound and thoughtful, but it all still comes from people who don't live in my world, who don't *understand* my world. So I have to take everything with a grain of salt and remind myself that they are coming from a hearing space whereas my art is being created from a Deaf place.

Yet Zuercher's gut instinct tells him to move forward. His efforts are being noticed far and wide, positively influencing artists all over the world – and for that he must keep going:

> It's very difficult to be the first in any field and have very few to no peers or mentors with the same identity whom I can use as an emotional, professional, and creative sounding board. I am blazing a trail and I often feel very alone, which is incredibly difficult. So, really, my experience in this industry has so far been more about projecting myself, my sanity and my emotional state, more than my art itself.

While one's gut instinct is extremely informative, the multi-hyphenate should contribute to other artists having a positive gut instinct when beginning a project. Simply take into consideration the artist one is working with, provide resources accordingly, and be willing to lead with an open heart.

Regulation

As covered in Chapter 5, "Workflow and Work Ethic," organization is imperative to the multi-hyphenate artist. Therefore, by asserting organization strategies, structure, and rules, one begins *regulation*.

Regulation is a set of rules one places on themselves to be able to effectively delegate work while respecting boundaries. It enforces a working structure that allows an individual, organization, or small business to function properly. It not only provides an artist with the correct expectations, but it prevents them from also abusing one's power. For example, during the COVID-19 outbreaks, many small businesses enforced a mask-wearing policy for customers to protect themselves, employees, and fellow customers. If they did not abide by these rules, they were asked to leave. The same goes for a multi-hyphenate enforcing a policy in their space. It protects everyone involved, so it must be laid out clearly from the beginning.

Policy, structure, and regulation are enforceable in something like a welcome packet, an introduction email, or an artist agreement. In a clearly mapped-out welcome packet, one might find information like office hours, cancellation/rescheduling policy, payment options, and more. The more distinct and specific, the better. For example, a photographer might provide a packet depicting the lay of the land for clients coming for a photoshoot. A director of programming at a cabaret and concert space like The Green Room 42[28] might send a packet of details so the performing artist can understand dressing room space, soundcheck details, and payment policy. In the midst of COVID-19, a company manager would regulate how the artists in a rehearsal room interact with each other and rehearse safely.

When it comes to small business and logistics, it's very important to create a workflow for oneself that makes sense and is easily manageable – especially when it comes to elements of a small business, like income. When dealing with income, it's important to regulate how it's being documented, saved, and spent. And when a small business is making a fair share of income, it would probably be in one's best interest to approach the next step of protection: incorporating.

Incorporating

Seventy percent of American businesses are small businesses. When establishing a new business, one should incorporate. By incorporating, one is formally establishing their business that will then be seen by the government as an official entity. This action ensures the protection of the business owners' personal assets. Who should apply to be incorporated and when? What are the benefits? How does this affect taxes? Should all artists incorporate? What is an LLC?

Artists tend to devote time to creating, but when it comes to staying on top of taxes, it's easy to scramble and find oneself unprepared. Staying on top of finances is going to be helpful in the long run, especially as a multi-hyphenate begins to cumulate a larger income from multiple projects. Employees of companies, or people who are paid with W-2s, don't need to worry about getting incorporated just yet. But artists who are self-employed, like the multi-hyphenate artist, should begin to consider if they are going to become an LLC (limited liability company) or a corporation.

Small businesses usually find themselves becoming an S-Corp or an LLC and should contact an accountant to help them figure out the right plan for their finances. Sean Maurice of MCR Tax Group[29] is an accountant based in New York who helps artists with their taxes.

"Taxes are like fingerprints," says Maurice.

> Everybody has one, but nobody is identically the same. Looking at the peers you work with – both can have two children, be in the same job, making the same money. . . . Person A gets a refund and Person B doesn't. It's totally different for each person. There's no blanket set rule for anybody in particular. You really have to consult with your accountant to get a better idea of what's going on because people *love* to share stories. People giving tax advice based on advice they got from their accountant is worse than social media because those rumors and the misconstrued advice is turned over in so many ways . . . it's not even funny.

Many artists in show business aren't aware that one can provide deductions to help lower taxes. With artists, expenses accrued during the year can be applied to hopefully lower tax payments. For example, if a videographer purchases a new camera and subscriptions to Final Cut Pro[30] and the Dropbox[31] business plan, these expenses can provide a tax cut, which means paying less. Yet, with changes in presidential administration comes changes that affect artists.

"One of the biggest things we lost under the Trump[32] administration was the SALT Taxes – State and Local Taxes," continues Maurice.

> Here in New York we pay probably some of the highest real estate taxes in the country – I think California beats us. They cap that at $10,000 and that includes your state withholding which they took out of your paycheck already as well as your local taxes – in NYC, it's your city taxes. So the combination of your state withholding, your city withholding, and your real estate taxes cannot exceed $10,000 and for most of us it does. That additional cap reduces the deduction. If you had $35,000 in taxes in

2018 and you had that same $35,000 in deductions when the law changed, that's essentially $25,000 worth of deductions that you lost which is essentially additional income because now you don't have those deductions to write off to help you reduce your taxes.

There's lots to learn in terms of taxes and artists. It's recommended to reach out to someone like Sean Maurice and help navigate the next steps. If there's *anything* to take away, Maurice recommends incorporating to offer protection in terms of lawsuits:

> I highly recommend that, if you're self-employed, you have to have that level of protection to cover your assets. So that way, if you're doing work under Sean Maurice, LLC, they can only go under what Sean Maurice, LLC has and not go after you personally. It doesn't mean someone will not try – but that's what the LLC and the corporations are there for . . . to protect your assets.

Protection

Ashley Kate Adams is the founder of AKA Productions, responsible for such productions as *Rules of Cool*[33] and the record label No Reverse Records.[34] Through her book and online coaching experience, #BYOP (Be Your Own Producer),[35] Adams is an advocate for the creative freedom of artists all over the world. But the learned priceless lessons she teaches to artists everywhere came at a high cost.

"There was absolutely a time I should have protected my art when I wasn't fully aware yet how to," Adams says.

> In 2016 I was the recipient of multiple horrific losses at once, my father's unexpected passing and a massive creative business loss. I willingly shared my story with a creative process, allowed it to begin, was not fully protected, signed over my rights and landed on the other side of the project with the ability to not have been fully present within that process because I made a series of uneducated choices under a lot of pressure which I encourage everyone heavily not to do. That situation was not a matter of life and death, but because I was not educated in the matter and I *was* going through a life and death scenario at the very same time in my personal life, I jumped into the deep end without anyone to save me.

Adam's story is not unique, unfortunately. It is known, simply because Ashley Kate has healed and understood the lesson, bringing this instance to all who seek her advice. Being taken advantage of in such a way is not rare. When these instances do happen, it can scare off a creator from ever working again. How many shows like *A Strange Loop*,[36] *Hamilton*,[37] or *Soft Power*[38] have we lost over the years because of situations like this?

The reason why show business is called exactly that is because there is a business element incorporated in the field – oftentimes outweighing the artistry. It is imperative that an artist hires a legal team to help guide them through the nitty-gritty of a contract. By no means does anyone want to give up the rights to what they've spent years creating, but that possibility is always a risk. While finances might not be everyone's favorite part of artmaking, negotiating contracts is certainly not fun either. Legal jargon can make a poetic genius go cross-eyed. Enter the entertainment lawyer.

Nicholas Rohlfing Law[39] is a transactional entertainment law firm representing a broad range of clients in the entertainment community including theatrical producers, composers, authors, collaborators, conductors, music directors, directors, choreographers, casting directors, dramaturgs and literary managers, associate directors and choreographers, actors, musicians, novelists, filmmakers, web designers, recording artists, and various rights holders. Rohlfing represents artists who have been associated with *Hello, Dolly!*,[40] *Hadestown*,[41] and *Hamilton*, to name only a few. He works with artists with teams of agents and managers, as well as artists who create by themselves – a perfect legal guide for the multi-hyphenate. So, when does one hire an entertainment lawyer?

"It's when you need one," Rohlfing says.

> Let's say that you're an up-and-coming cabaret singer and performer and somebody wants to manage you, and they say, "We think we're a good fit . . . we get along – here's the contract," I would say that immediately that would be a point where the bells would go off. When somebody hands you a contract, they're handing that to you because they want that relationship to be dictated by the words on that page. So for you as the recipient of that contract to say, "I'm going to trust that this is going to be fine and I'm going to sign, though I don't quite understand," you're doing yourself a great disservice because a contract handed to you tends to benefit the person who handed it to you. At that moment, you need someone to look over it for you.

While agents and managers have the ability to go over a contract, they might not be able to do so with the same capacity of an entertainment lawyer. Plus, many artists feel

pressured to make a decision that can lead to premature commitment. Rohlfing says,

> Agents often say they'll take a look at it, but there are a lot of stories where I look at something I get from an agent and I want to make some sort of revision because it's not as protective as I want it to be for the client. So many artists want to please and get to the part with the art and they don't want to make waves. They feel rushed. There are instances where there is pressure on the artist to make a decision. When that artist is unrepresented there is a lot of leverage from the other side. Something they would say is, "We really need to know by the end of the day." I think it's intimidating often for an artist. What I say is, if you're beginning a relationship that is a business relationship to some degree, as my wife Heidi says to young artists in this business all the time, "you are the president of your own company." So you get to say when you're ready to make a decision to do a particular thing. You get to take a breath. You get to consult with your team, be that your husband, or your friend who's an agent, or your next-door neighbor who's a lawyer, or your lawyer you have hired – you get to say yes or you get to say no. You're in charge of your own career.

While getting a **GRIP** on one's artistic protection helps to preserve finances, relationships, and intellectual property, it also helps with the overall image. Even with a strong social media presence, Wes Taylor[42] is very careful about what he shares with his audience.

> When I had just gotten to the city, I was in a lot of long running shows, fortunately, but I was getting bored and stifled. I would just start making these sketches or web series or whatever. To me, I just wanted to keep creating and producing more content: putting it out, putting it out, putting it out. In hindsight, I look back and I say, "Ugh, a little more discretion. A little bit less!" Because now you're everywhere and a lot of it. . . . I don't *love*. That's okay because I was younger and I was figuring it out – but it's all there now.

In the 21st century, protection can be as large as contract negotiations and as small as censoring oneself on social media. With social media dominating the way humans connect with each other, it's effortless for anyone to open TikTok, record a video, and post it – whether the information is true or not. Social media is an extremely useful tool, but many use it to harm rather than help. Artists should always be in search of a better world, but is the content being posted a true reflection of who they are as a human being? Is every single opinion worth posting on Twitter? What is one's intention with their

Figure 8.7 Wesley Taylor gets his wig applied (designed by Charles G. LaPointe) and prepares in his dressing room backstage of Spongebob Squarepants on Broadway at The Palace Theatre. Costume design by David Zinn. Michael Kushner Photography

content and are they truly protecting themselves and their artform with what is being posted?

"I always think about when I was a kid, I'm glad YouTube wasn't around because I would have destroyed myself before I even came on the scene," Taylor continues.

> I think a lot of times that less is more. We're talking about social media – we're talking about all the ways in which we put ourselves out there. In my writing, in my art, in the way I present myself – a lot of times I'm learning that the older I get that less is more. Keep it more mysterious. Keep them wanting more, rather than giving it all out for free – not playing all your cards, showing all your hands. Keep stuff at bay so that people actually want what's out there and what else you have to say.

Protecting one's art is, in turn, protecting themselves. While there are many practices to protect oneself, the only way to go through the lengthy yet necessary process is to believe in themselves. One must acknowledge that they are worthy of protection – that their voice deserves to be respected and their place in the world is secure. One must understand that the amount of work they've put into their creation deserves a place in the sun. To execute years of hard work and begin to experience the positive attributes of doing so, only to believe one is not worth it is what's called **imposter syndrome**.

Imposter syndrome is the idea that an artist's efforts are not legitimate, that their ideas, perspective, and products are fraudulent and not worth respect. It's quite a mindset to be in after devoting countless years and limitless energy to a project or art form. All of a sudden, when it's time to deliver, imposter syndrome prevents one from doing so. It's devastating – and prevents the artist from boarding the Satz train, resulting in missed opportunities. Imposter syndrome in multi-hyphenates can occur because it's not rare that self-taught or born out of natural talent proficiencies are added to an identity, while others who identify as that proficiency studied their whole life to act as such. There will be many artists lurking out there judging someone else's journey, therefore contributing to one's bout of imposter syndrome.

When identifying imposter syndrome, one might be saying things and asking questions such as

- "I am not qualified to do this."
- "My voice does not deserve to be heard."
- "My point of view is not worth sharing."
- "Why would anyone want to experience what I've created?"
- "I didn't go to college for this, so why am I doing this?"
- "What is everyone saying about me?"

It's never too late to discover a new art form or way to express oneself, and as discussed, it takes self-reflection, time, and practice to be able to appropriately add a hyphen to one's identity. With lists like Forbes 30 Under 30, it seems as though there is a time limit on success – that success found in one's later years in life isn't as important or impactful. Multi-hyphenates must navigate the world with gusto and commit to the way in which they want their artistry to be seen by the world – taking the time they need to exist confidently.

Christina Bianco[43] has had many conversations with herself about how to identify in show business. She identifies as a singer-actor-impressionist-writer-creator-producer but has fought hard to be seen as such.

"It's only recently that the industry is taking me seriously as a writer-creator-producer," says Bianco.

> I've been working for so long writing, creating and producing my own content – for stage and screen – but audiences and press have always assumed someone else was doing all of that work. It's taken me ten years to realize that I need to take pride in all my work and that it's not egotistical "diva behavior" to call myself a multi-hyphenate. It's just the truth. Taking ownership of that has already helped me grow and brought me new opportunities.

Imposter syndrome is not an easy concept to shake as it directly attacks a person's purpose, preventing them from forward motion. But forward motion is exactly what the multi-hyphenate needs to commit themselves to. By applying elements such as access, work ethic, workflow, failure, boundaries, and protection, one can begin to *navigate* through the industry whole-heartedly, existing as a decision-making, meticulous, and courageous multi-hyphenate.

Figure 8.8 Christina Bianco photographed at Holmdel Theatre Company. Michael Kushner Photography

EPISODE EXCERPT

ERIN KOMMOR

Rise on NBC

MENTAL HEALTH IS FIERCE • *EPISODE 4*

Erin: I wish everyone would just go to therapy. Our country . . . our world would be so different.

Michael: Can you tell me how mental health and therapy . . . I wasn't planning on talking about mental health and therapy, but I'm obsessed because that is key to being a human being but how has that played into your business as an artist? How has that helped you discover all of these facets of yourself? How has that helped you become a better multi-hyphenate? How has that made you a better Erin?

Erin: So I went to some weird, interesting stuff growing up and I didn't go to therapy for a while because I didn't need that . . . I'm a tough girl.

Michael: I can go through it on my own, I can figure it out.

Erin: Yea . . . I wear eyeliner and cut my own hair, like, don't mess with me. And then basically a couple years ago a bunch of things happened . . . I basically had a breakdown, I guess I'd call it that. And I realized all these things I had been suppressing and, most of all, I wasn't allowing myself to feel anything that I should have been feeling from a long time ago. So it takes a long time to go through it, and navigate through the pain, and let go of the layers of blah, blah, blah . . . but, no, I think without therapy I wouldn't know myself . . . and also that's a combination of therapy, of yoga, of healing as opposed to ignoring trauma. But I think that does show up in my work because as an artist you're not separate from your work – like you are your instrument, you know – and by healing myself and by healing myself I can be honest with the characters I play.

Michael: Did you find you were able to draw from those experiences with Rise?

Erin: Oh yeah – but also . . . yeah, that was hard because . . . we're both empaths, you know that . . .

Michael: Yeah, 100%.

Erin: And I got a little too attached and empathetic towards my character and yeah... it was dark. I would do ten takes and be sobbing every single one and I would just have to go home and make dinner and I was just like, "But what about Sasha? Is she okay?" I got way too attached and then my therapist was like, "You have to schedule in time to decompress because your body, when you cry, doesn't know you're acting. It just knows you're experiencing an emotion. And you have to let it pass through you. You can't just snap in and out." Like what we do is not normal. So you have to schedule time to let it go and then transition back into your normal life. And I was not doing that. I was just like *pants heavily* and then like . . . my head exploded.

Michael: That's fierce. But that's an amazing example of how therapy has helped you. I love that tool.

Erin: All the tools. We don't know the tools until someone is like, "Here's a tool."

Michael: Right, it's just giving us a toolbox – that's what therapy is.

Erin: I love a tool box.

Michael: We love a toolbox, honey.

Notes

1 www.saksand.com/
2 www.tinascariano.com/
3 www.dimlywit.com/obsessed
4 www.kmentertainment.net/feels-like-home-with-tina-scariano
5 www.kmentertainment.net/
6 www.beowulfborittdesign.com/
7 http://soffer-namoff.com/
8 www.stephenmarklukas.com/
9 www.actorstrainingcenter.org/team
10 www.imdb.com/name/nm9884396/
11 www.imdb.com/name/nm0614682/
12 www.imdb.com/title/tt7562112/
13 https://variety.com/2021/legit/news/pose-star-jason-rodriguez-arraygency-talent-agency-bipoc-queer-trans-creative-1235034306/
14 www.arraygency.com/
15 https://broadwaypodcastnetwork.com/dear-multi-hyphenate/52-jason-rodriguez-agencies-in-the-theatre-industry/
16 www.johnpmcginty.com/
17 www.ibdb.com/broadway-production/children-of-a-lesser-god-515596
18 www.ibdb.com/broadway-production/king-lear-519767
19 https://en.wikipedia.org/wiki/Glenda_Jackson
20 www.linkedin.com/in/bryan-campione-3968944
21 www.playbill.com
22 www.rogerqmason.com/aboutme
23 https://broadwaypodcastnetwork.com/dear-multi-hyphenate/51-roger-q-mason-wig-the-fck-out/
24 https://martigcummings.com/
25 www.garrettzuercher.com/
26 www.deafbroadway.com/
27 www.hunter.cuny.edu/graduateadmissions/program-requirements/school-of-arts-and-sciences/arts-humanities/playwriting
28 https://thegreenroom42.venuetix.com/
29 https://opencorporates.com/companies/us_ny/3162175
30 https://en.wikipedia.org/wiki/Final_Cut_Pro
31 https://en.wikipedia.org/wiki/Dropbox
32 https://en.wikipedia.org/wiki/Donald_Trump
33 www.imdb.com/title/tt4267820/?ref_=nm_flmg_act_9
34 www.noreverserecords.com/home
35 www.ashleykateadams.com/byop
36 www.playwrightshorizons.org/shows/plays/strange-loop/
37 https://hamiltonmusical.com/new-york/home/
38 https://en.wikipedia.org/wiki/Soft_Power_(musical)
39 www.nicholasrohlfinglaw.com/
40 www.ibdb.com/broadway-production/hello-dolly-507877
41 www.hadestown.com
42 https://en.wikipedia.org/wiki/Wesley_Taylor
43 www.christinabianco.com/

EXERCISE 9   DM-H

WRITE A WELCOME PACKET

Small business owners not only have to be impeccable with their services, but they also have to run a tight business. Setting clear boundaries between yourself and a client, collaborator, or fellow artist is not only smart; it's required! Why not set up the intention for a safe, enjoyable experience by sending out a welcome packet that clearly spells out all expectations.

Materials

A journal or computer
A pen

Step 1. Write a personal introduction. Some clients may be nervous for the service you're offering, like if it's for a headshot session or vocal coaching.

Step 2. Provide location. Many people can get lost in new areas, so provide multiple clear directions to get to your space. How does the client get into the building? Is it wheelchair accessible? Don't leave details to chance.

Step 3. Include protocol. This is where one should include specific information that promotes healthy boundaries. If you are bringing someone into your home, where do clients leave their shoes? Is there a puppy who will greet the client at the door? How long do the sessions run? What if the client is running late? Is it a requirement that a client is vaccinated from COVID-19?

Step 4. Policies. Is there a deposit needed? What about a cancelation policy? What happens if a client doesn't show or needs to reschedule? How does one pay? What is your Venmo information?

Step 5. Expectations for after the session. What if it's a session where a client gets something tangible like photos, videos, a wig, or a costume? When can they expect it? How do they receive it? What are the final steps?

Have fun with this and leave nothing to chance! Lay it all out there in the Welcome Packet. Once the client receives it, they can make the choice to abide by the rules or not follow through with the appointment. Either way, you've protected yourself and you can continue to make wonderful art.

PART III
NAVIGATION

"When its working at its best, I think of theatre as really responsible and relevant storytelling with an eye on the impact you seek to have not only on the audience, but the audiences audience."

– Jen Waldman, Episode 43, "The Titanic Leader"

"Networking opens so many doors for so many to change the careers of so many. But how do we widen the funnel for those that are qualified or more qualified but don't know the people in charge?"

Felicia Fitzpatrick

BLACK HISTORY IS NOW

Chapter 9
Networking Versus Netweaving

DOI: 10.4324/9781003254744-13

Ali Ewoldt prepares as Christine in the
The Phantom of the Opera

Career Connection
Press Representatives

O&M.[1] Polk & Co.[2] Boneau Bryan Brown.[3] Matt Ross Public Relations.[4] The Press Room.[5] These are just some of the leading press offices that dominate the theatre industry. What is the purpose of a press representative, or 'press rep'? A press rep serves as the connection between actor and/or theatrical piece and the press outlets of the world like the *New York Times*,[6] *People*,[7] TV spots, interviews, social media influencer accounts, blogs, and vlogs to name a few. They help control the narrative of how the public views the musical or play by deciding what features and outlets might support ticket sales of the show.

Press reps are often unsung heroes of the theatre. They are salaried, and they don't get paid extra to show up to the theatre to help guide an interview or monitor a photography session on location. There are companies that focus on musicals or plays as a whole, and personal press reps who just focus on the image of a single artist. Ways to join a press office are usually located on the website of these businesses. Unsure how to find them? *Here's a tip* – look at a page in the *Playbill* of a Broadway or off-Broadway show and find where the cast and crew are listed. The press rep will be listed as 'Press Representative.'

"Yes, you can make a career out of being a press rep," says Ryan Ratelle of RRR Creative.[8]

> You can make a decent living wage. For me, what attracted me to moving on and wanting to do other things – beyond the fact I am a creative individual who wants to be doing different things – there's a ceiling. If you're a press agent on Broadway who doesn't want to go on and open their own firm, you're a press agent on Broadway. You're making the same amount of money, doing the same thing forever. You're working on different shows, which is exciting but there's no upward mobility.

So, when is it time to move on? Michael Jorgensen[9] is a communications strategy expert, focusing on public relations publicity campaigns. He is involved with a project from the early stages all the way to completion, even onward. After receiving his Masters in Classical and Contemporary Art from the Royal Conservatory of Scotland[10] in Glasgow, he came back to the United States and began an internship with Transport Theatre Group,[11] which he booked from a Skype interview from overseas. On top of this internship, he accepted a second internship with O&M. Jorgensen grew inside O&M rising from intern to assistant to leading on shows on Broadway – that is until the pandemic happened. After massive furloughs throughout the industry, Jorgensen found himself being laid off and staring into all the possibilities of what comes next:

Come very early March, it started with one email saying, "I know of someone looking for press, but I work for a company that doesn't let me do external things . . . might you consider it?" And then a couple of days later, another one came. I think it was within the course of the first week and a half, I probably had four different meetings – and that was before Jorgensen PR was even a thing! It was just people reaching out.

Michael realized that before long, he would need to start taking the steps to make his business official. This included officially setting up his business, establishing his company name, a logo, creating a website, social media – and keeping relationships in good standing.

> I made the phone call to my previous employer just saying, "Hi, hope things are well. I don't know what things are looking like for you, but because I was laid off I had to take on some gigs just to make ends meet." I want to keep good relationships everywhere.

As soon as his first project and his social media were announced, Jorgensen kept booking projects to represent, including the off-Broadway musical *A Commercial Jingle for Regina Comet*,[12] written by Alex Wyse[13] and Ben Fankhauser.[14]

Press reps are there to help connect the show to the world around the theatre industry by considering the overall campaign of the show. Depending on where the show is along in its process, who's in it, and the types and numbers of requests from outside sources vary depending on the situation. These requests can be from a *New York Times* feature to Tony campaigning all the way to an ensemble member eating a specific food for a new blog. Some theatrical experiences take more work to get press to bite, while other shows have journalists clamoring to get their piece. In the summer of 2021, when live theatre like cabarets and concerts began to reopen, landing a press feature was somewhat easier because there was less to cover. Once Broadway began to reopen just a few months later amid the Delta variant outbreak, press outlets became understaffed and over-inundated with requests . . . many of which could not be met. Press is a direct reflection of what the world is experiencing in that moment.

When push comes to shove, the press rep serves as the middle person, and they are incredibly helpful to younger content creators and artists who are wanting to connect with a show on Broadway. As they are part of the creative team, the show's specific press office is listed on every poster, every *Playbill*, and on online databases like the Internet Broadway Database.[15] Each press office usually has its contact emails on its websites, so go forth and prosper.

Bob the Drag Queen,[16] winner of Season 10 of *RuPaul's Drag Race*,[17] says:

> I'm just being social. I never thought about 'networking.' The term feels like I'm forcing myself to be social and hang out with people . . . networking is the best when hanging with people you enjoy.

Networking is the idea of extending resources and social connections through actions such as gatherings, events, and groups, hoping to further one's degree of opportunity – yet there is often a distaste for it. Perhaps it's the seemingly cold, corporate feeling that turns people away. Or it's the idea of feeling like one has to sell themselves. Show business is more networking than one would think; it just *looks* completely different. One could argue it's more fun, more interpersonal – and sure, one can compare it to a corporate experience, but that doesn't mean people enjoy it. In fact, artists still loathe it even though there's much more wiggle room to network at one's speed and in a more relaxed environment.

"I wouldn't, couldn't consider myself a pro at networking," continues Bob.

> After I didn't recognize someone, they said we met three times . . . and I said, "Really!?" I don't think you have to be a good person to network, but I believe there are good people who are just bad at networking.

When networking, an artist can run into a myriad of run-of-the-mill questions that seem disingenuous and skim the surface. Of course, not everyone who asks these types of questions is painfully forcing themselves to act interested, but chances are the person asking these questions doesn't want to be there just as equally.

> "So, what have you been up to?"
> "We really need to get a drink or something."
> "Have you booked anything lately?"
> "How was your quarantine?"

Everyone knows how everyone's quarantine went. Not only was it plastered on Facebook that one has started *The Great British Baking Show*[18] over for the third time, but their knitted socks also looked awesome and their virtual game nights were a smash.

> I *hate* networking when it feels forced, planned, or disingenuous. To me, there is nothing worse than being put in a setting where you are *told* to Network.

I would much rather have it derive from life moments and experiences, spontaneous interactions and new connections,

says Ryan Mac,[19] who toured the United States as the Fiyero understudy in *Wicked*.[20]

Have to do something. *Need* to do something. Many artists feel as if they are stuck to partake in the same rigmarole in one specific way. Sure, being an artist takes intense work and dedication – but efforts change as the generations change. Networking has become an effortful struggle to find connections. And when it's forced, is it genuine? Probably not. Whether it's because of the lack of connection or the ability to be able to cancel an engagement with a simple text message the day of, networking is not a sought-after experience.

Artists sometimes don't want to do it, they sometimes don't know how to do it, and most times they avoid it at all costs. Networking over the years has moved away from the ability to actively expand circles of creativity and instead now focuses on a social climbing attitude that often ends with a selfie or a follow on Instagram but no genuine connection or active plan to engage. Collectively, society is simply missing one element: interpersonality.

On the Broadway Podcast Network show *My Broadway Memory*,[21] stage veteran Ann Harada[22] shared the story of how she made it to Broadway. Initially, she started as a Production Assistant for a producer on a show called *Sleight of Hand*,[23] which ran on Broadway for a week at The Cort Theatre. She met the agent of the lead of the show, invited them to her cabaret, and the agent then signed Ms. Harada. She then booked *M. Butterfly* on Broadway as a performer.

Harada says,

> I remember personally dropping off a promotional postcard at their office to invite them. We used postcards a lot back then. One of my biggest jobs for the producer was running around the city delivering messages in person. She thought it made the correspondence more urgent and special. She'd write "By Hand" on the envelope. I guess that's where I got that idea.

With the dawning of the age of social media mixed with the US idea that quick success is the best success, younger artists are expecting to become stars immediately. It's certainly not a bad goal, but even after one becomes a viral sensation, capitalizing and expanding on that process is part of the long haul. Folks must remember that, whether or not it's because of phoning it in or being the over-eager beaver, it doesn't matter if it's a

Figure 9.4 Ann Harada on set between takes of *Indoor Boys*. Source: Michael Kushner Photography

college student or Tony winner, networking affects everyone yet still turns *many* people off. Yet while networking puts such a distaste in many people's mouths, it's an entitled experience to be able to have such an aversion. Networking is a reflection on privilege and access in the industry. Because the theatre industry promotes a who-you-know experience, networking is a part of that, making it all the more difficult for decentered people to network and extend their social and resource circles.

Felicia Fitzpatrick[24] was Playbill's first-ever director of social media and creative strategy and first black female department head. Fitzpatrick is known as a "pioneer of Broadway social media, revolutionizing Playbill's social engagement and storytelling strategies during the time Broadway was shaping its own digital landscape" (feliciafitzpatrick.wordpress. com). Throughout her career, not only has she experienced microaggressions in networking regarding race, but she also took note of how people responded to her age, saying:

> Because I'm light-skinned, I realize I have more privilege compared to those who are dark-skinned. I have

experienced racial microaggressions, but for me, a lot of it was about age. Broadway is an industry built on tradition and longevity, and I started in the industry when I was 23 years old. Being a young, bubbly woman talking about how social media could help Broadway – I was scoffed at and wasn't always taken seriously. Yes, I can have a Beyonce dance party, but I can also lead a social media marketing strategy meeting.

It's a question that dives into the privilege required to be a part of the theatre industry. Many theatre programs in colleges have built in networking systems that create a safety net for recent graduates to transition smoothly into the industry. But what if one can't afford college? Or move between cities? Or is facing a type of prejudice based on who they are as a human being?

Networking should be inclusive, equitable, engaging, joyous, and proactive. Actors establish their characters' objectives on stage, the same applies to multi-hyphenates by establishing their 'Why.' Networking is not immune to this. When networking, the driving questions are, What is the objective one has for themself? What does one want to achieve? and How can the goal be achieved?

Theatre practitioners have to reframe the mindset.

Inspired by a conversation with Broadway actress and musician Catherine Porter,[25] shifting the term networking to *netweaving* has more active attributes and a positivity associated with it. 'Working' perpetuates that this is a mandatory effort in excelling in a career. It's cumbersome and can be a meat-market, social-climbing nightmare. While **netweaving** is the idea that in a professional networking situation, all are worthy of being seen while intertwining possibilities to create and see each other.

There is a fine line between networking and netweaving. Is one making these connections to advance oneself, or is one creating an environment where everyone can succeed? What establishes the difference is the individual's intention. So, how do intentions get shifted so folks can become netweavers? According to the Backstage article "How to Change Your Mind About Networking,"[26] the answer is that netweaving is about three key elements:

- **Building an ensemble:** What good is that business card in your pocket if one never plans to use it? When netweaving, folks must search for the active attributes that get them excited to use an email address. Are there key words in their conversation? Do they have mutual life experiences? Does the person remind you of your mother? Whatever the reason, artists need to ponder: Can one see themself creating with this person?
- **The creative experience:** Is one engaging with a person whose work they admire? Or are they a recent college grad looking to team up with someone else? Folks need to engage and figure out ways to interweave their artistic efforts. They need to assess if they can help someone, and how they can help them.
- **Lasting impressions:** Simple question: Is this a person one can see themself creating with 20 years from now? Folks can't see into the future, but they can follow impulses. Remember – even when risking failure – when one leaps, the net will appear (Kushner, Backstage).

Another deterrent to networking is that one feels it's a massive undertaking and the future of one's career lies within one interaction. This is false. Netweaving is all about micro-movements. When folks are speaking with someone who is working on a project and they want to be involved, they must plant that seed. If they have the goodies to make their experience better, they should share them. It's

not social climbing, it's not using someone – it's stepping up and delivering. Other active micro-movements are email introductions, "plus one" invitations, being a guest on a podcast, pro bono work for nonprofits or organizations, and – just like Ann Harada – a good, old-fashioned postcard delivered by hand will do.

Yet sometimes, it's not the micro-movement, but a full-out explosion of energy that gets an artist noticed. When discovering she wanted to explore the media world in addition to her love for theatre, Felicia Fitzpatrick relied on her theatre experience when applying for her first internship as DoSomething.org's[27] first social media intern. After graduating from the University of Texas[28] with a BA in theatre and dance with a concentration in African American performance, Fitzpatrick responded to their job listing with a creative idea and not knowing *anyone*.

"I made an enthusiastic theatre kid video," Fitzpatrick says.

> The application instructions said to tell them why I deserved this internship in only 140 characters, like a tweet. Because I talk a lot, I made a video and linked to it in those 140 characters. I focused on social justice, being a social butterfly, but then and then paid homage to Janet Jackson[29] in the *Nasty*[30] music video. I filmed it at 1am in my dorm room with my roommate sleeping next to the camera.

Ultimately, networking is old-fashioned, stale, and surfaced, while netweaving builds ensembles and opportunities tailored to one's personal speed. Artists need to remember to take a breath, change their mindset, be themselves, and find ways to connect.

According to an article by Scott Frotheringham on healthline.com, "it can take anywhere from 18 to 254 days for a person to form a new habit and an average of 66 days for a new behavior to become automatic."[31] So, flipping this mindset isn't just that – it's about applying it and figuring out ways to make netweaving work for each individual experience. Netweaving is so much a part of showbusiness, that it should be practiced alongside studying craft. Some theatre programs have netweaving opportunities built in their curriculum, but many students seem to graduate and then are thrown into the wild.

Although Fitzpatrick studied theatre in college, she decided to venture into media because she was intimidated by the effort and resources needed to pursue a career as a professional artist, saying:

> My personality couldn't swing the hustle that comes with the artistic life. I knew it wasn't going to be wig

caps and mics all the time. So I went the editorial and media route. But of course, theatre found me after I began working at DoSomething.org full time. I saw *An Octoroon*[32] by Brandon Jacobs-Jenkins[33] and it made me deeply miss theatre. I started looking on playbill.com/jobs and applied to the Social Media Manager position. No Janet Jackson video this time, but I used graphics to catch their attention. From that, I became the first Social Media Manager for Playbill, then Director, and it's a big responsibility to supervise such a big platform. I hope I brought a fresh perspective and I'm so glad they were open to hiring someone from outside of the theatre industry."

Upon asking actress and musician Alexa Lebersfeld[34] if she felt her BFA Musical Theatre program helped her with networking, she says:

Not at all. We were taught how to audition professionally in the room, and that's about it. I felt very unprepared to tackle life in NYC in general, outside of the audition room itself. This mindset is really a deterrent, because I go into the audition room, feel very strong, and then don't book the gig. Then I go, "I am following the 'steps' and not booking the jobs, what am I doing wrong?" I sit there analyzing the audition itself, when maybe it is more that I don't have the outside relationships to book jobs and collaborate more frequently. I need to remember that the audition itself is just *part* of the process, and not the main, or sometimes only, focus.

Lebersfeld brings up some incredible points. Many times, the audition is not the only thing that determines if an artist books a job or not – which can be supremely frustrating. People often say they know a director who once said, "It's great that they're talented – but do I want to get a beer with them after rehearsals?"

There's an interesting mentality and expectation when it comes to this – yes, artists should have the talent and skills to be able to tell the story appropriately, but they are also expected to be the perfect friend. Is that fair? While many regional theatres across the country have a "summer camp" or getaway kind of vibe, an artist shouldn't be expected to crack open a beer if they don't want to. Artists balance many things in life including raising families – and a job shouldn't be determined by whether a director or producer wants to have fun with them.

So, how do younger artists like Alexa Lebersfeld and Felicia Fitzpatrick, both with different proficiencies, skill sets, and backgrounds, enter the business feeling supported and less alone? For those just beginning their careers and are able to

attend a conservatory or college, look for programs who not only will make one stronger artists and humans but will also allow an artist to graduate with a safety net of graduates to connect with. This is known as building an ensemble, or group of people whose work and work ethic is trustworthy and who's Why statements all align. The ensemble is not reserved for the rehearsal room but should permeate all aspects of one's life such as love, creation, and mental and emotional support. Building an ensemble is one of the greatest gifts to come out of netweaving.

Beth Schaefer,[35] owner of French Woods Festival for the Performing Arts,[36] has seen her campers use each other in professional endeavors. By nature, the summer camp encourages children to build an ensemble of friends and artists that often lasts a lifetime.

"Over the years we have had many of our campers and staff go on to careers in the arts," says Schaefer.

Broadway star Andrea Burns[37] was asked to perform in one of her first off Broadway shows by her friend from camp whom she met when she was a teen. That friend grew up to be composer Jason Robert Brown.[38] Casting directors who spent time as campers or counselors often ask us to visit camp to run auditions for professional projects and producers have been kind enough to help us bring campers en masse to big shows on Broadway. We are an environment where we attract creative people who make things happen and those people find each other at camp.

In 2008, Brown later would come back to French Woods, casting a few campers in his production of *13* on Broadway.[39]

So, what happens when the industry falls apart, say, like in a global pandemic? Networking and netweaving rules change *drastically*. And – it gets harder. So, what does an artist do next? ***Reach out.***

Carly Valancy,[40] the founder of the *Reach Out Party*, read Molly Beck's[41] book *Reach Out* and was inspired to do just that. After being inspired to reach out to someone new every day for 100 straight days, Carly noticed her networking circle expand.

"There are so many versions of gatekeepers and so many rules – that I thought, how beautiful is this? There are all these fantastic things happening . . . and it's all *me*," says Valancy on Episode 34, "The Reach Out Party"[42] of *Dear Multi-Hyphenate*.

I started sharing stories and after one hundred days of straight reach outs, my entire life looked so different and it was based on the idea of storytelling and sharing these stories, hearing these stories, and encouraging other people to do the same. I thought, oh wow, there's a whole community of artists who need this desperately.

There's a popular phrase, "save it for a rainy day" – 2020 was that rainy day. But it taught artists that one doesn't need to save it for a rainy day – as long as they are prepared and motivated, it's always appropriate to contact the email on business cards and *reach out*. But before one does, ask yourself, *"Why* am I reaching out?" Don't allow Zoom correspondences and post-pandemic moments of engagement to be as objective-less as those pre-pandemic conversations during networking. Remember one is now *netweaving*, or promoting a goal to complete something.

This may sound stressful to contact someone after a lengthy pandemic has halted the work of many. First of all, breathe. Nothing is possible without breathing, plus, it will help gather thoughts and find a center of gravity. When feeling focused, open the computer and begin to work. Even if an artist does

one thing for their career every day, that is still 365 things completed in one year. Kudos to them; that's no small feat.

Now – think of who to reach out to. Are they an artistic director? A designer? Representation? A head of an MFA program? Whoever it is – each correspondence should feel genuine, interpersonal, and again – like a problem is being *solved*.

"I was lucky to apply to Playbill and make it in," says Fitzpatrick on her reaching out experience.

> I didn't know anyone in the theatre world who could make an introduction for me. Networking feels so essential in this industry – it's all about relationships, and if you don't know people on the inside, it's harder to get through the door. So how do we widen the funnel to invite in those who are qualified but don't know the people in charge?

If this all seems overwhelming, that's okay. Remember that netweaving is all about the micro-movements. Start from

Figure 9.5 Alan Seales (left) and Dori Berinstein (right), the co-creators of Broadway Podcast Network (BPN), make a speech at the launch party of BPN at Sardi's in New York City. Source: Michael Kushner Photography

a place that seems less scary, more manageable, and more definitive. One step at a time.

A common theme between artists during the pandemic was how and where one can tell their story – a question that continued once the industry reopened. With COVID-19 regulations, artists who are COVID-19 long haulers, and finances being incredibly tight, the industry looked very different from March 2020, such as the way we produce in-person theatre and theatre adjacent creations. With virtual programs blossoming all around – many artists began to figure out ways to connect with audiences like going "live" on social media, holding virtual readings, and creating podcasts.

The podcast has been around since before COVID-19, with the origin word showing up in an article for *The Guardian* by Ben Hammersley.[43] Throughout the years, it has been a medium where so many download their information and ingest while commuting, cleaning the house, or exercising. During the COVID-19 pandemic, podcast popularity grew to outstanding numbers, with not only more people listening to podcasts but creating them as well. According to Alan Seales,[44] cofounder of Broadway Podcast Network,[45] "There were 17,000 new podcasts started every week in 2020. The median 30-day download per episode caps at 120."

That is certainly an overabundance of podcast creation – many of which the creators stopped after only a few episodes. So, while it seems that podcasts are all the rage, it doesn't mean one has to create one to tell their story. One can just *reach out* to their favorite podcaster and see if they will have them as a guest. It might seem scary, and sure, there's plenty of room for rejection. But what if the answer is yes? What if they welcome one on the show? What if they say no, but they figure out another way to help? Who truly knows until they try? With such a ballooning of podcast growth in this short time – many hosts are looking for guests with stories as well. If one has a specific project they are working on, one may be able to find podcasts, interviews, and press outlets to be a part of. Hiring a press rep may allow one to be introduced to a bigger pool of potential collaborators.

Yet even if one is not financially able to build a team, they still can take it upon themselves by creating marketing materials that will help them get seen, like a press release. A press release is a useful tool that reveals a particular event, show, or announcement in hopes of getting picked up by a press outlet like a news source. Press releases tie in all the information one needs to buy a ticket. They are a call to action and contribute to part of the multi-hyphenate make up, the paper trail.

Reaching out to new, growing podcasts is an easy way to practice self-pitching skills, broaden networking circles, and implement marketing tools like press releases. These smaller reach-outs serve as training wheels for the larger reach outs. Such efforts of netweaving will ebb and flow as the years go on, but there is one thing that is certain – netweaving as a whole isn't going anywhere. The need to engage and connect is embedded in a human's DNA. But isn't it interesting that networking, an opportunity for genuine human connection, actually repels people? During the COVID-19 pandemic, so many artists stepped back from the industry to gain control of their personal lives and rightfully so. But during that time, showbusiness shifted and adapted, embracing virtual theatre – promoting the continuation of storytelling. How did people create these opportunities? By also adapting their netweaving skills.

Is it more difficult to sell a story when there are fewer opportunities to perform and there's an active public health crisis? Absolutely. Is it frustrating to have to start over just as one was getting used to the twists and turns of the industry? Yes. But never has the artist ever been one to run out of ideas and give up. One must advocate for themselves and continuously figure out new ways to show up.

Now that a virtual element of theatrical storytelling has been integrated so deeply into the fabric of society, the element of virtual theatre and creation is not going away. So how does one reintroduce themselves into such new and rapidly changing world? Netweaving extends itself into the world of social media. While it might not seem like netweaving, likes, comments, interaction – it's all a part of it. Presenting oneself on social media can be a downright scary, yet freeing, and completely random experience but conquering it is entirely possible.

One just needs an idea, an audience, and a point of view.

PENNYWILD

Choreographer, DJ, Music Producer, and Digital Marketing Director living in Los Angeles by way of New York City.

AN ARTIST'S GUILT • *EPISODE 41*

PennyWild: Dance informs music and vice verse. Whether it's a generative or reactive force, they go hand in hand, everybody knows that. When you hear a song your impulse is to start moving to it – that's kind of the whole nature of the beast. But then from a logistical standpoint, I felt like I was kind of able to beat the system in a weird way because I feel like I have been landing gigs that I am last in line to actually get but because I know the person who needs a choreographer through my music career and they say, "Hey Penny, one of my clients needs a choreographer . . . I know you're a choreographer. Are you interested or do you know someone who is interested?" And if it's something I feel is right for me, then I'll make a pitch and submit and see if I can finagle my own creative lens to land the job. But I feel like if I was going through this the traditional route, like for example I am represented as a choreographer with an agency in LA, but you know, sometimes they submit you and you'll get the gig or you won't and they'll look at your credits and they'll look at your reel and they'll look at your age and your experience. But 95% of the gigs that I've gotten as a choreographer, I've just received an email from someone who saw me DJ somewhere or something and I mentioned I was a choreographer and then they saw my Instagram and then they're like, "We want to work with you cause we know you. Because if we liked your music, odds are we will like the other stuff that you do. If we just vibe with you as a person then we want to be in the room with you, we just want to be on set with you." And then vice verse – DJ gigs that I have gotten, I will have choreographed for an artist and that artist needs a DJ to open for them on tour. And then it's like, "We know Penny from the DJ thing!" You talk about cross pollination a lot . . . that's kind of what I've seen on the horizon is a lot of the cross pollination and I feel like I was so hindered by the idea that I wasn't the best at one thing . . . that I'm not the world's best choreographer, I'm not Los Angeles' premiere choreographer, I'm not Parris Goebel. But I also feel like I'm not Calvin Harris. So that was really discouraging me for a long time because I felt like if I wasn't the best at one trade, I was just going to kind of be mediocre throughout all and this would be the frequency – it would be super, super mundane. But then as the years go by and you really season those things that you're good at – and you get really good at those things, then there are certain people that really appreciate and vibe with the fact that you are versatile. So, it's kind of an ever changing journey. I sometimes do wish that I just focused on music production and was like just putting out bop after bop and those would go to radio and I can start touring.

At the end of the day, as much as that's like a pipe dream to be amazing at one thing, I just know myself and I'm never going to be satisfied if I do one thing. I have to continue to get my feet into all these different things otherwise I don't think I'll be satisfied... I don't think I'll be complete.

Notes

1 www.omdkc.com/about/
2 www.polkandco.com/
3 www.boneaubryanbrown.com/
4 www.mattrosspr.com/
5 www.thepressroomnyc.com/
6 www.nytimes.com
7 www.people.com
8 https://rrrcreative.com/
9 https://jorgensenpr.com/
10 www.rcs.ac.uk/
11 http://transportgroup.org/
12 https://reginacomet.com/
13 https://en.wikipedia.org/wiki/Alex_Wyse
14 www.playbill.com/person/ben-fankhauser-vault-0000121939
15 www.ibdb.com
16 www.bobthedragqueen.com/
17 https://en.wikipedia.org/wiki/RuPaul%27s_Drag_Race
18 www.pbs.org/food/shows/great-british-baking-show/
19 www.ryanmacofficial.com
20 https://anastasiathemusical.com/
21 https://broadwaypodcastnetwork.com/podcast/my-broadway-memory/
22 www.broadwayworld.com/people/Ann-Harada/
23 www.ibdb.com/broadway-production/sleight-of-hand-4470
24 https://feliciafitzpatrick.wordpress.com/
25 www.last.fm/music/Catherine+Porter
26 www.backstage.com/magazine/article/how-to-change-your-mindset-about-networking-72468/
27 www.dosomething.org/us
28 www.utexas.edu/
29 https://en.wikipedia.org/wiki/Janet_Jackson
30 [[Endnote Data Missing]]
31 www.healthline.com/health/how-long-does-it-take-to-form-a-habit
32 https://en.wikipedia.org/wiki/An_Octoroon
33 https://en.wikipedia.org/wiki/Branden_Jacobs-Jenkins
34 www.alexalebersfeld.com
35 https://frenchwoods.com/important-staff-bios.htm
36 www.frenchwoods.com
37 https://en.wikipedia.org/wiki/Andr%C3%A9a_Burns
38 http://jasonrobertbrown.com/
39 https://en.wikipedia.org/wiki/13_(musical)
40 https://carlyvalancy.com/reach-out-party
41 https://msmollybeck.com/
42 https://broadwaypodcastnetwork.com/dear-multi-hyphenate/34-carly-valancy-the-reach-out-party/
43 www.theguardian.com/media/2004/feb/12/broadcasting.digitalmedia
44 https://broadwaypodcastnetwork.com/hosts/alan-seales/
45 https://broadwaypodcastnetwork.com

Reference List

1. "FELICIA Fitzpatrick." *Felicia Fitzpatrick*, feliciafitzpatrick.wordpress.com/.
2. Kushner, Michael. "How to Change Your Mindset about Networking." *Backstage*, 20 Jan. 2021, www.backstage.com/magazine/article/how-to-change-your-mindset-about-networking-72468/.
3. Frothingham, Scott. "How Long Does It Actually Take to Form a New Habit?" *Healthline*, Healthline Media, 24 Oct. 2019, www.healthline.com/health/how-long-does-it-take-to-form-a-habit.

EXERCISE 10 DM-H
CREATE A PRESS RELEASE

Press releases are incredibly helpful tools to document the official information of a project and its creators. They can announce a new film or release details for a long-awaiting release of a project or reveal the cast and creative team of a new musical. They also contribute to adding to one's paper trail, adding to one's multi-hyphenate identity.

If one is not working with a press team – how does one create a press release? What is the information that needs to go into

it? By following this easy-to-fill-in guide, one will be able to plug in their specific information and then send it to various news sources.

In this exercise – wherever bold, simply plug in the information that pertains to a project or announcement. If the information does not pertain to the specific project, feel free to skip it or edit it however one sees fit.

Materials

Access to computer

Step 1. Prepare the email. Make sure there is a direct contact to someone at a news source. Usually, a journalist's email can be found on the website of the source. The subject should be

FOR IMMEDIATE RELEASE: **Insert the press release headline.**

In the body of the email, one should include a very short and personalized letter to the press contact. It could read as follows:

Dear **name of journalist**,
Name of person sending press release, here. I received your email from **mention personal connection/where you found it**. Thank you so much for taking the time and considering this press release. Please reach out with any questions. If you need any more information, don't hesitate to let me know. Thank you!

Step 2. Separate the personal part of the email and the press release with a divider, like so:

FOR IMMEDIATE RELEASE

Step 3. Include the press release. The press release can be written in the body of the email or in a Google Doc. Remember to include any graphics that should be a part of the press release like logos or headshots.

Date
Names of producers in accordance with **names of companies**, announces the new **type of project**, **title of project**, set to open/be released on **date**.
Insert two- to three-line bio about the project.
List any confirmed creative team or cast involved with the project.
Next, mention any sort of production history here.
Then, list all the social media and website information.

Step 4. Send out the press release. Make sure all the information is correct, including spelling. If you are sending out the press release to multiple sources, make sure the person being acknowledged in the beginning matches the email.

If one is asking a source to run the press release exclusively, it is not recommended to send the press release out to multiple sources at once. If it's run as an exclusive, that means the news source is the only one with the story. Be sure to include that request in the personal part of the email.

PRO TIP: Unsure of a news source to send a press release to? Some outlets are extremely exclusive when it comes to content. Thankfully for BroadwayWorld, they are incredibly user-friendly and accessible when needing a press release. One can find an up-to-date email for the BroadwayWorld News Desk by visiting their website. It's not completely guaranteed, but BroadwayWorld has been extremely supportive by publishing press releases for artists and their ventures – all while publishing Breaking News in the Broadway industry.

Chapter 10
Social Media

"Social media is a tool. So, it's all about how you want to use it. And I use it for business purposes because it was the way to get my work out there as a writer and a way that sometimes the system would not acknowledge me. And it worked."

Douglas Lyons

DOI: 10.4324/9781003254744-14

Alan Seales, co-creator of Broadway Podcast Network

Career Connection
Podcast & Radio

The joy of participating in the theatre is that anyone, again given the proper access, can find their corner of the sky. In the 21st century, there are more opportunities to reach an audience far and wide, thanks to video and audio content downloadable right on one's phone. These opportunities span a lengthy list of prerequisites and passions, serving different purposes, and catering to a multitude of communities. The theatre industry's outreach via podcast and radio programs don't only come in large numbers but are free to low cost as well.

Artists find ways to communicate with an audience through multiple forms of artistry, and the creators of Broadway Podcast Network (BPN)[1] were able to do so through a pandemic. Despite podcast oversaturation, the Broadway community was able to rise above it and use it as a way to communicate with the world.

One day in 2018, Alan Seales[2] was searching for Broadway-related podcasts but found little to no results. After starting his own podcast, *The Theatre Podcast*,[3] he and Broadway producer Dori Berenstein[4] launched BPN in 2019. During the pandemic, not only did BPN prove to keep the lights on Broadway, but it also proved to be a community for the artists themselves.

"Thinking back to my time as a professional actor, one of the things I miss most is the family you develop during the run of a show," says Seales, cofounder of BPN.

> Applying that same mentality to the success of a company like Google, where I worked for over seven years before co-founding BPN, it again comes back to a sense of family. Fundamentally, if you want to go to work, you're going to be better at your job. BPN continues this tradition. We want everyone to feel like family. Podcasts can sometimes be deeply personal and honest, and BPN needs to be a safe space for everyone.

Some of Broadway Podcast Network's highlighted band of artists include Donna McKechnie,[5] Tonya Pinkins,[6] Josh Lamon,[7] and more. One will find podcasts such as *The Wrong Cat Died*,[8] *BroadWaysted*,[9] and *Dear Multi-Hyphenate*.[10]

"Part of the joy I personally experience, and see in my team, is the love we all share for the stage and creating new works and new experiences that equally bring the same passion and joy to others," continues Seales.

> We are all part of the community for a reason, and share the same drive to be involved in the process that brings so much joy to the world. In quarantine during the COVID-19 Broadway shutdown, this was more necessary than ever. We continued to produce, create, innovate, and keep the connections alive.

Julie James[11] of *Broadway Names with Julie James* on Broadway Sirius XM Radio[12] hopes not only to entertain her listeners but to educate them as well.

"What I would love to believe is that not only do we provide this entertainment, which at the heart is what this radio station is supposed to do," says James.

> But where we take it further is by featuring a lot of the artists, creators, not just celebrities. It's always fun when you get an ultra-famous person to feature, but it's also really fun to roll back the curtain on theatre makers – when you get to talk to a composer, a director, a costumer – there are so many different people that create these villages in every theatre, not just Broadway. We've featured Cody Renard,[13] the stage manager. We've recently featured a Broadway bartender! They're certainly not responsible for creating the show, but think about their value and how interesting their job is. Unlike a restaurant or bar, they serve all their people in a few minutes. How do they keep their cool? How do they keep their accuracy in making a drink and counting money?
> "I would like to think the showtunes can't be discounted. I would love to believe there is someone listening asking, "What is that? What is that show?" Darren Criss[14] told me he became obsessed with *Purlie*[15] because he had never heard *Purlie* and heard it on the station. I think especially for a certain generation, hopefully there's an educational component of "What is that?" and not only in terms of what is that music, but is there someone out there wondering "Who conducted that?"

Thanks to creators like Alan Seales and Julie James, who create and open up worlds from behind the microphone, theatre lovers everywhere can feel closer to show business. By creating this insightful environment, it could very well possibly inspire the next multi-hyphenate from *anywhere* around the globe.

As networking becomes netweaving, there is an added element in the 21st century that will only grow and become a larger part of one's life – and that's social media. Believe it or not, social media can lead to more than just popularity – it can lead to one's work heading to Broadway.

"I used to be a reality TV casting producer, so I was scouring Instagram every single day and reaching out to people that I could tell had what we were looking for," says Rebecca Michelson,[16] creator of 11 O'Clock Creative.[17]

> But, if you're not posting those things – how would we know? I always tell people, your entire being these days takes place in the six squares on your Instagram. Obviously, Instagram is changing but if someone wants to look you up quickly, they are going to go to Instagram and they are going to look up your name. So, if you just keep in mind the things that mean the most to you – whether or not that's personal or professional – and you always make sure those things exist on those six squares on Instagram, that is your brand.

. . . or at least until another app comes, whichever the trend.

Whether or not one agrees an artist should have a brand, today brands are very much a part of the artist persona. A **brand** is an overall, marketable image that is unique to each individual artist. With Instagram, TikTok, and Twitter, many artists cling to the image which fits them, refraining from creating posts that aren't a part of their brand image. Keeping to a brand cultivates followers and fans who are actively interested in engaging with what's called an **"influencer"** or one who has a strong social media presence. While it seems like influencers are much more in the television/film world, it's simply not true. The Broadway community relies on influencers to help sell tickets or a special event to an audience. Influencers can be found at opening nights and posing on the red carpet, so they can post the photos on their social media, hopefully encouraging ticket sales. While having more followers certainly matters, having the verified blue check next to one's name certainly helps as well.

How does this work? A marketing and branding company like SpotCo[18] might reach out to influencers on social media and send them a curated package to enjoy and post about on social media, therefore engaging in promotion. When *Schmigadoon*[19] aired on Apple+,[20] certain influencers were sent a box of artisan cookies that contained special flavors concocted especially for the show. The filmed version of *Come From Away*[21] on Apple+ also had a similar experience with influencers receiving a box of *Come From Away*–specific goodies to help promote viewership.

Angela Fisher is the founder of Neufluence,[22] an entertainment and influencer marketing agency that collaborates with brands and organizations to build awareness and generate revenue by partnering with mega and macro creators and opinion leaders.

"Social media allows us to connect with and build relationships with anyone from around the world," says Fisher.

> It has democratized celebrity by removing the barriers to entry for those looking for fans and notoriety and it's allowed us quick access to learn anything we want. While social media provides us with a conduit to communicate that prospect [and] has its positives and negatives (harassment, bullying, racism), however, through social media, we are able to have discussions as well as express thoughts and ideas.

While many find social media detestable, it at least serves as a *tool*, like a three-dimensional business card. While one can't directly write to someone on a business card, one certainly can on social media. In terms of netweaving, adding each other on social media immediately helps one discover more about the other. Business cards can't do that.

As discussed in Chapter 9, "Networking Versus Netweaving," reaching out is a large part of the multi-hyphenate experience: acting as a key element in the success of artists who are creating their own work, and social media plays a massive part. Sometimes artists have representation such as agents, managers, or press representatives who do all the emailing and reaching out for them. And other times, a multi-hyphenate is working on their own, not having to rely on anyone but themselves.

While having teams is, of course, helpful in a myriad of ways – such as delegation – sometimes multi-hyphenates have to adhere to a pace that might be faster than the other team members. It could be weeks before someone sends out an email that needed to be sent out yesterday. If an artist prefers to work at their own hustle, in today's world folks can call upon subscriptions like IMdBPro,[23] where one can find contact information for a specific artist. Plus, with the accessibility of social media, artists usually do check their private messages.

Douglas Lyons[24] is no stranger to multi-hyphenation. On top of performing on Broadway, he is also the writer of the musicals *Polkadots*[25] and *Beau*.[26] His journey to Broadway as a writer was speedy. Why? A direct message on Instagram.

"With *Chicken and Biscuits*,[27] it'll be three years from first draft to Broadway, which is kind of rare," Lyons says.

> "But it's also proof, I believe, that the system that is not-for-profit and the ways shows have to function and maneuver is being debunked with this entire voyage. I actually slid into the DMs of Hunter Arnold,[28] who's now

the lead producer, and was like, 'Hey man – I think you should read my work. It seems like after *Hadestown*[29] and *Once on this Island*,[30] you do very edgy and forward thinking material.' And in quarantine and after eight months of badgering him, he actually read it and sent me a message like, 'You're really great . . . we should try doing something together."

After some meetings over Zoom and figuring out which project fit, *Chicken and Biscuits* had a lead producer and the journey to Broadway began. Lyons continues:

> Social media is a tool. So, it's all about how you want to use it. And I use it for business purposes because it was the way to get my work out there as a writer and a way that sometimes the system would not acknowledge me. And it worked.

While agents and managers usually reach out on behalf of their client, what if a multi-hyphenate does not have that representation and must reach out on their own? Even with representation, it doesn't mean they do all the work for their client – the client is still expected to hustle and build connections. It's okay to take up the responsibility, as long as it's done correctly. While this might be intimidating, especially if one is emailing a high-powered executive or A-list celebrity, remember *why* one is reaching out in the first place. And what's the worst that can happen? They say no?

The 'ask,' or a direct message or email, must be crafted carefully and without breaking boundaries. There is an art to the perfectly crafted 'ask.' Let's break down what a strong reach-out might entail.

Overall Tone

Without apologizing for one's presence, this whole email is basically saying, "I come in peace, I'm trustworthy, and I'd love to collaborate with you." While sending an email is not taking up too much space, it still is using personal information (even if it is posted on a public forum) to send a request, so be respectful of that. Keep in mind time is of the essence. Chances are they don't have time to read a novel. Keep it clear, keep it quick, and keep it friendly.

The Common Denominator

Usually a person, this opening line stops them from asking, "How the *heck* did they get my email!?" Humans can be very

private, so if the person connecting you is trustworthy, there's a chance you may be as well. Here are some ways to establish the common denominator:

- *We both are represented by Ryan at RRR Creative*[31] *and he was comfortable enough to forward me your email address.*
- *My aunt Lizzie is your friend from college, and she said to reach out to you!*
- *The Press Room*[32] *forwarded me your email address and speaks so highly of you.*

A Warm Salutation

Even if one is a big fan of the subject's work, it doesn't necessarily need to be said in the initial reach-out. After introducing oneself, try something more approachable like:

- *I'm an admirer of your work and it thrills me to have the opportunity to reach out to you.*
- *I'm coming to you with an exciting ask, and the prospect of working with you is extremely special.*
- *It's always been a great goal of mine to work with you and I'm hoping this may be a way!*

A Concise Background

Next would come a short bio, potentially 50 words or less. The writer of the 'ask' should pick three notable credits that reflect their Why statement. The statement will help figure out which credits will be appealing to the person one is reaching out to. There's nothing to be too heady about, just keep it concise and impressive. The objective would be to help them understand that they both belong in the same creative space. There are a few different ways to phrase it:

- *Now, a little bit about me . . .*
- *I'd love to introduce myself as I'm sure we have a few people and projects in common.*
- *Just in case there's something that interests you, here is some information about me.*

A Clear Intention

Here are the meat and potatoes of the email. This is one's specific 'ask.' Delicately, one must form this section where it's not condescending, desperate, or needy. Let it come honestly, with good intention, and the heart will follow. Some ways of phrasing this follow:

- *I'm working on a SAG-approved short film titled* The Story of Deb. *You were the first person I thought of to play the role of Deb.*
- *During the COVID-19 pandemic, I finished a play that I'm excited to share. I'll be producing a Zoom reading of my piece and I'm hoping you would lend your time and talents. Obviously, compensation will be provided.*
- *It's with great excitement that my web series is in preproduction. Seeing as we always try to find a project to work on together, and we're looking for coproducers, this may be an opportunity for us to finally come together.*

Initial Information

This is simply a short (50 words or less) bio of the idea, plot, or meaning of the piece. Keep it simple and quick, like riding an elevator and the idea has to be conveyed by the time you get to the lobby. For example:

- Pretty in Pink *is the untold story of Regina George*[33] *and how she became the leader of the Plastics. The feedback we've received from producers have been incredibly encouraging, with David Merrick*[34] *calling our show, "Electrifying, daring, and accessible for everyone."*
- Sigh No More, *the new musical version of* Much Ado About Nothing,[35] *combines a pop/rock score with the traditional instruments used during the Elizabethan era. We had a sold out run downtown and the* New York Times *claimed the show to be "nothing short of invigorating." Nothing has been done like this before, and we are so excited to share this project with you.*

More Information

Again, keep this short. This is an option for the potential collaborator to learn more on their own time. This is when to include an EPK (Electronic Press Kit), YouTube links, Google Drive links, anything to paint the picture. An EPK is usually a graphically designed PDF containing all the specific information for a project such as titles, creative teams, production history, proposed budget, target audience, and anything that will help a potential team member learn more.

If the extra information is an external link, make sure it is hyperlinked into the body of the email for convenience. Here's how one could phrase this:

- *I've attached an EPK for your perusal. In that document, you'll find all the information you need to know about this project. It was fun to make, so I hope you enjoy browsing it!*
- *My cowriters and I had an awesome night of our songs at Feinstein's/54 Below, so please check out our YouTube playlist by clicking here.*
- *While the complete draft isn't done, I've attached a PDF of what is completed for you to read over.*

Optional Communication

Because one is encroaching on personal space by using a private email, it's always good to acknowledge it and provide other options of communication. One can do this by using the following:

- *Please let me know if you'd like me to reach out to someone on your team to further the conversation. I have no problem shifting the conversation elsewhere.*
- *If you'd like to discuss somehow other than email, please let me know and we can schedule that accordingly.*

Call to Action

This is when the 'ask' begins to wrap up and the ball is put in the recipient's court. The reach-out job is done, and now it is up to them to take action. Kimberly Faye Greenberg,[36] otherwise known as "The Broadway Expert"[37] encourages the artist to sign off noting that they will follow up in a certain amount of time.

"The person you reach out to may just be busy and hasn't had an opportunity to reach out to you yet . . . or even just maybe forgot to get back to you," Greenberg says. "As a person who is a multi-hyphenate and balancing a lot of plates, don't be afraid to follow up with those who you need or want to try to make a connection with."

There should be no threatening element to the call to action such as "If I don't hear from you I'll call your reps!" A gentle, reassuring call to action may be the following:

- *I understand our schedules are very busy during this time. If I don't hear back from you by the end of the month, I'll gently reach back out to you!*

- *Because this is time sensitive, I'll follow up if I don't hear back by the end of the week.*
- *Thank you so much for taking the time to read this email. While I hope to hear from you, in the case that I don't, I'll reach back out in a few weeks.*
- *Truly, it is so exciting to introduce myself and my project, so thank you for reading this email and I look forward to hearing back from you soon.*
- *I look forward to hearing back from you. I'm here with any questions you may have!*

A Sign-Off

This is simply one sentence or thought to close off the email. Some possible choices follow:

- *With admiration, Barbra.*
- *Again, thanks so much! Kaisha.*
- *Looking forward, Sean.*
- *Remember to include your pronouns! Why is this important? By doing so, you are allowing the space for a trans/ nonbinary person to safely do the same.*

Why is this format often successful? Looking at the through line, the sender doesn't apologize for taking up any space nor do they give any option for the receiver to say no. In the sign-off, it's about looking forward to a next move, even if the receiving artist does say no. And if they do say no, at least it's an answer, and the party involved can move on and find another way to achieve their goal.

While 'asks' are usually sent via email, if an email isn't necessarily the vibe of the artist, it is perfectly acceptable for an artist to "slide into each other's DMs" on Instagram, Twitter, TikTok, and so on to begin a collaborative experience. Even for professional inquiries, social media is becoming a main source of communication – even the first step in the vetting process of hiring someone. Fortunately, or unfortunately, an artist can either be approved or rejected for the job based on social media alone. It has been known for artists to lose out on auditions simply because they don't have enough followers on social media. Whether or not one finds that a negative or positive thing, it's simply the truth as to what is happening in audition rooms.

> For years, influencers have cashed in on an explosion in corporate advertising, as brands turned to online personalities and digital platforms to help create marketing buzz for their products. Advertisers spent

$6.5 billion on influencers in 2019, up from $1.7 billion in 2016, according to global data from the Influencer Marketing Hub,

according to an article written by Wendy Lee and Anousha Sakoui in the *LA Times*.[38]

With social media deeply ingrained into society, one's online presence is important. Strong social media presences have a mix of passion, knowledge, accessibility, approachability, and authenticity. If a following is formed, it's because that influencer has a point of view that positively affects a group of people. Users look to social media for inspiration, tips, levity, and ways to make their day to day lives easier – which was incredibly sought after during the bleakness of the COVID-19 pandemic. The pandemic was a dismal time as many artists felt they were experiencing the pandemic alone. Some performed a mass exodus from their city back to their parents' house, as many couldn't make rent. Some left the industry altogether. Some sought out higher education. And some took to creating social media, shifting to an online experience inspiring other artists to keep creating.

This shift kept artists relevant all while building an audience through creating **content**. Content is influential video, photo, audio, or text which is published on social media. Has this word ever existed in the industry before social media? Tony Award winner Randy Graff[39] (*Mr. Saturday Night*,[40] *City of Angels*,[41] Original Fantine in *Les Miserables*[42] on Broadway) recalls when content had no part in the industry.

"Back in the days of the covered wagons, when I was coming up, the word 'content' was not in the lexicon," says Graff.

> It was called "self-promotion." You self-promoted with the help of a personal publicist, who got you interviews via newspapers, television and radio. I had a personal publicist for both *Les Mis* and *City of Angels* . . . a young fellow just starting out named Chris Boneau.[43] His office was the size of a closet, and that closet grew into the biggest theatrical publicity office of Boneau/Bryan-Brown Inc.[44]
>
> I think social media is great for actors who want to self-promote and be seen and are looking to grow their fan base. Casting directors dive through YouTube to discover young talent. It gets problematic for me, when it is *required* and put in a contract. A friend of mine who had no interest in going on Instagram, was contractually obligated to do so for a Broadway show in order to promote the show.

By reaching these wider audiences through producing content, artists began to have conversations based on comparison, how to prepare for auditions, headshots, common mistakes to avoid, and advice to college students. When posting such content, one usually attaches a hashtag in the comment section, which serves as a type of category. To put into perspective the outreach that *one* app like TikTok has, by May 2022, compare the following hashtags with the number of views:

- #art – 281.8 billion views
- #actor – 31 billion views
- #comedian – 22.7 billion views
- #theatrekid – 5.5 billion views
- #broadway – 4.7 billion views
- #theatre – 4.8 billion views
- #musicaltheatre – 4 billion views
- #audition – 3.1 billion views
- #actorslife – 1.2 billion views
- #directorslife – 6.2 million views
- #multihyphenate – 4.6 million views
- #auditionlife – 9.6 million views
- #artistinspiration – 2.1 million views

So, what do these numbers mean and what do they translate to? How is this relatable to a multi-hyphenate artist?

"The idea of creating content is meant to be fast-paced," says theatre TikTok influencer Kaisha Huguley,[45]

> It's meant to be easily digestible so people can just absorb the information and go on to the next thing. It's meant to be something that can grab someone's attention and hopefully they take something from it. I think one of the ways content can help sell art is to hook people in – for example an Instagram reel or TikTok video, saying "Hey! Do you need x, y, z?" Kind of introducing the piece of art and telling people why they need it because a story that might resonate with me, may not resonate with my wider audience – so explaining up front this is the benefit you will get out of seeing this thing, or experiencing this thing, is a way that content can help sell art.

Not only can social media help sell a product, it can provide income. On TikTok, if a user has more than 10,000 followers, they can apply to the Creator's Fund which allows the user to garner an income based on follower interaction. Yet sometimes, artists are asked to compromise their intentions when producing content. Evan Wittstock,[46] also known as Sierra Mist, went viral building an audience on TikTok by creating artistic videos of his makeup transformations into famous characters like Ursula from *The Little Mermaid*.[47]

"November rolled around and I filmed my first one just for fun," says Wittstock.

> Initially for me it started out as a way to share laughs with my friends when the whole world was falling apart and we couldn't see anyone. And then I kind of accidentally turned into being a content creator, which I wasn't necessarily planning on. Now that I have this substantial following on TikTok, I've been getting reached out to by lots of brands and people who are trying to push their product and sell stuff. In the beginning I was like, "That's so cool! I want to do that." But then I realized that I don't want my TikToks to become product pushing. I don't want to watch that, so I don't want to do it myself! I think about it like doing one-man theatre in front of my iPhone. A lot of what I put into my videos is what I learned from going to theatre school. Punctuation with props, physical timing, comedic timing, having the transitions go with the music – especially if it's a TikTok that has music, I want it to feel choreographed.

In true multi-hyphenate form, Wittstock recalled his Why to help him take his next steps in terms of content creation. While Wittstock's social media fame came from something unexpected, other creators joined to find a following and broaden their audience.

Remy Germinario[48] studied musical theatre at New York University.[49] He spent years auditioning at appointments scheduled by his agent and managers, equity principal auditions, and equity chorus calls. Eventually, he began to activate his sense of agency, establishing a healthy boundary between the productions he auditioned for, simply because he found another performative art form he found joy in: comedy. By discovering comedy, he only showed up to the auditions which fit his purpose as well as his interest.

After developing a comedic voice, Germinario joined Maude, a house team at Upright Citizen's Brigade,[50] and began frequenting comedy clubs like Stand Up New York,[51] Broadway Comedy Club,[52] Caveat,[53] and Greenwich Village Comedy Club,[54] to name a few. Germinario found himself throwing comedic (and figurative) spaghetti against the wall. Here and there on social media, he'd have some shared sketches – but nothing widely viewed. Until a chance encounter that proves that if you have an idea, follow it. Joining TikTok, Germinario threw on a couple of wigs and started doing what he knows to be tried and true: impersonating Food Network[55] chefs. He found the TikTok algorithm worked in his favor and soon found his videos receiving worldwide attention. Not before long, celebrity

Figure 10.3 Comedian Remy Germinario performs a socially distant set during Stand Up New York in the Park in the summer of 2020 in Central Park, New York City. Source: Michael Kushner Photography

chef Ree Drummond, the Pioneer Woman,[56] found his videos, followed him, and began to engage with likes and comments.

"I was sitting on the couch and screamed," Germinario says.

> As a comedian at my level, you don't expect the person you're impersonating (who is very well known) to have seen your material. It was validating because it was clear she had a great sense of humor and saw that I was doing this out of love and in jest. Having her stamp of approval meant a great deal and inspired me to continue this content.

By chance, Germinario found himself packing his bags for a road trip he had planned months before the connection happened. Taking a slight risk and possibly facing disappointment, he reached out to Drummond mentioning that he'd be driving through Oklahoma where her ranch is located, and where she films her show on Food Network. Lo and behold, they met, even creating videos together that would satisfy the

fans Germinario has been gathering. But that's not all, after a *single* post from Drummond on Instagram, Germinario noticed his followers skyrocketed from 2,500 to 17,000 in less than a day. *Why is this so important?*

"Having a jump in social media presence means you have more of a platform to share your work," Germinario says.

> Having a bigger audience gives me a bigger motivation to produce content, whereas content creating was quite a bit of work, for not enough reward. In the comedy world, producers and club bookers like to hire comedians who have followers and credits.

Huguley, Wittstock, and Germinario all use the same app and yet have wildly different experiences. This is extremely reflective of the multi-hyphenate experience. But how does one start and begin to make waves and build an audience? Again, in terms of access – having the most professional video and recording equipment costs money. But Rebecca Michelson of

11 O'Clock Creative says all it takes is one's face in a post on social media:

> I try to put an introduction about myself in my feed once in a while. I try to get my face in my stories. I always try to recommend to people who are scared to be more themselves on Instagram to start with Instagram stories. Put a Q+A box up. Have people ask you questions. Get in the stories and put your answer right to camera. You'll notice a lot more engagement in your posts when putting your face in your posts instead of pictures of the sunset or the reading you just went to. Show us what your day looks like. So many are small business owners – if you make a product, show us how you make it. Have someone interview you about it. There's a lot of easy ways to get into it without having to invest in professional video.

In response to the industry's intermission – was this shift to social media simply to hold us over, or have we entered an age where art is blending into content? On April 13, 2021, the Twitter user @KyWilliamsDraws[57] tweeted, "Art being called content and artists being called content creators has to be one of the worst things to happen in the art space in years." While there are honest intentions to entertain, broaden brand and audience, and garner income – social media comes with a lot of confusion. Anyone can make an account on social media, so oftentimes space is taken up with bullying, false information, or catty behavior. Just because there is a plethora of content being flung into our phones, does not make it good or impactful or true.

According to *The Atlantic*,[58]

> Pew [research] finds that Americans have deeply divergent views about fake news and different responses to it, which suggest that the emphasis on misinformation might actually run the risk of making people, especially conservatives, *less* well informed. More than making people believe false things, the rise of fake news is making it harder for people to see the truth.
>
> (Graham, theatlantic.com)

So how does that affect those in show business? On a micro level, if anyone can create an account, so can artists – which means people from all corners of the world are sharing their 'audition techniques' or 'top ten things to avoid in an audition room.' While everyone has their perspective and understanding of the industry, is everyone meant to teach or impart wisdom? And while one audition tip might work for one person, it certainly will not work for everyone. Is this the show business industry's version of *fake news*?

Multi-hyphenates are constantly ebbing and flowing between releasing content and creating art. As many multi-hyphenates are one person bands, they are responsible for not only creating art but also figuring out ways to market their art – and social media is free and easy to do so, a direct correlation to access. Plus, with new artists finding access to the industry through engaging on apps like Instagram and TikTok, social media is probably not going away anytime soon.

"I don't think social media will go away because it has become too entrenched in our lives," continues Angela Fisher. "We are always on social media and the platforms have features that are designed to keep users engaged. I am curious to see how it will evolve and which platforms will remain popular."

As social media continues to ebb and flow just as the multi-hyphenate does, it would be in the best interest of someone to do their best to promote awareness, kindness, and honesty – three attributes that never go out of style. Social media can be an extremely toxic and painful place; so one must do their best to make their contributions helpful.

Since social media is not going anywhere, instead of allowing social media to become a cancerous place, it can be used for good – something that multi-hyphenates should strive for. As multi-hyphenates are problem solvers, social media can be a massive tool to do just that. When one solves problems and does so passionately and with purpose, they can commit to socially responsible artistry – art that can change things for the better.

DJ Pennywild,[59] is a music producer, DJ, director, and choreographer living in Los Angeles. Taking the music and choreography world by storm, she has found a strong balance between creating art, having a social media presence and inspiring others. PennyWild says on Episode 41, "An Artist's Guilt" on *Dear Multi-Hyphenate*,[60]

> Even though what we're doing can seem very trivial, and very niche, and very self-serving – that at the end of the day it really is doing right by the world and putting out art that helps other people go through the things that they're going through in their life and it gives them an escape. But I think if I can be doing something that's not only serving me and having me grow into the best of my capabilities and allowing me step into my power – I'm also going to be producing the best work, and then by proxy, delivering that work, putting that work out into the Universe, and then hopefully somebody that's consuming it can find joy in their life. It can be an escape for them or it can inspire them. I think that most of the art that I'm a fan of inspires me to get off my a** and finish that song I was working on.

EPISODE EXCERPT

KAISHA HUGULEY

Performer and faculty member and director of Diversity & Cultural Creative Initiatives in the Office of Equity, Diversity, & Inclusion at AMDA in NYC.

CREATING ON TIKTOK • EPISODE 36

Kaisha: I think that a platform like TikTok, it's really challenging not to compare yourself to the other things that you see – especially as an artist because you want your art, you want your creations to be top level, high quality, all the things. And so, when you're seeing these creators who literally . . . some of these videos, I'm like how do people create this stuff? I'm like what are you guys using to edit your videos!? I'm literally in awe of some of the things I've seen – so I agree that it is very challenging not to compare yourself and to stay motivated to stay on your own journey to create what it is that you feel you should create.

Michael: It's wild because TikTok is 15- to 60-second story telling and the multi-hyphenate, even though more and more people are talking about what a multi-hyphenate is . . . it has always existed . . . but now younger artists are starting to realize that they can be one too . . . and that is okay.

Kaisha: Yeah!

Michael: I think if you have to explain to your parents, or your uncle, or your aunt that you're going to go to New York and be an actor, you might as well throw in, "Actually, I'm going to be an actor-photographer-producer-writer." Watch them faint. But, you know what? Might as well kill two birds with one stone, right?

Kaisha: Right! Exactly.

Michael: I just think that TikTok is really good, and I can't believe I'm saying this because last week I was saying, "I'm never getting on TikTok!" And now here I am constantly trying to figure out how to broaden my identity with it. But, I think so far it's been really good. I'm reaching a lot of new people that are fans and are able to express themselves in a way – I think in anything we do need an objective, right? There's a reason why we're doing it – and I think my relationship with TikTok is that I'm giving people a safe space, people that don't normally have safe spaces to create for themselves or others and giving them a platform to do that. Have you sort of found what your 'Why' or what your objective or what your purpose on TikTok is?

Kaisha: You know . . . I'm still discovering it. I have been in this kind of consistency challenge with myself to make sure that I'm posting everyday during December. I just want to get at least like 3 to 4 videos up everyday, no matter what . . .

Michael: Everyday!? 3 to 4!?

Kaisha: Yeah. Everyday. I'm trying. Not perfect, but trying.

Michael: Well, let's hold each other accountable. Let's do that because I didn't know 3 to 4 was a thing.

Kaisha: You know what's so crazy? People recommend that you post 6 to 7 a day if you really want to grow . . . and I'm like, "Who has time to post 6 to 7 TikToks?" Yes... so I'm like 6 or 7 is a lot for me, but I can commit to 3 to 4. So we can definitely hold each other accountable.

Notes

1. www.broadwaypodcastnetwork.com
2. https://broadwaypodcastnetwork.com/hosts/alan-seales/
3. www.thetheatrepodcast.com/
4. www.dramaticforces.com/about/
5. www.donnamckechnie.com/
6. www.tonyapinkins.com/
7. www.joshlamon.com/
8. https://broadwaypodcastnetwork.com/podcast/the-wrong-cat-died/
9. https://broadwaypodcastnetwork.com/podcast/broadwaysted/
10. https://broadwaypodcastnetwork.com/podcast/dear-multi-hyphenate/
11. https://juliejamesonline.com/
12. www.siriusxm.com/channels/on-broadway
13. www.codyrenard.com/
14. www.darrencriss.com/
15. https://en.wikipedia.org/wiki/Purlie
16. https://rebeccajmichelson.com/
17. https://11oclockcreative.com/
18. www.spotnyc.com/
19. www.imdb.com/title/tt11808942/
20. www.apple.com/apple-tv-plus/?itscg=10000&itsct=atv-0-apl_hp-pmo_lrn-apl-avl-210916
21. www.ibdb.com/broadway-production/come-from-away-510272
22. https://neufluence.com/
23. https://pro.imdb.com/
24. www.ibdb.com/broadway-cast-staff/douglas-lyons-491388
25. https://broadwaylicensing.com/shows/musicals/polkadots-the-cool-kids-musical/
26. www.beauthemusical.com/
27. www.ibdb.com/broadway-production/chicken-biscuits-531921
28. www.tbdproductions.com/theatricals-who-we-are/
29. www.hadestown.com/
30. www.ibdb.com/broadway-production/once-on-this-island-514926
31. https://rrrcreative.com/
32. www.thepressroomnyc.com/
33. www.imdb.com/title/tt0377092/
34. https://en.wikipedia.org/wiki/David_Merrick
35. https://en.wikipedia.org/wiki/Much_Ado_About_Nothing
36. www.kimberlyfayegreenberg.com/
37. www.thebroadwayexpert.com/
38. www.latimes.com/entertainment-arts/business/story/2020-04-17/coronavirus-has-wiped-out-these-influencers-brand-deals-but-are-finding-new-ways-to-engage-online
39. www.randygraff.com/bio.html
40. www.ibdb.com/broadway-production/mr-saturday-night-532890
41. https://en.wikipedia.org/wiki/City_of_Angels_(musical)
42. www.ibdb.com/broadway-production/les-misrables-4443
43. https://en.wikipedia.org/wiki/Chris_Boneau
44. www.boneaubryanbrown.com/
45. www.kaishahuguley.com/
46. https://finance.yahoo.com/news/drag-queen-pulled-off-cruella-191100793.html
47. https://en.wikipedia.org/wiki/The_Little_Mermaid_(1989_film)
48. www.remygerminario.com/
49. https://tisch.nyu.edu/
50. https://en.wikipedia.org/wiki/Upright_Citizens_Brigade_Theatre
51. www.standupny.com/
52. www.broadwaycomedyclub.com/
53. www.caveat.nyc/
54. https://greenwichvillagecomedyclub.com/
55. www.foodnetwork.com/
56. www.thepioneerwoman.com/
57. www.twitter.com/KyWilliamsDraws
58. www.theatlantic.com/ideas/archive/2019/06/fake-news-republicans-democrats/591211/
59. www.pennywildmusic.com/
60. https://broadwaypodcastnetwork.com/dear-multi-hyphenate/41-pennywild-an-artists-guilt/

Reference List

1. Lee, Wendy, and Anousha Sakoui. "Macaroni Recipes and Hand Washing Videos: How Influencers Are Adapting to the Coronavirus Crisis." *Los Angeles Times*, Los Angeles Times, 17 Apr. 2020, www.latimes.com/entertainment-arts/business/story/2020-04-17/coronavirus-has-wiped-out-these-influencers-brand-deals-but-are-finding-new-ways-to-engage-online.
2. Graham, David A. "Some Real News about Fake News." *The Atlantic*, Atlantic Media Company, 12 June 2019, www.theatlantic.com/ideas/archive/2019/06/fake-news-republicans-democrats/591211/.

EXERCISE 11 `DM-H`

PITCH A PODCAST

Podcasts are great for artists to connect with an audience and discuss specific topics through an exploration of daily practices, philosophical questions, and/or entertaining stories. As multi-hyphenates, explaining a topic clearly continues to promote a holistic and definitive artistry. Creating a podcast may seem easy, yet the step-by-step process is not only convoluted, but there is no one process to follow. As Alan Seales, the cofounder of BPN, mentioned – 17,000 new podcasts were started every week in 2020 and the median 30-day download per episode capped at 120. Yet so many of these podcasts didn't last longer than a couple of episodes . . . So why go through a lengthy technical process just to give up?

Materials

A journal or computer
A pen

All it takes are answers to the following questions:

1. What is a topic that brings me joy and allows for exploration and multiple perspectives?
2. Who is the audience I'm trying to reach?
3. What is my objective and what do I want my audience to understand?
4. Who are the guests you would interview?
5. Are there any other podcasts that are similar in topic, conversation style, and special guests?

Once you ruminate on these questions, think about how long you can keep this podcast going. Is there longevity in the topic or is it a limited series? Creating a podcast should never feel like a chore – it should illuminate the spirit from within and call for genuine connection to your guests and your audience.

Dorothy Petersen applies Tony nominee L Morgan Lee's wig (designed by Cookie Jordan) while preparing for A Strange Loop on Broadway

Chapter 11
Comparison May Not Be the Thief of Joy

DOI: 10.4324/9781003254744-15

Paige Turner as Mother from Ragtime

Career Connection
Alternative Spaces (Concert, Cabaret, and Drag)

A basement underneath the hottest disco in town. A stage on the fourth floor of a modern hotel. A swanky jazz club with roots connected to the music movement of the 1920s. An old-fashioned cabaret space where the Stonewall riots[1] began. A piano bar on Restaurant Row.[2] A theatre down the stairs of a midtown cafe. Cabaret spaces have their own energy, their own image, and their own rules. They are well known, highly frequented, and a friend to all who step inside. These spaces have just as much life, breath, and secrets as a Jewel Box theatre. If Broadway is the heart, cabaret spaces are the nerves.

Jim Caruso[3] made his Broadway debut alongside Liza Minnelli[4] in *Liza's at the Palace!*[5] in 2009. He is one of two talent bookers at Birdland Jazz Club,[6] a jazz club in New York City that's been swinging since 1949, and has committed himself to *Jim Caruso's Cast Party*,[7] a wildly popular happening that has brought Broadway glitz and urbane wit to the legendary Birdland in New York City every Monday night since 2003, according to its website.

"To me, the concept of cabaret is *Theater With a Two-Drink Minimum*," Caruso says.

> And "theater" can refer to most anything! Music, comedy, revue, burlesque, monologue . . . you name it, I've cheered in a cabaret room. At its best, cabaret is an intimate, up-close meet-and-greet with a performer you want to know better! Other than the cover charge, I'm not sure the idea has changed much over the years.

Cabaret spaces have been around since the 1920s. Acts would feature song, dance, and drama. They were, and still are, led with an MC, like we know of the character the Emcee in Kander and Ebb's[8] *Cabaret*.[9] While not in a top hat and cane, today one would experience Susie Mosher's[10] in-your-face (and in-the-moment) comedy interweave throughout her evening *The Line Up*,[11] also at Birdland Jazz every Tuesday night in the downstairs space. Her brilliant mind allows for hysterical musical comedy improvisational moments that leave the audience in stitches. While Mosher creates hysterical moments in her show and provides electric entertainment, these evenings prove to be extremely helpful to Mosher's mental health.

"I've been doing cabaret for as long as I've been performing – which is about 40 years," says Mosher.

> I suffer from pretty severe anxiety. I literally have to take beta blockers because I get such anxiety, it's like a rushing sound in my ear. I can't even

focus and it's very debilitating. In doing *The Line Up*, because I don't have to remember anything – everything I do is right off the cuff – that alleviates my main source of anxiety, which is that I'm going to forget my line or not know what I'm doing, which is the actor's nightmare. Doing *The Line Up* has freed me from that anxiety, which is a huge gift.

Piggybacking off what Mosher shares, the art form of cabaret takes different shapes and sizes and serves different purposes for all involved. What types of experiences do cabarets offer for a creative and an audience member?

- They offer a safe space for an artist to test out new material like songs, monologues, characters, banter, jokes, and stories.
- They serve as a useful netweaving environment for actors, musicians, technicians, writers, directors, producers, administration, and more to mix and mingle.
- Because these performances are personal and supremely more intimate, the audience feels more connected to the performer, especially if they are of star status.
- They allow new, younger producers to learn about the industry and methods of production. The fixed environments provide a cushion for the producer, so they may be able to take risks and learn from their mistakes, if any.
- They allow green performers who may have just graduated from their programs to introduce themselves to the industry. Self-produced concerts/cabarets at spaces like Feinstein's/54 Below[12] and The Green Room 42[13] are perfect for an artist to invite an agent or manager in hopes of building a relationship together.
- They allow the performer to check in with themselves apart from the costumes, the sets, and the glitz and glamour of a production.

Randy Graff[14] had begun to fall in love with the art of teaching and had taken a step back from performing. When approached to perform a solo show at Feinstein's/54 Below, Graff found herself having anxiety over returning to the stage. This opportunity allowed her to learn a new meditative tool that proved to be so effective that she would pass on to her students.

"When I learned about the *Inner Child*, I was getting ready to do my solo performance show at 54 Below," says Graff.

> I had some performance anxiety because I hadn't been on stage in a while and I had never performed as myself, so there was some fear and vulnerability there.

I saw a friend who is a composer and music director, but also works with actors and performance anxiety. He understands it from being in it. He gave me this tool that I was so ripe for, which is why it worked for me. Before you go on stage, put your hand on your heart, and imagine yourself as a little kid who is scared, anxious, nervous, etc. . . and that you, as an adult, can take care of them with three little words. *I got you*. I would say it every night before I went on stage. I would stand in the kitchen at 54 Below, with my hand on my heart and quietly speak to my little kid. "I got you." And it totally calmed me down and empowered me. Try it. It works!

It doesn't matter what one's accolades are – whether or not one has a Tony Award or just graduated from college, these cabaret spaces serve as incubators of personal growth. Jen Sandler[15] started her career in theatre and fundraising in special arts and development and joined the producing staff as an Original Program Producer at Feinstein's/54 Below. She is responsible for creating and casting electric nights of original programming that entertain the patrons of the basement turned cabaret space of the famed Studio 54.[16]

"I look for things that are different, that aren't just *54 Sings Blink 182*,[17] as fun as that would be," Sandler says. "I look for things that are exciting, that will turn things on their head, that you can truly only see for one night and want to see again because it's so special."

Sandler experienced a very modern type of networking when she produced *I Wish: The Roles That Could Have Been*[18] alongside Alexandra Silber.[19] Note: The powers, tactics, and results of networking were explored in Chapter 9, "Networking Versus Netweaving."

"She made a tweet where Alexandra said she wanted to have a concert where performers would sing from roles they

couldn't do for any reason, and her example was Little Red Riding Hood," continues Sandler.

I tweeted her and said, "Hi! I don't know you but this is a really good idea and we should talk." Jennifer Ashley Tepper,[20] the Creative Producer of Feinstein's/54 Below introduced us and it's now a series at 54 Below. We just did a post-pandemic version and discovered that as much as the show is about seeing performers in ways you've not seen, it's also about welcoming a better and more inclusive theatre community as the theatre comes back.

Cabaret continues to prove to be a massive learning experience for all involved, all while creating memories that are not replicable. Cracks, forgotten lyrics, emotions, even drunk performances are forgiven in a cabaret space – forgiven, but certainly never forgotten.

"I grew up seeing every single act possible," reminisces Caruso.

That included Bernadette Peters,[21] Manhattan Transfer,[22] Joel Grey,[23] Chita,[24] Liza, on and on. Don't tell them, but I secretly recorded every show. I'd play those cassettes endlessly, learning the songs and studying what made the acts so great. To this day, I see as many concerts as I can . . . Broadway folks, jazzers, cabaret divas, country, pop . . . I'm open to everything. I learn from the best and I certainly learn from the worst. It's a good way to build a point of view so that you can craft your own show! Don't hire someone else to do it! Grab yourself a killer musical director that "gets" you, and start creating!

Alexandra Silber ✔ @alsilbs · Dec 3, 2018 ···
Dear @jenashtep, please produce a concert in your living room where people sing the roles that passed us by, JUST so:
1. @alexwyse can be the Artful Dodger
2. @mykalkilgore can sing "I just can't wait to be king"
3. I can be Red Riding Hood—my Into the Woods destiny of yesteryear

Figure 11.2 A screenshot of a tweet made by Alexandra Silber which began the collaboration between Silber and Jen Sandler, creating the Feinstein's/54 Below concert *I Wish*. Source: Michael Kushner Photography

Figure 11.3 Al Silber (right) and Brian J. Nash (at the piano) sharing a laugh on stage during *I Wish: The Roles That Could Have Been* at 54 Below in 2019. Source: Michael Kushner Photography

Figure 11.4 Jim Caruso admires historical photos that adorn the dressing rooms of the famous Birdland Jazz Club. Source: Michael Kushner Photography

On the opposite end of the spectrum, when the efforts of web series can take months, even years to complete, drag is an ever evolving, impulsive, and of the moment art form. The art of drag has a long, beautiful, and complicated *herstory*. Constantly challenging the role gender has in society, Trans, nonbinary, and cis-gendered members of the LGBTQIA+ community have contributed buckets of blood, sweat, and tears fighting for equality and inclusion.

The mere existence of a queer artist is a protest. Whether it's Marsha P. Johnson[25] and Sylvia Rivera[26] being the brave trans women of color to ignite the Stonewall Riots, a new drag queen with a thirsty wig and cliffhangers stepping on stage for the first time, or the winner of *RuPaul's Drag Race*,[27] these moments bear the weight of those lost, those here, and those to come. Queer activism is art, and while it's often comedic, fierce, campy, or runway-ready, the theatricality is etched in its movement.

Since 2006, Paige Turner[28] has been sweeping Hell's Kitchen in New York City with her hysterical shows influenced by her Broadway background. Daniel Frank Kelley[29] approaches Paige Turner like a character – his

commitment to her specifics is something that makes Paige Turner a staple in the New York City, Provincetown, and Puerto Vallarta scenes. Kelley has been on Broadway in *Parade*[30] and *Footloose*,[31] as well as national tours and regional theatres all over the country.

"I had just come off the role of the Emcee in *Cabaret*, very gender bending and kind of a drag role in many ways," Kelley says.

> I decided how much I loved entertaining and not chasing the role. I decided that I would just do drag full time, but in my own way, and see what would happen. Drag is definitely the gimmick that got my talent noticed. I always believed in myself and my talents, but this told people to watch.

And watch, they did. Kelley's Paige Turner would sell out bars, events, and holiday shows to name a few. Kelley even began to incorporate his producer brain and created a mammoth event known as *So You Think You Can Drag*,[32] which took over the off-Broadway theatre complex, New World Stages[33] on Thursday nights in the fall. New

World Stages contains five theatres underground in New York's theatre district. After the standing performances would take their bows, the New World Stages crew would transform the lobby by installing a runway stage and clearing the common area so hundreds of people could attend the show. Kelley's producing efforts would sell out nights, create a community, and have established the careers of many successful queens.

"I definitely draw from past theater experiences and apply them to everything I do in drag," Kelley continues.

> I am not big on contests in general and think they can be extremely unfair; however they do serve a function for many reasons and a lot of good can come from them, especially self-discovery for the contestants. When New World Stages responded to what I do as a drag performer, they asked me to help develop a contest. This was my chance to create something I'd want to see, make it a contest that had a theater producing and backing it, which right away allowed me to make things happen in a way that hadn't been done before in NYC. It was a perfect fit and it launched over 100 drag queens, many who went full-time and many who ended up on *RuPaul's Drag Race*.

With the rise of drag arts, even a course on the hit reality television show *RuPaul's Drag Race* taught by Joe

E. Jeffrey[34] at the New School,[35] queens are becoming proficient in managing their own micro-environments tapping into finding talent, creating shows, navigating press, and selling tickets. What was once radical underground ball culture, dominated by daring and artistic Black and Brown lives, has become mainstream – a popular question for straight cis-gender out-of-towners is, "Where can I find the best drag show?"

While drag is political for some, Marti Gould Cummings[36] takes it to the next level. Cummings is a drag artist, television personality/producer, and political figure. Cummings acknowledges that their prowess for politics had been fueled by their Drag Artistry. In 2021, Cummings ran for District 7 NYC Council[37] as the first nonbinary candidate. While unsuccessful in achieving the vote, their work is not done, and their fight is just beginning – already publicly acknowledging plans for future elections.

"Being a drag artist really prepared me for activism and politics because so much of drag over the years has been linked to various movements for equity and equality," they say. "Drag and my work in the theatre has helped me to not only understand myself better but to understand others and has provided a voice that I didn't realize I had."

"I wanted to be an astronaut – I wanted to go out there," says Cynthia Henderson,[38] dreaming of the possibilities.

> But I couldn't because I have asthma, though it never dampened my fascination with existence itself. Because I am so small in *comparison* to the world around me. I can't possibly be that important. I'm a tiny speck in regards to how small our Universe is. Yes, I have my postage stamp spot in this world, but beyond my postage stamp, if I am going to be a global citizen and respectful to this industry, I have to be mindful that my aesthetic is not the only one out there.

Henderson's perspective is a view of comparison that doesn't hold her back but propels her into the stars. Believe it or not, comparison is certainly the thief of joy – if it's used *incorrectly*. When used correctly, comparison can be an informative and useful tool. It doesn't have to be abusive, and it *certainly* doesn't have to be self-harming.

"I used to love a good comparison story of myself," Dani Stoller[39] says.

> Both ways. "I'm better than they are and they are better than me." Now I'm like – there's room for *everybody*. I'm a big Yogi person and everything is of service. Everything. Everything we do is of service. If you don't get something, that's okay. Be in service. If you see a show that a friend of yours would be good for, let them know. That's of service. You have to constantly act like there's enough for everybody. As soon as you act like there isn't, that is when nothing will happen for you.

Paving one's own road is always difficult and sometimes the end doesn't seem in sight – especially when jealousy and envy are born out of comparing one's journey to another. Overcoming these factors is the bravery it takes to be a multi-hyphenate – and the only way to shut it down is to work from the inside.

"Every artist that has ever lived on this planet has dealt with envy or jealousy in some capacity," says Wesley Taylor.[40]

> It's very human. It's also a complete waste of time and energy. And ultimately, it's very unproductive. But knowing

that doesn't make it easy. I will say when I'm fully consumed by a project that is getting me out of bed in the morning, challenging me and inspiring me, then I struggle a lot less with comparing myself to other people. It's when I'm not creating or when I'm waiting for something to happen. Or not dreaming, not writing, not doing something that's propelling me towards the next thing and I'm just on social media . . . that's when that Green Eyed Monster shows up.

Ah, the green-eyed monster. Shakespeare wrote about the green-eyed monster in both *The Merchant of Venice*[41] and *Othello*,[42] referring to jealousy. Whether one is jealous or the victim of someone with jealousy, the green-eyed monster has affected us all. While avoiding these negative experiences is nearly impossible, it's controllable. The ability to manage the green-eyed monster comes from managing expectations. To others who have yet to understand the multi-hyphenate within themselves, it might seem as if one is taking creative opportunities from others. Not everyone will understand the multi-hyphenate experience – but the multi-hyphenate does not have to explain their process to anyone but themselves. These deniers are simply viewing the world through a very small scope.

To deny a creator's existence for making new art *and* getting paid for it is merely a reflection on one's comparison of what they know to be true. Perhaps one day a multi-hyphenate will hire that person and maybe then will they sing a different tune. Just like RuPaul[43] says, "If they ain't paying your bills, pay them no mind." That's the G-rated version, but it still rings true.

In Chapter 8, "Get a GRIP," Wes Taylor mentioned that if social media had been around while he was younger, he would have ruined himself before he even got on the scene. While this is certainly true of the type of content one puts out there – social media is designed for users to share only the best parts of their lives, making it easy for one to measure their successes based on what they ingest while scrolling through Instagram, TikTok, or Facebook.

Anthony Norman[44] (HBO's *Mare of Easttown*,[45] *The Prom*[46] on Broadway) shares his distaste for social media. Norman often taps out of social media simply because he gives himself over to it too much.

> I just recently gave a good friend of mine my Instagram password and had her change it because I was looking at it way too much and it was serving me no purpose other than maybe making me feel good every now and then if I posted something, or if I posted a story that I thought was funny or someone else thought was funny. It was so come and go. . . . Instagram just never made me feel good. At the end of the day it never made me feel good.

I was less productive with it. And anytime I ever had this conversation with someone, 90% of people's responses were, "Oh, it doesn't do that for me." I didn't ask you! I'm just telling you what it does for me, you fool – you *clown*.

Everyone's relationship with social media varies. While it's easy to hide behind a phone and judge someone else, it's just as easy to stare at the screen and judge oneself. Navigating social media, one must remember that anyone can post whatever they want on social media. One can have received seven different "nos" throughout their day but has the power to post a picture throwing it back to when they received an award or had their first rehearsal for their third Broadway show. It's rare for people to post about their failures or the mundane. The oversaturation of positivity and self-hyping prove to be just as toxic as reveling in self-pity.

Since there is a visual and audio element to social media posts, comparison is not just about a gorgeous picture in Greece or another gym selfie – it creates comparison in an industry-specific way, directly affecting confidence in skills and proficiencies. If there was an artist dreaming of singing in a concert at 54 Below and someone else kept posting video after video of the concerts they were in, how does that make one feel? Potentially left out. Or what about a headshot photographer who sees a client they just worked with shoot with another photographer immediately after?

It's normal for people to make up their own narratives. Maybe that performer produced the evening and cast themselves. Maybe the headshot client loves what they got with the first photographer, but the second photographer reached out and offered a free shoot? The spiraling one causes themselves after immediately placing the blame on themselves is not helpful. Marc J. Franklin,[47] former principal photographer and photo editor of *Playbill* magazine,[48] has found a healthy relationship with comparison by instilling boundaries between himself and social media:

> I try to avoid [comparison] as much as I can. Comparison is inevitable, especially with social media where it is easy to become absorbed in likes and follower count. For me, a lot of the work to keep comparison at bay is simply being aware of it. Then, I try to turn that awareness into action – I log out of social media when I need to. I remind myself that my job is to make photos and not to acquire a certain amount of views. I revisit work that I've created that makes me proud. I make a project in a way that makes me feel confident. I remember that my own voice is worthy and valuable.

So – how can comparison be turned into something more positive? Comparison can be used to incite inspiration, an action plan, and results.

"Wow! I want their career," one might say.

"I saw the most aspirational play the other night! That's the type of work I want to produce," a budding producer might exclaim.

"There's no one compared to me on your roster, which is why you should represent me," an actor might say to a potential agent.

While the origins aren't clear, it is said that *comparison is the thief of joy*. Sources speculate Theodore Roosevelt[49] or Mark Twain[50] to be the original speakers of this phrase, though it was taken and placed in the syllabi of teachers and professors all over the world. As an artist, one has the privilege of not only expressing joy but also causing joy. When joy is taken away, efforts become heavy and mundane – ultimately risking an artist to try less and less. Remember the for-now job? Why would someone commit themselves to something when it's not joyful? After surviving a pandemic, humans owe it to themselves to find joy in whatever they do – even while fighting for a cause.

Comparison is a useful tool to guage one's abilities regarding auditions, job application, skill/proficiency set, artistic decisions, and more. It can help a manager and client come up with a specific plan when it comes to shaping a career. It can help one assess their purpose. Comparison, with the removal of emotion, creates awareness. Yes – an artist should always believe in their talent, but the tv, film, and theatre business is exactly that . . . business. Therefore, skill set must be at a certain level for it to be applied. If an artist responds positively to a breakdown or job opportunity, it's their responsibility to be able to deliver accordingly.

Many in the industry look at themselves as a 'product,' while others find that word disparaging. Whether it's a song, a set design, a costume, a monologue, and so on, if an artist produces something with the hopes of it being ingested by an audience, it becomes output. However, one looks at it – a product, wares, art, a commodity – releasing this output into the world is a precious experience. It holds years of commitment, money, and emotion, all risking rejection. It's a lot to ask someone, and yet, that's the price for putting art into the world.

In the tv/film and theatre markets, there is an over-saturation of supply, with not much demand, especially post-COVID-19. Something that never goes out of style is a multi-hyphenate's secret weapon: point of view. A multi-hyphenate must be able to sell, or at least, present their work through individualistic eyes. In doing so, comparison is helpful for understanding the uniqueness of one's output. One must respect what has already been done, what is happening now, and what needs to happen next. The three elements which help this exploration process are the three I's: **identification, individuality, and inspiration.**

Identification

Artists who have dominated showbusiness walked so future generations could run. Therefore, identifying the work done in years past is an educated way to move forward with fresh eyes. By committing to thorough research and understanding the work that precedes art today, one can keep building upon an idea or completely disregard it and try something new. With the internet at society's fingertips, almost anything is researchable. YouTube has become an incredible tool for an artist's growth.

"Whenever I go into an audition," says Colleen Ballinger,[51]

> if I have to have an accent for something, if I have to look a certain way, if I have to have my hair done a certain way – the first thing I do is search hairstyles in the 1920s. Or how to do a southern accent. I did *Waitress*,[52] and you bet your butt I was looking up southern accents on YouTube before flying to New York City. It's endless resources for education and inspiration. It even helps me clean out my washing machine!

Sammi Canold's[53] 2019 production of *Evita*[54] at City Center Encores![55] in New York City was certainly different from the original brought to Broadway by Hal Prince.[56] Prince, the Broadway producing and directing mogul responsible for productions such as *The Phantom of the Opera*,[57] *Fiddler on the Roof*,[58] *Cabaret*,[59] and more, is also responsible for the groundbreaking original production of *Evita* in 1979 starring Patti LuPone[60] and Mandy Patinkin.[61] Because Cannold was able to identify Prince's work by watching the taped original production at the New York Public Library,[62] she was able to make her own choices and implement her specific point of view. She notes there is *no comparison* between her and the 21-time Tony Award–winning Prince.

"He is Hal Prince," says Cannold, lighting up about the legendary director and producer.

> The majority of folks, I think, coming to see the show at New York City Center have some preconceived notions about *Evita* because of what Hal did. I can't be blind to that. I have to take into consideration what has happened before and figure out how to honor it while also building up it and moving forward. I saw Hal Prince's production at the New York Public Library and it has always been my *Evita* north star in the sense that it is iconic and definitive. I never had any desire to compete with it because Hal is my hero. I was 25 years old – the same age as Eva[63] when she met Perón.[64] I have a very specific vantage point on this story.

At the time Cannold directed *Evita*, a first-class production of *Evita* had never been directed or choreographed by a woman. It

Figure 11.6 Jason Gotay, photographed for The Dressing Room Project, prepares in his dressing room backstage at New York City Center before a performance of Cannold's Evita. Source: Michael Kushner Photography

was important to bring to the table her experiences through a lens based on how she navigates the world. She was also able to bring Argentinian collaborators onto the team and include their perspectives that perhaps haven't been unlocked in the past.

"That was in no way to disregard the work of the past," she continues,

> but rather to build on it. Our production looks quite a bit like it is the grandchild of [the original] production because it takes place in a black box – it is very Brechtian[65] stylistically speaking – so it was really about paying homage to what Hal did.

In Cannold's production, she placed a number of Easter eggs to pay homage to Prince. Prince had been very vocal throughout his life about future productions of his work not being carbon copies, but rather directors having their own point of view and building on it – something that could not be done without identifying Prince's iconic work.

"I think that is a very generous thing to say," continues Cannold, "and also was very freeing for me to not feel like I

stepped on the toes of this great master, who is part of the reason I'm a director in the first place."

Using identification is also a useful tool for a team of agents and managers. By coming up with a branding statement. A **branding statement** is different from a 'Why' statement, having less of an objective and sharing more about the type of work one would like to commit themselves to by using imagery or likeness. Say an actor comes up with a branding statement such as "I have the exuberance of Mel Brooks[66] and the vulnerability of Timothée Chalamet.[67]" Right in that sentence, the actor is identifying themselves as having these two polar opposite personalities, which help establish a helpful visual for anyone interested in casting the actor. By looking at this statement, this actor probably has a range that allows them to do the broad comedy of Mel Brooks material as well as the simple, day-to-day pathos similar to Timothée Chalamet's body of work. Identifying the positive attributes an actor has helps the manager or agent establish a plan between themselves and client, and helps the manager build their clientele roster.

"Comparison as it relates to 'typing' is a real thing and necessary since I have a small company," Carole Dibo[68] of Carole Dibo Talent says. "For instance, if I am considering bringing on a new client, I don't want them to be the same 'type' as someone I already have."

Individuality

Frances Ruffelle[69] won the 1987 Tony Award for Best Supporting Actress in a Musical for originating the role of Eponine in *Les Miserables*.[70] When listening to any rendition of *On My Own*, it's hard to get Ruffelle's hauntingly beautiful vocals out of one's head while picturing the drenched waif dreaming in the Parisian cobblestone streets. Ruffelle identifies her uniqueness by removing emotion when it comes to comparison, allowing for freedom in creativity.

"I think comparison is a very useful tool," Ruffelle says.

> I have always learned by watching others. I've learned from their brilliance and I've learned from their mistakes. I don't compare my voice to anyone else's . . . it's mine and I know it's unique. I'll leave it to others to compare my range and tone . . . and they do!

Upon moving to New York City and having a lengthy run of her one-woman cabaret, *Frances Ruffelle LiveS in New York*[71] at The Green Room 42,[72] the freedom she found through comparison has allowed her to connect with an audience on a more personal, and specific level. Ruffelle often supports her friends by frequenting cabaret and concert spaces around New York – ultimately providing a useful education in her efforts as a multi-hyphenate.

> For me, watching people's one-person shows has been the perfect lesson. I set myself a challenge to create a unique piece. In doing so, I've developed into a writer-director; writing and directing one-person shows for others. I'm now writing scripts, plays, and films. Writing has become my passion and has given me so much happiness and fulfillment. To me, that is a success.

Even after one creates one of the most legendary characters in the musical theatre canon, wins a Tony, and moves on to a lengthy and admirable career – an artist never stops evaluating their relationship to art. Such evaluation also helps more straitlaced thinkers begin to connect with their individualism. For Colleen Cook,[73] she has begun to connect to the "in-between" – something her corporate background never allowed her to do.

> I love being surrounded by talented people and watching their process. It is fascinating to me probably because

Figure 11.7 Frances Ruffelle performs a number from atop of a chair during her one-woman show *Frances Ruffelle LiveS in New York at* The Green Room 42. Source: Michael Kushner Photography

my brain doesn't work in the same way. One of my friends said to me, "You always think in black and white, your involvement with these artists helps you see some of the gray." After many years in a corporate setting, there is something very freeing about working on projects that never feel much like "work" at all. There is definitely a rush after the completion of a successful artistic project; seeing and feeling the energy of an audience responding to it. Your work often ends in a shared joy and that is something very different and fulfilling for me at this point in my life.

Inspiration

"I think there is a thin but dangerous line between inspiration and comparison, but at their root, each of them comes from a place of examination," continues Marc J. Franklin of *Playbill*.

As an artist, it is important to be knowledgeable of other artists and their work. I get so much excitement and so many ideas from looking at the talent from those artists, whether they are in my field or beyond. But I think the other side of that "inspiration" coin is measuring myself against others. Art is not a competition. At its core, art is creative expression – everyone is on their own journey and are creating from a place that is solely theirs. For me, that abundance of perspective and vision is what makes art so thrilling.

He is certainly correct – art is *not* a competition. Whether or not this energy was instilled in students getting their college degrees and subjecting themselves to a cut program, or it was the way hungry performers would sabotage each other to reach their way to the top. Art belongs to everyone, and it's certainly more enjoyable when it's celebrated instead of envied. That celebration must come from within. Celebration creates an environment in which there is space for everyone – ultimately eliminating the negative aspects of comparison. Celebration gives back joy to the artist.

Christina Bianco[74] has built a career based on celebration. Her impression skills found her off-Broadway in *Forbidden Broadway*,[75] as well as being featured on the *Ellen*[76] show and providing vocal talents to *RuPaul's Drag Race*. She believes she has been able to do so because of how well she knows herself. By using different aspects of comparison, Bianco was able to make headway in her career not only as an actor who does impersonations but also an actor who performs material that doesn't require impressions. Bianco recently graced the stage in a rave-reviewed turn as Fanny Brice[77] in *Funny Girl*[78] at the Théâtre Marigny in Paris.[79]

"Early on, I noticed that no one's opinion was the same," says Bianco.

My versatility clearly confused them. But I was told that I had to be a clear type and fit into a pre-existing box so that casting and creatives would know what to do with me – so I tried to do just that. When I got out of college I compared myself to other popular performers and tried to be like them. The problem was, I *wasn't* like them. I was trying to force a character onto myself. Therefore, no one behind the table knew what to do with me and I didn't get cast. I'd get callback after callback but my talent didn't matter because I didn't know who I was. It took me a while to realize that I didn't need to follow a template. It's ironic that being cast in *Forbidden Broadway*, playing twenty characters and doing impressions is what led me to that realization, but it gave me an outlet to be all the varied things I really am! More importantly, it gave me confidence. It's hard to pave your own way but if you have a skill or talent that gives you an edge or makes you "different," you should take every opportunity to make the most of it. Now, we live in a world where kids are changing their face in photos with filters and apps – or getting plastic surgery to look the way they think they should. More than ever, it's important to remember that being an individual will make you stand out, make you special and make you whole.

Comparison is about understanding one's place in the world, not their relationship to the other's inhabiting it. It's about a **point of view**, something irreplaceable and unduplicatable. Just like failure, comparison is a concept that needs to be readjusted with a positive spin. When embraced and used for good, it's incredibly educational and eye opening. Every single artist on this planet has a point of view that is unique. An artist's voice is like a fingerprint. Inherently, one doesn't have to try to be different – it's in a person already. Working through comparison is not to take stock of how successful one is or how many jobs they have – that awakens the green-eyed monster. Keep the monster at bay by identifying preceding works of art, taking note of what makes one an individual, and always staying inspired to take the next step. The green-eyed monster won't bother anyone anymore.

For a multi-hyphenate, the possibilities are endless, from understanding Why to navigating social media to comparing one's place in the world. And by comparing oneself in relationship to the world around them, they will find one aspect that is imperative to a multi-hyphenate identity. Artists have a responsibility to create with passion and purpose. By doing so, they positively affect the community, create opportunity, and keeps tradition alive. Multi-hyphenate artistry is not just to be in the spotlight – it's to solve problems and connect to a bigger picture. Therefore, it forms a type of art that is the core of the intention of the multi-hyphenate: **socially responsible artistry**.

EPISODE EXCERPT

L MORGAN LEE

Obie award-winning actress, theatre maker, and photographer. She is most known for her performance in the Pulitzer Prize-winning musical, A Strange Loop which garnered her a Lucille Lortel nomination and the distinction of being the first openly transgender actress to originate a role in a Pulitzer Prize-winning piece of theatre.

THE PERCEPTION OF THE MULTI-HYPHENATE • *EPISODE 46*

Michael: What do you have to say to younger artists that might not know their worth just yet? When did you start to find your worth in charging for any service, any artistry you have -- not just photography but all of your hyphens?

L Morgan: Mmm – I am not the best at that. Money is such a leave it on the coffee table as you leave thing for me. It's such a weird subject. I am getting better. I am getting better on the acting side of it. In terms of photography – quite frankly I could be charging more than I do. I want to look out for the artists who don't have a lot of money. There was a photographer who is one of the big names in the headshot game, who at this particular point was charging I believe it was $1300 or $1400 for headshots. And this photographer said in an interview when someone asked, "Your headshot sessions are pretty expensive, they're over a thousand dollars – how do you feel about that? Most actors don't really make that much to be able to pay that." And this photographer's response was, "If you can't pay $1500 for headshots, you're not an actor." And it sent fire through my body thinking of the number of some of the best actors I know who have not been able to make money enough to pay for $1500 in headshots in years because whatever reasons . . . they aren't being seen, they don't have representation. Whatever the case. They are doing lots of projects but they don't have enough to be able to swing $1500 for a headshot so for this person who is dealing directly with actors on a regular basis – overbooked and overbooked – to be able to say you're not an actor if you can't pay $1500 for headshots, it was like crazy to me. And so I never wanted to turn into that. I think as a result of that, I've always tried to keep myself in a place where I know that I am being compensated fairly and not sort of taking advantage at all. That has been a journey because I've gone up, I've gone down. I've played with numbers – I've kind of played around a little bit. It's about your worth, as you said. It's about what do you think that your product is worth? I think that, yes, for instance, I could charge a little bit more but I don't feel like I need to because my spirit is involved in the game and I want to be able to know that I can do a session and I can make enough that my soul is happy. I might not be going, "Yes! I got $1000!" I might not be doing that. But I know my soul is happy. I know that person, still had to likely work to get the amount it took to do that shoot. I think advice to young people would be try and see. Your first run out of the gate, you might ask for too much and you'll realize very quickly hat you're asking for too much. It's also smart to research. It's smart to look around at other photographers and when you're able to see what their rates are, just start to look at the quality of work that you're putting out and the quality of work that those photographers are doing and start to compare what your rate is in the mix of them.

Lee is the first openly trans woman to earn a Tony Nomination. She was nominated for A Strange Loop on Broadway.

Notes

1 https://en.wikipedia.org/wiki/Stonewall_riots
2 www.timessquarenyc.org/locations/dining/restaurant-row
3 www.jim-caruso.com/bio.html
4 https://en.wikipedia.org/wiki/Liza_Minnelli
5 https://en.wikipedia.org/wiki/Liza%27s_at_The_Palace . . . .
6 https://birdlandjazz.com/
7 www.castpartynyc.com/
8 https://en.wikipedia.org/wiki/Kander_and_Ebb
9 www.ibdb.com/broadway-production/cabaret-3348
10 www.susiemosher.com/
11 www.timeout.com/newyork/music/the-lineup-with-susie-mosher
12 www.54below.com
13 https://thegreenroom42.venuetix.com/
14 www.randygraff.com/
15 www.linkedin.com/in/jensandler
16 https://en.wikipedia.org/wiki/Studio_54
17 https://www.blink182.com/
18 https://54below.com/events/i-wish-4/
19 http://alexandrasilber.squarespace.com/
20 www.jenniferashleytepper.com/
21 https://en.wikipedia.org/wiki/Bernadette_Peters
22 https://manhattantransfer.net/
23 https://en.wikipedia.org/wiki/Joel_Grey
24 https://en.wikipedia.org/wiki/Chita_Rivera
25 https://en.wikipedia.org/wiki/Marsha_P._Johnson
26 https://en.wikipedia.org/wiki/Sylvia_Rivera
27 www.imdb.com/title/tt1353056/
28 www.paigeturnernyc.com/
29 www.ibdb.com/broadway-cast-staff/daniel-frank-kelley-508893
30 www.ibdb.com/broadway-show/parade-6926
31 www.ibdb.com/broadway-show/footloose-10038
32 www.imdb.com/title/tt7641136/
33 https://newworldstages.com/
34 www.gaystarnews.com/article/this-professor-brought-the-whole-season-11-cast-of-drag-race-to-his-class-about-the-shows-impact/
35 www.newschool.edu/
36 https://martigcummings.com/
37 www.martiformanhattan.com/
38 www.ithaca.edu/faculty/chenderson
39 www.danistoller.com/
40 https://en.wikipedia.org/wiki/Wesley_Taylor
41 https://en.wikipedia.org/wiki/The_Merchant_of_Venice
42 https://en.wikipedia.org/wiki/Othello
43 https://en.wikipedia.org/wiki/RuPaul
44 www.anthonyjnorman.com/
45 www.imdb.com/title/tt10155688/
46 www.ibdb.com/broadway-production/the-prom-518117
47 www.marcjfranklin.com/
48 https://playbill.com/
49 https://en.wikipedia.org/wiki/Theodore_Roosevelt
50 https://en.wikipedia.org/wiki/Mark_Twain
51 https://en.wikipedia.org/wiki/Colleen_Ballinger
52 https://waitressthemusical.com/
53 www.sammicannold.com/
54 www.nycitycenter.org/pdps/2019-2020/evita
55 www.nycitycenter.org/
56 https://en.wikipedia.org/wiki/Harold_Prince
57 https://us.thephantomoftheopera.com/
58 www.ibdb.com/broadway-show/fiddler-on-the-roof-3513
59 www.ibdb.com/broadway-production/cabaret-3348
60 www.pattilupone.net
61 https://en.wikipedia.org/wiki/Mandy_Patinkin
62 www.nypl.org/
63 https://en.wikipedia.org/wiki/Eva_Per%C3%B3n
64 https://en.wikipedia.org/wiki/Juan_Per%C3%B3n
65 https://en.wikipedia.org/wiki/Bertolt_Brecht
66 https://en.wikipedia.org/wiki/Mel_Brooks
67 www.imdb.com/name/nm3154303/
68 www.actorstrainingcenter.org/team
69 www.francesruffelle.com/
70 www.ibdb.com/broadway-production/les-misrables-4443
71 www.timeout.com/newyork/music/frances-ruffelle-live-s-in-new-york
72 https://thegreenroom42.venuetix.com/
73 www.holmdeltheatrecompany.org/post/bww-interview-executive-director-colleen-cook-reflects-on-the-past-present-and-future-of-holmdel
74 www.christinabianco.com/
75 https://en.wikipedia.org/wiki/Forbidden_Broadway
76 www.ellentube.com/
77 https://en.wikipedia.org/wiki/Fanny_Brice
78 https://en.wikipedia.org/wiki/Funny_Girl_(musical)
79 www.theatremarigny.fr/

EXERCISE 12

CAREER STEALER

DM-H

The awesome thing about show business is that thousands of artists have paved the way for a new wave of artists to share their stories. Understanding the artists who have come before us is educational and informative.

Why did those artists find success? What made them stand out? What if you could take three artist's careers and steal them? While that sounds harsh, this is purely for fun!

Materials

Journal or computer
Pen

> **Step 1.** Make a list of artists you find similarities with. These artists can be with us or have passed on and can span any type of medium or proficiency. The format is loose – think of this like a journal entry.

> **Step 2.** Next to each name, write the similar qualities you share with this person. Then, write the qualities that are attractive to you and would like to inhibit. What are they like in interviews? Have they said anything that inspires you? What is the through-line of their work?

> **Step 3.** Now write the moments in their career which excite you. Did they originate a character that's on your dream role list? Did they design multiple iconic costumes? Do they write moving and beautiful indie films?

> **Step Four.** Brainstorm the ways in which you can apply their traits or attractive qualities to your work and your daily practices.

What happens when you start to keep these things in mind? Perhaps you start to focus on landing the type of work they made popular. Maybe it'll make your artistic efforts more specific, and it'll help you decide which auditions or interviews to go on. While this exercise isn't meant to cause one to imitate another's career, it's simply meant to set goals and help create specificity.

Chapter 12

Passion, Purpose, and Socially Responsible Artistry

"I cannot overestimate the power and satisfaction of being a world builder. I think every artist should try it until they succeed at it. Socially responsible artistry for me means telling your specific story and trusting that there is an audience for it and they will find it."

Tonya Pinkins

DOI: 10.4324/9781003254744-16

Career Connection
Activism

Joel Grey in the 2019 Easter Bonnet Competition

Within the theatre, television, and film communities there are many ways to donate one's time and talents, directly impacting a human in need. Whether it's selling collectors' items at the Broadway Flea Market raising funds for Broadway Cares/Equity Fights AIDS or sleeping on the street in solidarity with homeless youth through Covenant House, one can easily call on this hyphen to connect not only with the industry but also directly change a human's life. For over 45 years, Covenant House New York (CHNY)[1] has been a leader in providing residential services to vulnerable homeless, runaway, and exploited youth. After years of dedication, Emmy and Golden Globe winner Rachel Brosnahan[2] serves as a board member for CHNY.

"People ask a lot how they can get involved outside of giving a donation," continues Brosnahan in Episode 13, "Covenant House: Get Involved" of *Dear Multi-Hyphenate*.

> If you are someone who has skills and resources . . . that you can volunteer, that's also a really, really valuable way to get involved. People are around to help young people build their resumes and to practice their job interview skills . . . there is always a need.

Pam Sondanto,[3] Covenant House's senior vice president of marketing and growth, sees the immeasurable ways Covenant House youth are positively affected.

"Volunteer roles filled by members of the stage and screen community range from board membership to creative arts programs. I don't think I am the right person to explain what someone gets out of donating their time, talent, and treasure to Covenant House since it is such an individual experience, but I can confirm that volunteers have reported back that their measurement of how valuable their service is to us comes in a variety of forms. For example, our LGBTQ+ programming has advanced because of this community. Our young people have greater access to the arts because of this community. Our residents have found new ways to express themselves because of this community. And, most importantly, our young people feel seen by this community.

As Sleep Out has been described, it is an experience you go through, not an event you go to. We are in the midst of preparing for the 9th Stage & Screen Sleep Out this August of 2021 and we continue to use this opportunity to invite new members of the community to get to know us and our youth in an authentic way. To date, this Sleep Out has raised nearly $2.5 million and last year more than 200 people registered from across the country, which was a 100% participant increase from the year before!"

#MeToo.[4] #BlackLivesMatter.[5] #BroadwayFightsBack.[6] Claim Our Space Now.[7] See Our Truths.[8] Broadway for Racial Justice.[9] The '20s have a reputation for *roaring*, and in the 21st century, things are no different. In response to the 2016 election, the rise of racism and anti-Semitic violence, a global pandemic, workplace assault, and criticism of unions, the need for change and accountability are not just wanted but also needed. Account after account, fact after fact, the commercial enterprise that is Broadway has proved to be stuck in a racist and traumatizing loop that perpetuates (whether consciously or not) harm toward marginalized and de-centered folks. All theatres on Broadway are still owned and maintained by white people in 2021.

"There's an intense myth that theatre is a progressive place so people think that it's going to be progressive," Tony-nominated director Leigh Silverman[10] says. "The pain for many people is realizing that it's a myth, realizing that it's a fantasy."

Society is led to believe that the theatre is an extremely inclusive, diverse, and equitable environment. That sad truth is, it reflects that of corporate America, just with a little more song and dance. But it's not *all* smoke and mirrors. In 2021, many members of the Broadway community came together to start advocating for more equitable and inclusive work environments, take action against senseless mistreatment of Black, Brown, Asian American/Pacific Islander, and LGBTQIA+ bodies and dismantle white supremacy.

In creating Claim Our Space Now, founder Marla Louissaint[11] went to her social media to share ideas for unity and intersectionality in her fight. In just one second, one passionate motion on social media ignited a movement rooted in purpose.

"In my network alone, I know of very talented people across the arts, across sciences, litigators, all kinds of people," says Louissaint.

> If you are a person who identifies as Black or Brown, you claim space for yourself unapologetically because that is what white supremacy continues to take away from us – the ability to claim space, our lives, our sanity – a lot of things we are not able to claim as other people with privileged identities have. And if you are someone of privileged identity, then you should hold space and elevate others around you. That was the preliminary vision for what Claim Our Space Now would become. After seeing a lot of people resharing and tossing infographics on social media, I noticed these things were not organized – this is what my computer science side of my brain was like. There has to be a more organized way of organizing national resources and information that can really change and re-educate folks in the opposite spectrum of what we have seen in colonized textbooks that we've been learning in. We launched a National Resource Directory[12] for the folks

we are planning to elevate within our communities – in Harlem for instance – and also for people to redirect funds to those organizations, safe spaces, and such that we have done intense, and still are doing, research on in order to inch over to the West Coast to cover as many states as possible with our 17 categories.

Art, action, empowerment, inspiration, change – it all starts with forward motion. As discussed in Chapter 5, "Work Ethic and Workflow," this is when potential and kinetic energy comes into play. The future of the theatre industry is hard to guage as it changes day to day, but with the multi-hyphenate approach, the artists of today are the ones who have the power. Change comes from more than conversation – it requires a force.

Privilege allows for an artist to be able to pick and choose the conversations in which they find themselves in. But privilege also equals access – which can promote positive change, even if it's a small correction or acknowledgment. Even if stating pronouns in a room full of cis-white people only affects one person, perhaps that will educate one person and they continue the practice in their hometown or implement that whenever they hold space. Micro-movements become macro-movements. These efforts grow into the types of theatre produced, the meetings taken, the money donated, the content posted on social media, and the outreach made.

Passion, purpose, and responsible artistry are key factors to navigating how one participates in show business in the 21st century.

Passion

In order for an artist to start making movements, they must listen to the depths of their soul, the impulse to press 'go,' and the need to create. Sometimes passion sets the flame. Sometimes it acts like a slingshot, keeping the energy focused but slowly gearing up to attack. Passion can be quick to react, but it can also fuel years of planning, training, and dedication. Whether the response is immediate or drawn out, passion dictates *when* a response is required.

Rachel Sussman,[13] Tony Award–nominated creative producer, educator, and entrepreneur committed to cultivating collaborative theatrical work built on trust and transparency, uses passion to inform when she produces a specific project.

"I think the foundational element is the undeniable passion and urgency," says Sussman.

> Why this and why now? Is it relevant and how is it going to be in conversation with the world around it? I think

in some way it becomes a guiding principle. Is this the moment to share this idea? The next number of steps is: is the production ready? But at first I have to be deeply, and undeniably passionate. Am I the right fit aesthetically and are my values aligned with what we're trying to do?

Sussman is an incredibly driven and ardent producer. She has served as the artistic producer of New York Musical Festival (NYMF)[14] and as coproducer on *What the Constitution Means to Me*[15] on Broadway. But Sussman's passion manifested her dream project, one of the commercial lead producers on a new musical *SUFFS*,[16] written by Shaina Taub,[17] which premiered at The Public Theatre[18] in 2022.

"It's a specific piece that *is* my heart," Sussman adds.

> I became interested in the movement when I was 12. I did a project in US History on Women's Suffrage. I went to my middle school library and there wasn't any information and ended up going to the city library. I thought, "Why aren't these stories being kept for me?" This narrative of this history has grown and evolved as I've grown and evolved. When I went to NYU [New York University] and had clarity of vision of the path I wanted to take as a producer, the

passion for this history reemerged and I realized, "You love this thing, this can be a project." I circled back and was like "Why now?" The suffrage movement's fraught legacy (and the white, male lens through which it's been recorded) impacts intersectional feminism as well as the ongoing fight for voting rights today. The 19th Amendment was really the beginning of a fight that is far from over.

As shared numerous times, the 'Why' statement helps a multi-hyphenate find their relationship to their art. But asking, "Why now?" helps find its place in the world.

Rachel is not the only creative bringing a piece to Broadway that is reaching deep within their soul. As stated in the previous chapter – with conversations held over social media, Douglas Lyons[19] had a speedy journey of just 3 years when getting his comedy *Chicken and Biscuits*[20] to Broadway, which opened October 10, 2021, just after the COVID-19 pandemic.

"I think it was passion and community," says Lyons.

> I think people saw themselves in the play and got behind it. Elliott Clayton Cornelius,[21] who's a Broadway actor but also producer, came to the fourth reading and was in tears. He was

Figure 12.3 Rachel Sussman photographed for *Broadway for Biden* on the lawn of Alexander Hamilton's house in Harlem, New York City. Source: Michael Kushner Photography

like, "Doug, I have to figure out a way to make this happen and help fundraise for the world premiere." And now he's a lead producer on Broadway. I think engaging people to make them feel like they're not just being entertained, but that they're being hugged changed the way people receive stories. That is becoming the thread in my work. Yes, you're going to see something that engages you but you're also going to feel a part of it in some way. And if along the way more people feel a part of it, there's going to be more champions to want to make it happen. And it's a comedy, which is rare when it comes to Black stories! I think the palette needs to be cleansed and I think this could cleanse it.

In the efforts of commercial theatre, it may seem like emotions like passion, empathy, and kindness are removed from any equation, but it's not the case. Passion can help bring productions to Broadway, like *Chicken and Biscuits* and the Tony-winning revival of Ahrens and Flaherty's[22] *Once on this Island*,[23] which opened on Broadway at the Circle in the Square Theatre[24] in 2017. The revival wound up winning the Tony Award for Best Revival of a Musical. Who knew that a little bit of netweaving and a little bit of passion would lead to an incredibly popular, Tony-winning revival? Ken Davenport[25] might not have known for sure but had an inkling.

> "The story of *Once on this Island* – and how it came to be – is I had produced the revival of *Spring Awakening*[26] which was directed by Michael Arden.[27] I thought it was such a genius production and it had gotten rave reviews – I just grabbed Michael Arden at the opening night party and I said, "What's next?" He said, "I'd love to do *Once on this Island*." I said, "I love *Once on this Island*!" So already there were two people who were passionate about this idea. So, then the passion has to become practicality. So, what a producer does, with a business mind, is say, "How can I take an artists' passion and start going down practical steps?" I think that's what a producer does . . . is support an artists' vision.

What is passion if it does not inspire action? Passion would then just be a fleeting impulse, which many people let fly by. This is a case where one can either hop on the Satz train or let it leave the station. Davenport did not let the opportunity pass him by and began to leap into motion:

> He said, "I want to do *Once on this Island*." I think he had the idea for years, in fact I know he did. But it hadn't gone there. So I did what I knew first, which was to reach out to Stephen Flaherty and Lynn Ahrens, who wrote it, the very next day. Stephen had been at the opening night of *Spring Awakening*. I said, "Can I talk to you about this?" They were intrigued. I called the agent. Then I had a meeting with Michael, Lynn, and Stephen to talk about Michael's

vision to try to convince them. Slowly, you start to talk about putting the pieces together. It starts with passion but then it very specifically has to get to a to-do list, just like anything else – building a house, whatever it is.

> It's not big steps, it's a series of small steps, which makes it seem a lot easier to do. If I had thought or imagined about how challenging it would be . . . *oh my gosh, a revival of* Once on this Island*? It's going to cost $8 million, we're going to have a goat, we have to get a theatre, and all this stuff* – I wouldn't have done it. But all that I thought when Michael said he wanted to do *Once on this Island* was "I'm going to call Stephen and Lynn."

Passion dictates action steps within the multi-hyphenate. Does one have the fire it takes to be a connector, to be the problem-solver, to be the leader? In doing so, one must examine their boundaries, their proficiency level, and their availability. While opportunities like this don't come every day, when it's right – it's *right*. If a project comes across one's table and they aren't able to commit, more than likely another opportunity will come. And by that time, somewhere down the line – after a little artistic growth that person might seize the opportunity and have a Tony Award–winning revival on their hands.

Passion also dictates where one provides monetary and emotional support. Colleen Cook,[26] who in Chapter 3 "What is a Multi-Hyphenate?" discussed survival jobs, and at one time served on the boards of three very different theatrical experiences: on Broadway – Roundabout Theatre Company,[27] off-Broadway – Out of the Box Theatrics,[28] and Holmdel Theatre Company,[29] a local New Jersey theatre that provides equity guest artist contracts.

> Theatre is one of my passions. I decided to become a theater board member a few years ago after my kids were grown and had more free time. There was a local community theater company that after 30 years was struggling a bit. A few people approached me to come on board to help out as I had been involved as a leader of many other volunteer organizations in our town. I agreed and my involvement has grown significantly since then."

Cook then continued, acknowledging her passion and taking action:

> A key commitment of any board member of any nonprofit organization always includes a financial commitment. This does not always mean personal financial donations – it could also mean working hard to fundraise for your organization. It also always includes a significant time commitment, so I only join boards where I feel a passion for what they are doing, what they are about, and who they are. As a board member, you have a responsibility to advocate for and promote your

organization while contributing to steering policies and practices for its future success.

Passion does not just dictate efforts in a professional setting. It is now starting to reshape universities, colleges, and training programs. The eradication of systemic racism and microaggressive, toxic behaviors in the collegiate setting is beginning to take form.

The statuesque graduates of Pace University's[30] musical theatre program created *See Our Truths* – and according to its YouTube channel, "*See Our Truths* was created to share individual and collective truths for the purposes of building community, healing through connection, and dismantling oppression in all of its forms. This is a movement that will be open to any person or group of people that has experienced oppression and finally want to take a stand against it and change it. Our platform will be dedicated to a current mission until we see the change we want." Sarah Hamaty[31] is one of the artists who donated her time to share her story. Her participation is spurred by the passion she has for the work *See Our Truths* has committed itself to. Her story is documented in Episode 11 of *See Our Truth's* YouTube channel.

I am fortunate enough to be a member of the community Grassroots organization *See Our Truths*, which developed a docuseries on Instagram and YouTube exploring the individual testimonies of current students and alumni of color from Pace University's BFA program. In these episodes, we are able to share, unfiltered, our experiences from the varied systems of oppression that we were on the receiving end of, from faculty and even other peers in this undergraduate program. The organization provides an opportunity to begin and continue healing by sharing your full truth and coming together as a community in solidarity. The freedom to speak through a tough experience that you perhaps pushed down in your memory to protect yourself, allows you to actually begin learning and moving forward. When you feel you are not alone, it can offer a sense of peace and can instill real strength and courage. In tandem with the video testimonials, the *See Our Truth* team crafted a concrete list of abolition requirements to offer to the university to create real, concrete change. I hope to see theater education that is equitable and considerate. I would love to see faculties that directly reflect the evolving student bodies with intricate, in-depth training and high moral standards. I want the beauty of the beautiful, fresh, innovative, young generations of artists reflected in the industry as a whole. This community at *See Our Truth* is a collective making that dream a reality.

Figure 12.4 Sarah Hamaty photographed at Power Station at BerkleeNYC during a recording session. Source: Michael Kushner Photography

Ultimately, colleges are beginning to change their relationships to their student body by giving the students a voice. K.O.,[32] Tony Award winner for their turn as Anita in the 2008 revival of *West Side Story*,[33] recalls what they experienced at the Cincinnati Conservatory of Music (CCM)[34] when they taught and studied there at the same time. Olivo says:

> One of the only reasons I was going back to CCM was because I was still working on getting the rest of my BFA. I got a Broadway gig before I graduated, so I left CCM when I was at CCM. I've still been trying to get back to get the rest of my BFA. I went back so that I could teach and also take class – so I was a student as well as an instructor."
>
> The new department head is someone who has been doing the work in terms of decolonizing himself. And the work that I see CCM trying to do is root out the racism in terms of policy, as well as individuals who don't want to have it changed. One of the things with predominantly white institutions is that you get to a certain level as a professor, you get tenure, if you have privilege. It's not easy to get. So, we have a lot of people with a lot of privilege who don't understand a different way of life, or different people from different backgrounds excelling and creating policy.

According to College Tuition Compare, "a student can spend $30,522 for undergraduate programs and $20,189 for graduate programs per year. That is on average, after all, with schools as low as Birmingham-Southern College at $18,900 a year and as high as Boston College at $60,202" (collegetuitioncompare.com).

"What I've been seeing is not only trying to encourage Deans and the structural parts of the University to undergo training," continues Olivo,

> but really giving the students a voice in a different way and letting them be part of the conversation when it comes to how their education will be administered. Is it perfect? Absolutely not. You cannot try to undo something as insidious as oppression in a matter of a year . . . but what I do see is once something happens, all-hands-on deck, and everyone is looking at what the policy is and if the policy can change.

Mei Ann Teo[35] notes that most of their insight and preparation to become an artistic director came from the students they have taught. A professor before their venture into artistic directing, Teo spent 2004 through 2011 as head of drama at Pacific Union College[36] and 2015 through 2018 as assistant professor of directing and dramaturgy at Hampshire College.[37]

"As a professor, I have learned so much from my students, and my students have prepared me," they say.

Figure 12.5 Portrait of Mei Ann Teo, former artistic director of Musical Theatre Factory, taken in New York City. Source: Michael Kushner Photography

> My students have sharpened the ways I think about the world. My students are the ones who taught me about Queer and Feminist Theory and care. My students are the ones who actually, in the process of learning and growing as an artist and as an educator, have prepared me to be an Artistic Director because they are on the forefront. They are the ones who are thinking about the world in a way that most boards are not.

At first, Michael McElroy[38] declined the invitation to join the University of Michigan's[39] faculty. "I said absolutely not because I didn't want to leave New York City," says McElroy.

> This is my home. As long as I can remember, my dream was to move to New York City and that's where I would build my life. When I got here, when I graduated college, and I walk these streets – I feel at home. I didn't want to leave that.

McElroy then noticed a shift and began to realize something he never thought would happen:

CoVid happened. Quarantine happened. What it did for me in that moment was expose New York City in a different way for me. Allowing me to see it through this quarantine space, I was able to shift and not feel like I *needed* to be here. I went, "Okay – well I've now been in New York when it was at the height of whatever I dreamed it would be and I've been in New York when it was completely barren of everything I came here for." Just because I was able to experience it in that way, opened up the thought that I could possibly do without it. I'll still have a home here – I could go away and come back. But as I've lost New York City for a year, could I lose it for whatever the length of this contract is? My answer was, "Yeah – I think I could." Now that I've existed here in that way, I think I can let it go in that way.

McElroy has affected the hearts of many people, including students in the New Studio on Broadway[40] in the Tisch School of the Arts at New York University.[41] In this moment in the industry's life, McElroy has found why it's incredibly important he finds himself in Ann Arbor, Michigan.

I love engaging with the next generation of artists. We're in a really integral place of the transformation of the next steps of what artistic training should be, or *can* be. And I feel like we're right art the precipice of it being something that it should *not* be and that we have to – across all of our artistic training programs – really be mindful in this moment about what we are giving up and how we empower this generation to step into the best of what artistic training should be. And if that is a space that I can occupy in this moment? That's why I need to be there.

It's in this instance that Michael intersects his passion with a *purpose*.

Purpose

Dramatically speaking, while passion acts as the inciting incident, purpose is most certainly the action. As an artist grows and begins their journey, it's natural for them to find their way on their own time. Passion and purpose are most often ignited out of a need or a want. It's a little like the chicken and the egg – which came first? But passion and purpose are not always ignited together, yet they must always exist together, for there is no way one can truly exist without the other.

To Marla Louissaint, founder of Claim Our Space Now, it starts with standing in someone else's shoes.

It reminds me of a speech from Angela Davis[42] where she mentioned that all it takes to get into the space

of activism, and you don't have to be an "activist" in quotes, but if you have a passion for the arts, a passion for education – all you have to do is care about somebody is to put yourself in their shoes. It's placing that energy not only in yourself, but also to elevate and spread awareness, spread love, and put light toward other people.

"I think that purpose is in the result," says Mel Herzfeld,[43] Tony Winner for Educator of the Year.

And being an artist is the journey. You don't realize that there is an art and technique to what you're doing. There is something very organic that happens as a performer, or somebody who designs, or creates and envisions something . . . that's the artistry. I think you find your purpose when you see the result of what you're doing.

It's a discovery. It's a discovery that this is what I'm really meant to be doing. It feels really good. It's like when you're riding a bike, and there's balance, and everything feels perfect. It's almost effortless. When artwork is effortless, effortless to the point where it always feels right doing it, even when you are working it through. When you are sensitive enough to feel that, that is the part of the realization that you are an artist.

While many artists create work while connected to a strong purpose, one does not *need* a purpose to begin creating. In fact – an artist can find their purpose from starting something artistic. Purpose is just one way an artist can ignite their vision. Purpose can be a gift bestowed upon the artist after its completion. Creating art requires patience – and congruently, finding purpose requires that as well. Purpose reflects one's sensitivity and empathy, which are two learned traits. It takes time to shape a point of view on the world, and a unique view on the world is how one can establish their purpose.

By committing to a purpose, one is willing to give themselves over completely. Purpose requires three elements:

- Time. One must take stock of the world around them, understanding where their voice has the most impact. Does one's purpose require immediate attention? Or must it marinate, building strength and clarity? What are the everyday efforts? What are the long-term investments?
- Courage. One must act as a voice for the voiceless. One must produce thought and perspective that has yet to be brought forward. Actions must be planned, uncomfortable questions asked, and demands must be met.
- Focus. One must be specific in their needs and wants, seeking out the people who will help elevate their cause. They must pay attention to detail, protect themselves legally, hold themselves responsible for action, and meet deadlines accordingly.

"I don't know if you go into art necessarily thinking that it should have a purpose," says BC/EFA director Tom Viola.[44]

> Like a hammer has a purpose. That hammer is going to put that nail into a piece of wood. I think art comes from a place of wanting to tell a story. Whoever is telling that story, or the components of that storytelling, is going to affect everyone involved. You don't necessarily know or anticipate how people are going to hear the story. I don't think it's about purpose, I think it's *about the doing*. And then you let the rest go.

Yet, when someone *does*, it can have a great impact. By taking up space, by centering marginalized communities, and by taking care of the other – these are just *some* ways an artist creates *socially responsible artistry*, an experience that is completely specific to the individual.

Socially Responsible Artistry

"Socially responsible artistry has to be art that is beyond the self," says Dr. Alisa Hurwitz.[45]

> It requires individuals to be aware of the systemic issues that are present that may or may not affect them as an individual, especially if they don't affect them as an individual because you have to do a little more leg work to be aware of what those are. I think that we cannot create art without acknowledgment and work towards dismantling the systemic issues that create oppression for our fellow humans. I think that means using the power that we have to dismantle that. That power can be white privilege, that power can be cis-gender privilege, that power can be non-Native privilege. If you really are committed to it, it means speaking up even if that means making waves.

The idea of socially responsible artistry is *deeply* personal. For every individual artist out there, there is a different meaning as to what socially responsible artistry means to them. The efforts can span a city, they can permeate the country, or they can be experienced in a classroom. Socially responsible artistry is not simply posting on Instagram and moving about the day. It's *active*, loaded with intention, and has the duty to uphold a vision for a better, safer world.

Aaron Simon Gross[46] started his life obsessed with Broadway, showing up to school only wearing his T-shirts that he bought while seeing shows. As a child actor, he moved between regional theatres in the South Florida theatre community, eventually splitting time between Florida and New York – landing a role in Maurice Sendack[47] and Tony Kushner's[48] off-Broadway opera

Brundibar,[49] and then originating the role of Archie in *13*[50] on Broadway. Gross went on to study theatre at Northwestern University.[51] His perspective of socially responsible artistry pertains to the regions – how theatres outside of major cities uphold a responsibility to serve their communities.

"By virtue of how collaborative theatre is, there is no catch all – there is no-binary," says Gross.

> If we zoom out and look at outreach and the regional theatre model – what if social responsibility was *all art was presumably better*? If the people who are making the theatre *know* the audiences it's being made for? What does it mean that a huge percentage of the regional theatres in this country are using artists being shipped in from New York City and leaving? How is it actually serving the community? What can you do within a production to try and combat that when hiring designers? When you're thinking about who's going to make up the cast? Thinking about who's going to direct the play? Social responsibility takes so many different shapes and forms based on ten thousand different things.

Franklin Trapp,[52] the artistic director of Forestburgh Playhouse,[53] is an example of what Gross points out. He engages in socially responsible artistry which positively affects the community surrounding his theatre. Trapp credits one key element in a successful and responsible relationship between regional theatres and their neighbors:

> Gain the trust of your people. And by your people – I mean your subscribers, your patrons, your donors, the other businesses in your area. You need to gain trust – and how do you gain trust? You have to be *very* present, first and foremost. A helicopter artistic director might not be trusted by the local community because there's no relationship there – you need to build relationships with your community. In addition to that, you need to gain trust by creating art that is enjoyed and appreciated by the community. Once they see that, they are more likely to open their wallets to help you continue to do that good work. So many things are coming out of the pandemic. We had a very successful fundraising year. For our size of theatre, it was successful. The reason was because we never rolled over, we never stayed quiet during the shutdown. We immediately went online and provided free education, free performances of cabarets – we had an outdoor concert series in 2020. We were constantly present, constantly posting and sharing, giving things out to people so they always knew where we were and what we were doing. I think that gained the most trust from my community because they were grateful to know we were trying the entire time and not retreating into a shell.

Retreating into a shell prevents growth. Around the country, theatre has the chance to incorporate voices, centering those who help flourish the communities around these regional theatres. Zi Alikhan,[54] director of the incubator DNA: Oxygen,[55] also believes his responsibility is expanding efforts to the communities around him. He is able to gauge this work by asking the question, Who *isn't* coming to his theatre?

> My whole mission with DNA: Oxygen is to create a space that genuinely generates belonging for the people that work inside the theatre, but also the people who are coming to a theatre – and not just asking who is coming to our theatre and how do we serve them, but really asking who *isn't* coming to our theatre . . . and how can we make work and shift our lens to make the lives of people who are yet not coming to our space better every day? There are a lot of metaphors about seats at the table. I think a lot of folks believe what we are doing is taking the table and kicking people out of seats and replacing people in seats at the table. What we are going to do holistically is just make a bigger table and to prioritize the sitting of people who have never gotten to sit at the table before, but also understand there is an abundance of room at this table and allowing scarcity models to perpetuate is just a product of supremacy – the first way to combat supremacy is to build a bigger table.

Similar to that of an artistic director, Tony winner Tonya Pinkins[56] views socially responsible artistry more specifically as acting as a world builder. Just like Trapp affects the world and community through his efforts with Forestburgh Playhouse, Pinkins recalls how her film *Red Pill*[57] does the same – just through a different medium.

"*Red Pill* was life-altering for me," says Pinkins.

> I cannot overestimate the power and satisfaction of being a world builder. I think every artist should try it until they succeed at it. Socially responsible artistry for me means telling your specific story and trusting that there is an audience for it and they will find it. Never let an audience tell you what your art should be. You as the artist lead the audience to see worlds they never imagined.

Pinkins also attributes socially responsible artistry as the *way* in which art is placed in the world, not just how. She acknowledges the clublike mentalities met when putting art into the world, which serve as barriers – just another way in which the industry must work on providing access to its artists.

> I did not and never planned to apply to the high-profile festivals because I knew they were invested in the inaccurate stories that drove my desire to make *Red Pill* in the first place. State-sanctioned organizations are in a circle of celebrating

everyone in their group and selectively choosing who to let in. It's the Capitalist, Scarcity, Exceptionalism model that is so dangerous to everything. I've been celebrated in those circles and it feels great – but a lot more than artistry goes into winning those awards. For the most part, awards require costly campaigns from those organizations.

Still, Pinkins perseveres by finding the appropriate places to share her film, such as the Hamilton Black Film Festival,[58] the Madrid Film Awards,[59] and the Independent Horror Movie Awards,[60] to name a few.

Socially responsible artistry also pertains to the position one puts themselves in to unlearn. Only after the senseless act of George Floyd's[61] murder, did many white people in the United States finally begin to acknowledge the ways in which they benefited from systemic racism, especially in the theatre. Unlearning to learn antiracist practices had become a priority for many humans in the theatre community. Broadway for Racial Justice fights for racial justice and equity by providing immediate resources, assistance, and amplification for Black, Indigenous, and people of color (BIPOC) in the Broadway and theatrical community at large. In doing so, they help create safe spaces throughout the theatre community for creativity and artistry to thrive. Coalitions and organizations such as Broadway for Racial Justice is not only an example of the positive ways in which change is being promoted in the industry, but also an example of the direction theatre is being approached in the 21st century.

Actor and producer Adam Hyndman[62] serves on the board of directors for Broadway for Racial Justice. "Broadway For Racial Justice is a reflection of theatre in the 21st century because it illuminates a future vision of transformation and solidarity," says Hyndman.

> The organization scaffolds diversity and inclusion that is intersectional, and believes that our greatest impact and potential lies in our interconnectedness as an ecosystem that disrupts and mitigates harm while ushering in belonging. It is about the empowerment of folks to bring their whole and supported selves to their work. That conceit is such an affirmation of the collaboration at the essence of theatre and artmaking. The theatre of the 21st century for me is a beautifully expressive and powerfully vulnerable one, and that can only happen when we uplift our community from a place of equity and respect.
>
> During the pandemic and during our nation's/industry's racial reckoning, I found myself being invited to many virtual rooms of affinity. We would process our perspectives and emotions together and use digital space to hold on to connection during these dark times. As a producer and a "doer", I naturally turned many of these spaces into

action-oriented brain trusts and strategy sessions. The Industry Standard Group[63] (which will be the first community fund for BIPOC folks to invest in commercial theater) was one of those off-shoot initiatives, and Broadway For Racial Justice was another forming initiative that I was invited into. I am very active as a board member and I curate/manage a couple of our engagement programs. It has been a space where I am able to galvanize community and strategize for support and radical care in the industry. I have a background in social work and life coaching as one of the hats in my multi-hyphenate bag, so this work meets my intersectional lived experience as a queer, multi-racial artist in a really generative and authentic area of contribution for me.

Socially responsible artistry is required of any multi-hyphenate. Because multi-hyphenates take up space, and a lot of space at that, they must be conscientious of the stories they are sharing, the duties they are performing, and the decisions they are making. By joining groups like Broadway for Racial Justice, or donating funds, or staying aware of the types of spaces one enters – socially responsible artistry is personal and must be a conscious part of our decision-making, even on social media.

During the COVID-19 pandemic, artists were creating virtual experiences on-camera, live podcasts, and talk shows on Squadcast[64] or Zoom. Every time one would open up their social media, there would be a new graphic advertising a show. While it is absolutely necessary to advertise one's creations, many did not pivot when yet another senseless hate crime occurred. These graphics took up the space needed to share resources protecting marginalized people, as well as information preventing the spread of COVID-19. So, how can one better keep their social media in check in hopes of a more socially responsible output into the world? One should ask a few questions before moving forward. In no way do these questions serve as a means to sell a show. Responsible artistry is *never* a sales tactic.

That being said, when one is getting ready to self-promote, they should possibly ask these three questions, listed from the Backstage Article, *How to Be a Socially Responsible Artist When Self-Promoting During COVID-19*,[65] published in November 2020:

- **What is the purpose of this post?** Will they receive a lesson, a sense of empowerment, or a type of healing? Can they respond to a call to arms? Why is this event/show being produced at this moment? Is a mirror being held up to society or providing a means to change or transform an audience? How can the event or show affect a more global outlook? Can one include a link in their livestream to provide donation resources? Can one choose an organization to work with? Can one create a free performance for an educational program or nonprofit?

- **Is this post self-focused?** Does this match self-focused energy, discussed in Chapter 2, "It's Not About You?" Is the post or creation just about furthering one's career? One should shift gears by taking a deeper look inwards to understand intention.
- **Is this post unaware?** Do these posts completely ignore world events? Is one's silence insensitive? Does one's voice amplify the disenfranchised and the marginalized? Is one simply matching public sentiment, not because of personal opinion but because it feels there's an obligation to? Art is important and people should witness it – but society also needs awareness, activism, empathy, and attention during the awakening everyone is collectively experiencing (Kushner, backstage.com).

It's possible to multi-hyphenate at any given moment, but what good is art if it's taking space from someone who needs it? Art is collective. It gives back to those who are ailing. It serves as a voice to the voiceless. But sometimes giving a voice to the voiceless might consist of listening, giving space, and lending energy.

To Tonya Pinkins, socially responsible artistry is about just that – art . . . accompanied by a very familiar lesson:

> Find your voice. Don't allow it to be diluted. Every time you create something from that you will be strengthened as an artist and as a human. Fail – fail gloriously. Those failures, those struggles, those obstacles are feeding the kind of art you make. Bless them *all*, without them you wouldn't be you.

When creating and engaging, it's easy to get in one's head. Simply do what's right; committing oneself to art that is about the other, the community, or an ensemble. When becoming a multi-hyphenate, bring people in to create the bigger picture. Multi-hyphenate art allows new and fresh perspectives. It allows stories that haven't been told yet to come to fruition. Why not allow fellow artists to be a part of that journey? By everyone working together, it ensures equitable, progressive, and inclusive environments for all artists to thrive.

The multi-hyphenate experience lives in every single artist. But just as the multi-hyphenate experience is about creating access in others – it's about creating access within oneself. Allowing oneself to be accessible to the vulnerability, the joy, the treachery, the stress, the exuberance of creating art is all it takes to get started.

Do not wait for anyone to give permission; find the permission deep within and simply jump.

The net will *always* appear.

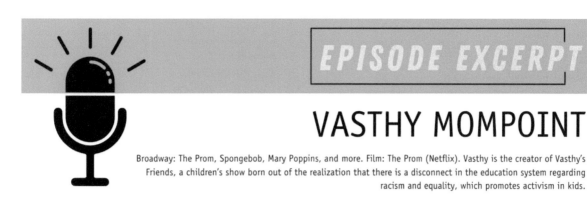

VASTHY MOMPOINT

Broadway: The Prom, Spongebob, Mary Poppins, and more. Film: The Prom (Netflix). Vasthy is the creator of Vasthy's Friends, a children's show born out of the realization that there is a disconnect in the education system regarding racism and equality, which promotes activism in kids.

FIND YOUR TREEHOUSE • *EPISODE 44*

Michael: Speaking of pandemic, you have been doing this incredible experience, show, called Vashty's Friends. Can you share a little bit with me about what Vasthy's Friends is, how it got started, who's involved, what it's for – all that jazz.

Vasthy: Yea! Well it started maybe three days after Broadway shut down. I remember I was at the time owner of a childcare company. I was like I want to find a way to keep our staff employed and I want to find a way to help these parents entertain their kids. This is when we thought it was two weeks. I was like, you know for the next two weeks (Oh, God) everyone's going to be inside and parents are going to have to work at the same time so let's do something. So I set my cell phone up on a pile of books and got my guitar out and played a song and read a story to kids and there we eight families there and I was like, "This is so cute, I'll keep doing it for the next two weeks." And then it kept growing and it kept growing and it kept growing – and then we had like 900 people registered for our events and our list and everything. It was going great – we had all these wonderful Broadway performers coming on, singing, teaching dance parties. And then at the end of May everything went *collapse sound* and we realized how crazy the pandemic really was, all the election stuff started getting nuts, and Black Lives Matter happened. During all of that stuff, I was going through a complete crisis because all of sudden, and what most Black people went through, all of a sudden your realize you're kind of living a lie for most of your life and just faking how much pain we've been in for so long. The main thing I noticed was from what our allies were writing and from what we were writing was that, for Black people, since we were talking about painful experiences since they were kids they didn't see themselves, they felt ignored – and allies going, "We literally didn't understand that it was like that." And so I was like, "There is a disconnect in the education system. There is a disconnect in a lot of places where we're not getting those things . . . where kids aren't seeing themselves in entertainment or in the world at all really . . . even though those people exist." And it's like we could make this not just a fun show for kids, we could make this like a kids activism show and do it through joy, and play, and fun. It went from, "Let's celebrate National Pizza Day!" to being like "We're going to do a Pride parade today!" Or we're doing a Juneteenth episode or Women's History Month. Or a Valentine's Day episode – it is a Valentine's Day episode but it features same sex couples and mixed race couples without saying, "Hey! We're a gay couple!" or "We're a mixed race couple" – just showing it as normal. And that we do. We just have these shows and we have all these people of different colors and races and being their authentic self and no one does it better than theatre people just going on there and doing their thing and being their authentic selves. The letters that we get from parents and kids' reactions are incredible. They just hang onto every single word.

Notes

1 https://ny.covenanthouse.org/
2 www.imdb.com/name/nm3014031/
3 www.covenanthouse.org/covenant-house-leadership
4 https://metoomvmt.org/
5 https://blacklivesmatter.com/
6 http://thetownhall.org/event/broadway-fights-back
7 www.claimourspacenow.org/
8 www.onstageblog.com/editorials/bipoc-students-expose-systemic-racism-within-pace-university
9 www.bfrj.org/
10 https://en.wikipedia.org/wiki/Leigh_Silverman
11 https://playbill.com/article/how-marla-louissaint-is-making-the-revolution-irresistible
12 https://nrd.gov/
13 www.rachel-sussman.com/about.html
14 https://en.wikipedia.org/wiki/New_York_Musical_Theatre_Festival
15 https://en.wikipedia.org/wiki/What_the_Constitution_Means_to_Me
16 https://playbill.com/production/suffs-off-broadway-public-theater-newman-theater-2022
17 www.shainataub.com/
18 https://publictheater.org/
19 www.douglaslyons.net/
20 www.ibdb.com/broadway-production/chicken-biscuits-531921
21 www.playbill.com/person/e-clayton-cornelious-vault-0000114968
22 https://ahrensandflaherty.com/
23 www.ibdb.com/broadway-production/once-on-this-island-514926
24 www.ibdb.com/theatre/circle-in-the-square-theatre-1106
25 https://kendavenport.com/
26 https://www.ibdb.com/broadway-production/spring-awakening-501403
27 https://www.ibdb.com/broadway-cast-staff/michael-arden-112033
28 www.ootbtheatrics.com/
29 www.holmdeltheatrecompany.org/
30 www.pace.edu/
31 https://broadwaypodcastnetwork.com/dear-multi-hyphenate/60-sarah-hamaty-everything-and-nothing/
32 https://en.wikipedia.org/wiki/Karen_Olivo
33 www.ibdb.com/broadway-production/west-side-story-481437
34 https://ccm.uc.edu/
35 www.meiannteo.com/
36 www.puc.edu/
37 www.hampshire.edu/
38 https://smtd.umich.edu/about/faculty-profiles/michael-mcelroy/
39 https://smtd.umich.edu/
40 https://tisch.nyu.edu/drama/about/studios/new-studio-on-broadway
41 https://tisch.nyu.edu/
42 https://en.wikipedia.org/wiki/Angela_Davis
43 www.cnbc.com/2018/06/11/parkland-teacher-melody-herzfeld-who-hid-65-students-got-10000-prize.html
44 https://broadwaycares.org/broadwayworld-interview-with-tom-viola/
45 https://counselingcenter.com/provider/alisa-hurwitz/
46 www.imdb.com/name/nm3697025/
47 https://en.wikipedia.org/wiki/Maurice_Sendak
48 https://en.wikipedia.org/wiki/Tony_Kushner
49 https://en.wikipedia.org/wiki/Brundib%C3%A1r
50 www.ibdb.com/broadway-production/13-480453
51 www.northwestern.edu/
52 www.fbplayhouse.org/management-staff
53 www.fbplayhouse.org/
54 www.zialikhan.com/
55 https://artistsrep.org/artist-development/dna-oxygen/
56 https://en.wikipedia.org/wiki/Tonya_Pinkins
57 www.imdb.com/title/tt11279862/
58 https://hbff.ca/
59 www.madridfilmawards.com/
60 https://filmfreeway.com/IndependentHorrorMovieAwards
61 https://en.wikipedia.org/wiki/George_Floyd
62 www.adamhyndman.com/
63 https://www.theindustrystandardgroup.com/
64 https://www.squadcast.fm
65 https://www.theindustrystandardgroup.com/

Resource List

1. "College Tuition Compare." *College Tuition Compare*, www.collegetuitioncompare.com/.
2. Kushner, Michael. "How To Be a Socially Responsible Artist When Self-Promoting During COVID-19." *Backstage*, Backstage, 19 Nov. 2020, www.backstage.com/magazine/article/how-to-be-a-socially-responsible-artist-self-promoting-covid-19-72119/.

EXERCISE 13

BUILD YOUR THEATRE PROGRAM

Imagine in a perfect world, the theatre program you would be the chair of.

Materials

Journal or computer
Pen

What majors would you offer? What kind of student would you accept? Where would it be? How would you pick your season of shows? How would you try to broaden outreach to the community around you? How would you make applying and attendance more accessible to prospective students?

Once you've thought about all these aspects, write a one-page, ribbon-cutting ceremony speech sharing your plans with the community, fellow staff, and incoming students who showed up to attend.

Objective: Coming up with an active plan to inspire others.
Tips: Keep it active. Keep it positive. Keep it inspirational.

Afterword
Creating During COVID-19

"Michael, enough with the negative energy," I thought. "Though the income is low, you are working – there is just a shift in what that looks like. The industry will fall back into place and headshots will be needed. For now, you're healing and now it's time to heal others. Just because Broadway is shut down, doesn't mean you have to be."

Michael Kushner, Dear Multi-Hyphenate

For those who have inspired me along my artistic process, I plan to take them with me every step of the way. Elena Garcia,[1] who wrote this book's Foreword, was my high school drama teacher. One of the lessons she taught us is that theatre can be made with a can and a stick. That's how I view my life and – *especially* when it comes to multi-hyphenating.

When I moved to New York City in October 2013, I sat in my room and took a breath. My room was the size of the bed, although to me, it was a palace. The overhead light was so dim; it didn't matter if it was on or off. I could open up my window and touch the bricks of the building next to me. It didn't matter if it was small and dark – it was my slice of New York City heaven. After I took it in, I went down to the theatre district to spread good intentions all over sacred territory.

After 7 years of hard work, little sleep, netweaving, and constant career building – on March 12, 2020, I had my last client before COVID-19 changed our lives. We hadn't lost members of our community yet, but somehow, I knew this was the end of an era. From now on, there will always be pre-COVID showbusiness.

This day had a vibe similar to the last day of school. While I was photographing Madeline, my client, images of the last day of second grade popped into my mind. I grew up in South Florida, Coral Springs to be exact, and there is almost always an afternoon thunderstorm that takes over the skies and passes just as swiftly as it came. According to my memory, there was always a full day with those torrential downpours on the last day of school. I would try to leave with all my construction paper creations cultivated throughout second grade, but the rain would threaten all the carefully crafted but fragile materials I had in my arms. While photographing Madeline, it was raining outside, and texts were coming in saying Broadway would be shutting down for two weeks. I was leaning toward postponing all my clients – as if to prepare for a little break. There was a strange levity. I was almost looking forward to this break we all had to collectively take together. Two weeks would fly by, right?

In the photoshoot, I had that immature, bizarre slap-happy feeling of running around, screaming like a banshee because you couldn't get in trouble by your teacher anymore. The clock was ticking down to that final summer break bell, the stickers were removed from your desk, your cubby cleaned out, and you didn't have to sit at your assigned seat. "So, this is what the room looks like from over here!" A clap of thunder. An unnecessary, dramatic scream that got your whole class laughing. No one cared. We were invincible while writing in each other's yearbooks.

While Madeline changed outfits in the bathroom, these claps of thunder became text messages from friends telling me that

their Broadway and off-Broadway shows were rumored to close. This wasn't so joyous like the days of the last day of school. Just like those Florida storms, scientists originally described COVID-19 exactly that way – it would leave us just as swiftly as it came. Eighteen months later, *Pass Over*[2] became the first show to reopen on Broadway, slowly ushering in the reopening of other theatres. But the storm has not yet done exactly that, pass over.

Madeline, a college student, had no idea what was happening next. I think she looked for me for guidance, since I usually have some sort of an answer – but this time I didn't. I was reminded of that moment in *Titanic* (1997),[3] when a woman from steerage asks Captain Smith[4] where to go . . . and he just stares at her. I was just as lost, just as scared, just as unsure. When Madeline left, I looked around my studio, finally sensed the heaviness, cried a bit, and sent some emails telling clients that we would be postponing their shoots. I had no idea the sickness I was about to see . . . or the sickness I was about to experience.

I have a weird relationship with illness. My stepmother Amy was diagnosed with amyotrophic lateral sclerosis (ALS)[5] in 2007, and I watched a popular, healthy, and influential woman of her community deteriorate. She passed away on July 12, 2021, after an extremely ferocious and lengthy battle. The disease took everything away from her – except her spirit, which is still touching everyone even after she passed on.

I am rarely ill. But when I *am* sick – I am knocked out. This time was different. About a day after Madeline's shoot, I started to become exhausted. I mainly thought it was because I had been hung over from an exhilarating, yet tiring spring season of work – but the exhaustion I had started to experience was debilitating. Danny Burstein,[6] Broadway legend who had later been interviewed by *The Hollywood Reporter*[7] about his COVID-19 experience had said, "It was when I was on my hands and knees in the shower that I knew it was time to go to the hospital."

I began to relate.

The symptoms I was experiencing jumped around. I had a fever, then I didn't. I had body pain, then I didn't. I had depression, then I didn't. I thought I just happened to get ill because I wasn't showing the exact symptoms of COVID-19, but then, just like Danny, I found myself on my hands and knees in the shower to catch my breath. On a full Sunday morning, I had a rehearsal with The Skivvies[8] and comp tickets to see the revival of *The Unsinkable Molly Brown*[9] starring Beth Malone[10] at Transport Group,[11] which hadn't shuttered yet. I was extra excited because it was my first *Playbill*[12] cover I had photographed.

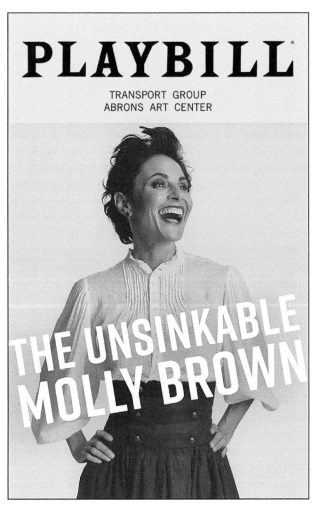

Figure Afterword.2. The Transport Group Theatre Company's *Playbill* cover of *The Unsinkable Molly Brown* revival. Source: Design by Playbill and Transport Group. Photo by Michael Kushner Photography.

It's a very American thing to push forward and execute plans one has committed to – even if they aren't feeling well. So, even though I was feeling ill, I still had pressure to carry out what was in my schedule – not because of who I was working with, but because of the pressure artists are expected to put on themselves. The rehearsal was for when I perform with The Skivvies at Florida State Thespians[13] in our Idina Menzel[14] number. I look forward to it every year. If I had been feeling well enough, it would've been a full and beautiful day. I tried to rally, but as I was in the Lyft heading to *The Unsinkable Molly Brown*, I was overcome with a feeling unlike anything I had experienced the past few days. I changed my destination to Mt. Sinai Hospital and missed the matinee. The show would close the next day.

I was dismissed from the hospital within 3 hours, being told I didn't have the virus but "just a bug" and to go home, stay there, and get rest. The next day I lost my smell and taste

– and *Forbes*[15] had just come out with an article saying that was potentially a symptom. I had the virus – and ultimately pulled through – while I watched so many others succumb to it. My 90-year-old grandmother had a month-long stay at Long Island Jewish Medical Center because of COVID-19 and came home virus-free. I thank the lucky stars every day for that.

As I write this, a long hauler, I am still battling bouts of exhaustion, body pain, shallow breathing – all in response to a blood clot that formed. When I was regaining my strength, my studio was collecting dust. The world was still shut down, and we kept moving Michael Kushner Photography[16] appointments to the next month . . . and then the next month . . . and then the next month. My studio became a storage unit. During quarantine, my fiancé and I were given a bike and guess where it lived – the studio. I've ridden it for a grand total of one time. *Why did we take that bike?*

Clientless. Workless. Bills. Illness. Life had changed drastically overnight. And now the circumstances have changed. Never in the history of theatre has the industry shut down for an extended period. Even after 9/11, Broadway reopened after two nights. Thousands of people were out of work, feeling hopeless, and even moving out of New York City entirely. When the industry was alive and thriving, there were always options to learn, be an intern, and experience. Now, there was nothing. It did feel like the end of the world. I woke up late, still recovering, with little to no energy. During the first few days, I would find myself saying, "What now?"

I made bread. I painted a portrait of myself in Elizabethan garb. I went on a lot of walks. To my fiancé's surprise, I even cleaned. As I tidied up my *Playbill* binders, I found myself taking a trip down memory lane, longing to be in a theatre. As I had flipped the pages a few times, I had realized that I have a distinct memory for every single *Playbill* I have . . . and I know everyone else does as well.

Almost immediately, I recorded a video of me flipping through a *Legally Blonde the Musical*[17] *Playbill*, adorned with signatures. As I flipped through, I realized so many of these people had become friends and clients. According to an Understudy slip that I kept, Lindsay Nicole Chambers,[18] a client and friend, had been on during that specific performance. It brought me such joy.

When I posted the video, Nikki Snelson,[19] original Brooke Wyndham and now Facebook friend, remembered our stage door encounter with my French Woods friends teaching her 2007 lingo like, "booked it," "loves it," and "struggle-juggles." My friend Tracey Mellon came up with all these phrases, and we couldn't wait to teach Broadway our language while meeting actors after the shows. It made our 15-year-old selves giddy. I remember during the song "Serious" the boy I had a crush on put his hand on my knee. I remember loving the show so much that we saw it twice in one weekend. Memories are so important in times like these, especially memories of being in the theatre.

Creating these videos lit a fire in me and dove into the virtual experience. I began teaching workshops. I started recording my podcast *Dear Multi-Hyphenate*.[20] I had begun to create again. Having something to look forward to was so helpful in the healing process.

Every night, the city would erupt in monstrous applause, cheering health care workers, banging pots and pans, and I knew it was 7 p.m. Another day has gone by and still, there was so much up in the air. I kept pushing myself to create but developed a sense of artist's guilt where I felt guilty for being able to find the motivation to create when others couldn't. Was I working or was I just trying to prove to myself the world wasn't ending? "Michael, enough with the negative energy," I thought. "Though the income is low, you *are* working – there is just a shift in what that looks like. The industry will fall back into place and headshots will be needed. For now, you're healing and now it's time to heal others. Just because Broadway is shut down, doesn't mean you have to be."

So, I began to push even further. I had the privilege of a booming photography company that was allowing myself to paint the bigger picture. While I was waiting for gigs as an actor, I was an employed photographer. During the first months of the pandemic I was unemployed but accompanied by resources that helped me push on. It's time to step up and let others know that now *is* an appropriate time to create. It is always appropriate to create – out of joy, out of pain, out of fear, out of the unknown.

On Facebook, the opinions were flying high – as usual – and something struck a chord in me. "Broadway is dead," an artist proclaimed after seeing their industry fold. I began to ask the question of why it's easier for someone to shout this on a public forum as opposed to doing what they can to save it? It's time for a revival, or a renaissance . . . and it starts with an idea, a reshaping.

As artists, we have two buttons in front of us. One is "Next" and the other is "Quit." When you're on the hardest level of the game, do you just quit and say, "Well, I tried"? No – you keep going. But this isn't a game. This is your career – and a tough industry, at that. Don't press the "Quit" button just because no one is there to tell you what to do. I watched many people press that button – which *is* perfectly respectable. Some artists really were dealt some terrible blows and maybe some were looking for an out for a long time – and there is

no shame in that. In fact, it's a reflection on the pressures we put on ourselves, just like I experienced when I had COVID-19 in March 2020. Even if the steam ran out – if we keep holding on, maybe I won't disappoint my family, my friends, and more importantly . . . myself.

But for the artists who left because it seemed like there was nowhere else to turn, there is always a community of people who need you, who need inspiration and positivity. When speaking about self-focused energy, I've mentioned being a responsible artist is someone who produces work that reflects and responds to the world around them. Here is where it is put to the test, and this is also where I was able to tie in my art with political action.

Just before the pandemic in August 2019, I participated in my third Sleep Out with Covenant House.[21] Every year, I raise funds and sleep on the street with the stage and screen community so that homeless youth doesn't have to. In no way do we simulate the homeless experience but rather demonstrate, in solidarity, our devotion to ending homelessness, especially in youth, and so many happen to be LGBTQ+. When we congregate for Sleep Out, there is usually some light programming, introducing Covenant House to the new participants, sharing how the raised funds have been used to create resources, and celebrating the beauty and individuality of the youth that are inhabiting Covenant House. During one of the presentations, a youth by the name of Chyna introduced a PowerPoint presentation she had worked on. She was nervous, and I would be too speaking to a group of people like Audra McDonald,[22] Rachel Brosnahan,[23] Stephanie J. Block,[24] and more. The PowerPoint focused on plans to use a photoshoot to de-stigmatize homeless youth. Of course, I approached Pam Sondanato[25] and immediately offered my time to help Chyna's vision come true.

Shortly after Sleep Out, in September 2019, the photoshoot titled *I Am Worth It*[26] was executed with brilliant leadership by Chyna. She directed me, established the shots, and communicated with her friends who I was photographing. I was careful to not make my privileged voice the loudest in the room. This was about Chyna's voice being amplified. The photoshoot would be split up into two parts: *I Am Not* and *I Am*.

During *I Am*, participants would show off empowering words painted on their bodies. These words showcased how they felt about themselves or what they wanted to become. During *I Am Not*, participants would show off words painted on their bodies that shared words that represent who they are not. These words have been used against them or in hopes of bringing them down. This moment was heavy, as horrific words were showcased on their skin. I was the one painting the words on their bodies, and it was a reminder that all my thoughts, actions, and words have consequences. Being a multi-hyphenate is being a responsible artist, and this is an example of when it's needed the most.

It wasn't my job to be melancholy or feel guilty at this moment – Chyna, Bless, and Janet did exactly what Chyna wanted. All three rose to the occasion and showed such strength and prowess. It was incredibly inspiring to watch these youth use art as therapy.

The photos were supposed to be celebrated in Covenant House's Gala *Night of Broadway Stars*.[27] But yes, COVID-19 hit. This gala was revisioned into an online presentation (quite seamless, I might add) and Covenant House was still able to raise funds, and possibly, even reach an even bigger audience than an in-person gala could. *I Am Worth It* had its own segment introduced by Andrew Rannells[28] and a cartoon created by StoryBooth,[29] complete with a narration recorded by Chyna herself. I was turned into a cartoon – and my geeky self was pretty chuffed about that!

The virtual gala served a purpose and kept spirits high, but still there were so many out of work. Business shut down. People moving out of their cities. No human contact. Zoom fatigue. It was the end of the world . . . and then it was May 25, 2020. George Floyd[30] is brutally murdered by three police officers and is subjected to torturous police brutality which sparks a country-wide outrage and a resurgence in conversations and actions regarding Black Lives Matter.[31] In the theatre industry, many are coming forward sharing the countless ways in which Broadway, the industry I am proud to be a part of, benefits from racism, transphobia, anti-Semitism, and more. It was an eye-opening moment to say the least.

I wanted to be the best ally. Pride month would begin just 5 days after George Floyd's death and with so much police brutality, systemic racism, and unfairness in the world – it didn't seem like there was cause to celebrate by posting selfies with mimosas on Instagram. I didn't want to control the narrative, but I did want to contribute allyship and be a part of the change we were all so desperate for. I started with a small action announcing my antiracist pledge for Michael Kushner Photography. It read:

> *A new equitable theatre industry is coming, and it begins with us. As a photographer, a producer, and performer I commit to unlearning to relearn and engage in anti-racist work. As I pledged to The Broadway Advocacy Coalition, I insist that spaces where I lend my creative talent must actively pursue the work of anti-racism.*
>
> *I have been demanding institutions to show us action plans on how they plan to support the lives of*

> *BIPOC. Holding myself accountable, I share with you my plans for an anti-racist environment. As reminder, with open hearts, we must work on this together. White clients agree to represent themselves free from "ethnic ambiguity," "hinting" and cultural appropriation. I will also commit to hiring more BIPOC hair and makeup artists. This is not a reflection on the talent of makeup artists I currently work with, but a recognition that it my responsibility to build equitable and inclusive workplaces. There is a common denominator in my clients: integrity. I learn from it everyday. I look forward to working with those who are engaging in change, unlearning to relearn, and craving for a space that is theirs – not borrowed.*

On top of releasing this statement, which was crafted with the help of Dimitri Moïse,[32] DeAnne Stewart,[33] and Shakina Nayfack,[34] I announced that if any client would want an extra edit from my studio, the extra edit fee would go to an organization of their choice, so long as it benefited Black lives. My 'Why' statement helped me make choices as an artist during this time. I was able to decide how I can help others solely by looking back at the one sentence that explained why I do what I do: I produce non-quotidian artistry that benefits the world around me.

I decided to keep going with art and allyship. With the permission of Chyna and Covenant House – I continued *I Am Worth It* and brought it outside the walls of Covenant House. After a call to arms on Facebook and Instagram, I asked my friends who both identified as being Queer and a person of color (POC) to meet me in Central Park for a photoshoot.

I eliminated the body paint element to keep it socially distant. Instead, we made signs that shared the *I Am* and *I Am Not* statements. I let the subject pose where they wanted, how they wanted, and I just asked questions. During the month of June, I released a photo per day on Instagram, complete with a caption explaining their choice of words or past experiences. The intention was to combine the pressing importance of Black Lives Matter and the original meaning of pride. Two of the participants used the photoshoot as an opportunity to come out of the closet. To me, it served a purpose – especially during a time when creating art felt like it was throwing it out into the ether, with no audience in the house. But that's the thing, there is always someone who is willing to listen and learn. Theatre is a state of mind, a reflection on life, a spark of possibility – not a period at the end of a sentence or how full the house is. And now, it is time to take the resources you've made over the years and reach out to them. How can you positively affect them? See how they need you, what you can collaborate on, and maybe, just maybe, it will fulfill you as an artist, all while getting compensated for your time.

Figure Afterword.3. Tuan Malinowski, actor and choreographer, jumps in the air with his sign while participating in *I Am Worth It*. Source: Michael Kushner Photography

Over the years, I have stayed in touch with Jessica Orleans, the principal from PS 281, a school I used to teach at when I had a for-now job. I worked with this school through Wingspan Arts,[35] who according to its website, "aims to enrich the lives of young people in and around New York City through multi-disciplinary arts education programs both in and out of the classroom." Their programs emphasize the value of theatre, music, visual arts, and dance while also using these art forms as tools for communication, personal growth, and self-expression. They treated me with respect and love and now I sit on their advisory board.

Orleans had become a friend. In the height of the pandemic, one day we were catching up and the idea of a virtual graduation ceremony came into conversation. I offered my services as a video editor and committed to creating a seamless graduation ceremony for PS 281. The hour-long ceremony debuted as a live "premiere" on YouTube, and all the families were able to sit down at the same time and enjoy the show. I used my artform, my knowledge of storytelling and dramatic structure, skills, and intention as a way to create income. Not only was I able to positively change lives, but I was also able to garner an income – just because of an email.

That actually seems to be the common denominator of most of my work. No one gave me permission to create. **No one gives a multi-hyphenate the permission to create**. Of course, we have to be responsible humans and respect boundaries, but it's okay to simply ask. By asking, or reaching out, one at least understands the possibilities and boundaries in place. You'll see that with a thought-out and personalized email, complete with an open heart and good intention, people are usually keen to collaborate. For some, all we have is creativity. It's simply the way we see the world. This is why art, born out of the accessibility provided by multi-hyphenating, continued to flourish – and maybe even inspire other artists to figure out the ways to create as the world began to reawaken.

Produced by Scrap Paper Pictures and NY Forever,[36] *The Great Filter*,[37] a play written and directed by Frank Winters[38] and starring Jason Ralph[39] and Trevor Einhorn[40] played off-Broadway at the Wild Project to a masked and vaccinated audience July 1–3, 2021, before moving virtual from July 26–August 26.

Figure Afterword.4. Jason Ralph in a production photograph from *The Great Filter*, which played Off Broadway at The Wild Project,[41] to three days of sold out, masked, and vaccinated audiences. Source: Michael Kushner Photography

Ralph, who starred in Netflix's *The Magicians*,[42] was inspired to take the new play about two astronauts as far as he could go. For all involved, it was a daring venture to see how theatre can still exist as we begin to heal from a pandemic.

"Well, if we're writing a play then let's try to put it up as much as we can," says Ralph.

So, we'll do a small production – we're in the middle of a pandemic so we won't be able to have an audience so maybe we can get some filmmakers and film it in a really cool way. We can do it on social media or put it on YouTube. That was our plan at the beginning, but as the world started cracking open and the city started opening up, people were able to be indoors and masked, and they opened up capacity to 30%. So we were like, okay now we should get a venue where people could be there. We started frantically searching for a theatre that could accommodate the new and ever changing protocols from the unions and from the city, which were constantly changing. The kind of HVAC system you need to have changed every week. We jumped theatres like three or four times just to find a place that could accommodate the rules, which is why we ended up at The Wild Project. I had not known about that theatre previously and it's an extraordinary space. I'm so glad we had to jump around in that way because it ended up being the best spot for the play – so sometimes these things just work out. As we were going along, we were able to have more and more audience until we could finally have 100% capacity, which is a huge win not only for us, but the city and the world. That process was really daunting and challenging, but also fun as we were trying to do something new and share something with the world. The world was also beginning to open along with us and so it felt like we were doing this thing together. We were right on the same pace as the city was as we were wanting to help open up and revitalize the city and give a hand to artists.

Projects like *The Great Filter* have always been produced by artists who just want to tell a story. Now, more artists have been opened up to the ideas of self-producing and self-creating, especially out of what was experienced during the pandemic. Even when everything was taken away, artists persevere and constantly figure out how to hold a mirror to society. These artists don't wait for anyone to give them

Figure Afterword.5 Michael Kushner, author of How to Be a Multi-Hyphenate in the Theatre Business Source: Michael Kushner Photography

permission. These artists are multi-hyphenates creating access for themselves to affect others. It's so much more than putting your hand in many different projects . . . it's making a positive impact solely because of your own artistic choices and agency.

The moment-to-moment occurrences of life provide more opportunity than we think – even when we feel everything has been taken away from us. We will always have ourselves, our stories, and our ever-changing perspectives. These are elements that will always survive and keep us not just as artists, but innovators.

While we are ever changing, so is our 'Why,' the driving force and the first step to multi-hyphenating. For me, before COVID-19, my Why statement was that I produced non-quotidian artistry that benefits the world around me. *After* COVID-19, my Why statement changed. I'm now an artist who **survived** a pandemic by accessing multi-hyphenate and non-quotidian artistry and skill, promoting community, interpersonality, and opportunity.

I am an artist. Who survived.
And you are, too.
Make it known.

EPISODE EXCERPT

THE SKIVVIES

The Skivvies are Lauren Molina and Nick Cearley, singer-actor-musicians performing stripped down arrangements of eclectic covers and eccentric originals. Not only is the music stripped down but the Skivvies literally strip down to their underwear to perform.

STARTING FROM SCRATCH • *EPISODE 2*

Nick: I think this is an interesting thing because back in the days when we were in college, I remember a triple threat being called an actor-singer-dancer – right? Or whatever order you wanted to order that in. And I think then when I first saw the John Doyle Sweeney Todd, in that era was called actor-singer-dancer-musician . . . which is like a quadruple threat, but I still think we're dealing with that hyphenate thing that you're talking about definition wise. And now I think everything has changed because that was before digital everything, right? So, I feel like that's what you're talking about and what everyone is now. I think you are more than a quadruple, a quintuple, a sextuple . . . whatever we're going for now.

Lauren: Sign me up!

Nick: I do feel like I'm all those things because you have to be now. I think of interviews that we listened to of Bernadette Peters on radio shows and they would ask her, "How has Broadway changed since you started out?" And she was like, "I don't even know what I would do." Because it is not the same game. And that's what I feel – The multi-hyphenate thing . . . I was in New York for two or three years, whenever year that was, when I first clocked it. We used to be triple threats and that was the multi-hyphenate and now it is what you're saying.

Lauren: Yeah, you're sort of expected to do so much more. As a performer, I feel like there's a lot more pressure to be good at everything. So that is one category of it – but even expanding upon it with The Skivvies . . . obviously not so many people are lucky to find a performer / collaborator to not create not only music, but sort of a brand together as far as the style, the tone, the marketing, the content. So, it has become more of a business aspect to it for us that I never expected as a performer – that I would have to think of it as a business, too. I feel like there's so many different elements of putting your thinking cap on and being like, "What am I good at and how could I use all of these different areas of my abilities and interests to form a career that is constantly morphing and constantly changing." I always say I throw a lot of balls in the air and I see what sticks, but that's truly what's happening. From my first big blowout with Sweeney Todd, that was my first big break, right?

Michael: Which I saw you in... and you were unbelievable.

Lauren: Thanks.

Nick: What did Patti LuPone say that time to you?

Lauren: Lauren, it's all down here from here. It doesn't get any better than this as far as the creative process in a Broadway show and not being the slave to commercial requirements of selling tickets because they were all about John Doyle doing his thing and he really set the precedent for what was possible and opened a lot of not only doors – that's so cliche to say – he was the gateway into all these other shows doing it on Broadway.

Nick: Well, he was my gateway drug. When I literally watched that show it was a gateway drug. I truly was like, "What can I do that is like this?" I had never seen anything . . . It inspired me more than anything, I think, than you'll ever know.

Notes

1   www.imdb.com/name/nm1470289/
2   www.passoverbroadway.com/
3   www.imdb.com/title/tt0120338/
4   https://en.wikipedia.org/wiki/Edward_Smith_(sea_captain)
5   www.als.org/understanding-als/what-is-als
6   www.playbill.com/person/danny-burstein-vault-0000056534
7   www.hollywoodreporter.com/lifestyle/arts/broadway-star-danny-burstein-his-harrowing-coronavirus-experience-strength-stillness-guest-column-1289839/
8   www.theskivviesnyc.com/
9   http://transportgroup.org/project/the-unsinkable-molly-brown/
10 https://en.wikipedia.org/wiki/Beth_Malone
11 http://transportgroup.org/
12 www.playbill.com
13 https://floridathespians.com/
14 https://en.wikipedia.org/wiki/Idina_Menzel
15 www.forbes.com/sites/judystone/2020/03/20/theres-an-unexpected-loss-of-smell-and-taste-in-coronavirus-patients/?sh=4bbf0ea95101
16 www.michaelkushnerphotography.com
17 www.ibdb.com/broadway-production/legally-blonde-423552
18 www.playbill.com/person/lindsay-nicole-chambers-vault-0000090232
19 https://en.wikipedia.org/wiki/Nikki_Snelson
20 https://broadwaypodcastnetwork.com/podcast/dear-multi-hyphenate/
21 www.sleepout.org/index.cfm?fuseaction=donorDrive.event&eventID=908
22 https://en.wikipedia.org/wiki/Audra_McDonald
23 https://en.wikipedia.org/wiki/Rachel_Brosnahan
24 https://en.wikipedia.org/wiki/Stephanie_J._Block
25 www.covenanthouse.org/covenant-house-leadership
26 www.covenanthouse.org/charity-blog/blog/i-am-worth-it
27 www.covenanthousenola.org/nochs/
28 https://en.wikipedia.org/wiki/Andrew_Rannells
29 https://storybooth.com/
30 https://en.wikipedia.org/wiki/Murder_of_George_Floyd
31 https://blacklivesmatter.com/
32 www.them.us/story/dimitri-moise-as-much-as-i-can
33 www.deanne-stewart.com/
34 www.shakina.nyc
35 https://wingspanarts.org/
36 www.nyforever.nyc/
37 https://deadline.com/2021/05/rachel-brosnahan-jason-ralph-trevor-einhorn-off-broadway-theater-the-great-filter-benefit-1234750949/
38 www.frankwinters.net/
39 www.imdb.com/name/nm4170268/
40 www.imdb.com/name/nm0251851/
41 http://thewildproject.com/
42 https://en.wikipedia.org/wiki/The_Magicians_(American_TV_series)

Glossary

Accessibility	the act of creating lucrative and equitable opportunities for collaboration, opening up space for decentered or marginalized folks, and forming outreach.
Advocacy	speaking up for oneself to promote positive change in an artistic setting, engagement, or experience.
Agency	the self-motivated act of permission an artist uses to protect themselves.
Artrepreneur	income garnering efforts usually more artistic than for-now jobs, incorporating artistic skill set and finding purpose within the theatre, television, and film industries.
Bandwidth	the capacity an artist has to be able to focus on or commit to a project at a given time.
Brand	an overall, marketable image that is unique to each individual artist.
Branding statement	a personal sentence for the artist, sharing more about the type of work one would like to commit themselves to by using imagery or likeness.
Boundaries	the act of establishing a safe distinction between oneself and another. That 'other' can be a person, a job, a habit, anything that might require an examination of distance.
Call to action	an idea meant to create engagement and stimulate response.
Content	influential video, photo, audio, or text that is published on social media.
Creative team	a group of people that make up the artistic decisions of the vehicle. In the team, one would find the director, designers, choreographer, musical director, director of photography, stage manager, and casting director, to name a few.
Cross-pollination	intertwining connectivity between the hyphens.
Delegation	when one assigns tasks to an individual or group of people.
Dominant proficiency	allows a multi-hyphenate to invest time or money on other projects.
Donated work	work without monetary compensation that feeds the soul and illuminates the spirit.
Free work	uncompensated work that insinuates the prospective client will benefit from the artist's expense, leaving the artist with little out of the experience.
Gatekeeping	separates artists from parity and inclusion, through the idea that people at the top of the food chain controls who gets what opportunity and when.
Grant	a significant fund designed to support the efforts of an artist. These sums of money are not meant to be paid back.
Hobbies	art or skill used as a way to relieve stress. Hobbies purposely don't become active methods of income or production so they can stay as pleasurable pastimes, not requiring deadlines or budgets.
Imposter syndrome	the idea that an artist's efforts are not legitimate, that their ideas, perspective, and products are fraudulent and not worth respect.
Incubator	a type of group or collective who focuses on the growth, process, and collaboration. While incubators might not produce the musical itself, they will commit themselves to the growth of a piece until the next step of production.

Influencer	one who has a strong social media presence, used to help sell tickets or a special event to an audience.
Intellectual property	legally protected work of art like a play, a book, or song.
Intern	an entry-level position, usually catered for someone who wants to learn about a new field or type of occupation.
Investment of time	one incubates a relationship by establishing integrity or trust which can take years, yet it promotes a trustworthy team to collaborate with.
Investment of money	putting funds into a project or experience to promote a return of funds.
Multi-hyphenate	an artist who has multiple proficiencies, which cross pollinate to help flourish professional capabilities.
Multitasking	active and swift switching between tasks.
Network	an artist's web of collaborators.
Netweaving	the problem-solving, active way one broadens their web of collaborators.
Opening night mentality	a mentality of immediately solving a problem in just a few steps by a specific and nearing deadline.
Producer	a person responsible to find a way to bring an artistic endeavor from the page to the stage or screen. They are responsible for growing the piece from an idea to a three-dimensional entity. They act as a CEO, or the chairperson of the board, or the president of any company.
Proficiency/hyphen	a larger, broader, and strengthened capability like performer, orchestrator, photographer, producer, writer, stage manager, electrician, designer, and more. Proficiencies are usually the broader spectrum of a skill set, and a career can be made out of just one of those artforms.
Reading	is a paired down theatrical experience where a writer, and usually a producer, shares their piece so they can get a better understanding of what they've created.
Regulation	a set of rules one places on themselves to be able to effectively delegate work while respecting boundaries, allowing an individual, organization, or small business to function properly.
Self-focusedness	a surfaced attention one puts on themselves in search of immediate praise. It is in the family of narcissism, can be born out of narcissism, can even grow into narcissism but is mainly misplaced intention.
Skill	a smaller, practiced effort, in service to the proficiency such as organization, Photoshop (photo editing), Final Cut Pro (video editing), social media, observational skills, sense of humor, comedic timing, self-awareness, sewing, roller blading, stage makeup, and more. They can be emotional, physical, tactical, and psychological.
Survival job/for-now job	an occupation helps an artist provide for themselves while committing themselves to an artform which might lack steady income. Provides an income so that the artist can pay rent, buy food, and engage in any of the fundamental steps that allow for a healthy day-to-day life.
Vetting	the act of downloading more information to help make a decision.
Why statement	a sentence serving as the foundation that strengthens an artist's point of view, in turn helping decision-making, commitment, and communication.

Index

Note: Page numbers in *italics* indicate a figure on the corresponding page.

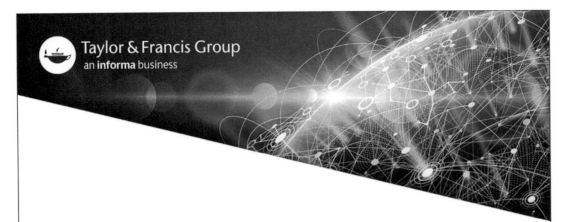